Also available from Bloomsbury:

An Anthropology of Architecture, Victor Buchli

Making Homes, Sarah Pink, Kerstin Leder Mackley, Roxana Morosanu,
Val Mitchell & Tracy Bhamra

Sexuality and Gender at Home, Brent Pilkey, Rachel Scicluna,
Ben Campkin & Barbara Penner (editors)

Queering the Interior, Andrew Gorman-Murray and Matt Cook (editors)

Caravans

Lives on Wheels in Contemporary Europe

Hege Høyer Leivestad

BLOOMSBURY ACADEMIC
LONDON • NEW YORK • OXFORD • NEW DELHI • SYDNEY

BLOOMSBURY ACADEMIC
Bloomsbury Publishing Plc
50 Bedford Square, London, WC1B 3DP, UK
1385 Broadway, New York, NY 10018, USA

BLOOMSBURY, BLOOMSBURY ACADEMIC and the Diana logo
are trademarks of Bloomsbury Publishing Plc

First published in Great Britain 2018
Paperback edition first published 2020

Copyright © Hege Høyer Leivestad, 2018

Hege Høyer Leivestad has asserted her right under the Copyright,
Designs and Patents Act, 1988, to be identified as Author of this work.

For legal purposes the Acknowledgements on p. ix-xi constitute
an extension of this copyright page.

Cover design by Adriana Brioso
Cover image © Andy Reynolds/Getty Images

All rights reserved. No part of this publication may be reproduced or
transmitted in any form or by any means, electronic or mechanical,
including photocopying, recording, or any information storage or retrieval
system, without prior permission in writing from the publishers.

Bloomsbury Publishing Plc does not have any control over, or responsibility for,
any third-party websites referred to or in this book. All internet addresses given
in this book were correct at the time of going to press. The author and publisher
regret any inconvenience caused if addresses have changed or sites have
ceased to exist, but can accept no responsibility for any such changes.

A catalogue record for this book is available from the British Library.

A catalog record for this book is available from the Library of Congress.

ISBN: HB: 978-1-3500-2992-7
PB: 978-1-3501-3245-0
ePDF: 978-1-3500-2993-4
eBook: 978-1-3500-2994-1

Typeset by Deanta Global Publishing Services, Chennai, India

To find out more about our authors and books visit
www.bloomsbury.com and sign up for our newsletters.

*For my daughters,
Ada and Hedvig*

Contents

List of Figures	viii
Acknowledgements	ix
Caravan and Camping Glossary	xii
Introduction: Standing Still	1
1 Caravans: 'These cupboards look like plastic'	17
2 Camp: 'You like to be visible'	37
3 Circumstances: 'Why don't we just sell the house, all our things and leave?'	59
4 Containers: 'You won't even see there's a caravan in there'	91
5 Community: 'We have found here what we can't find at home anymore'	117
6 Conclusion: Troubling Temporalities	141
Epilogue	151
Notes	152
References	165
Index	175

List of Figures

Figure 1	'Permanent' Caravan at Camping Mares (photo by Terje Tjærnås)	8
Figure 2	Row of Caravans at Lake Camping (photo by the author)	13
Figure 3	Caravan in the Making (photo by the author)	22
Figure 4	'Wood' Interior (photo by Terje Tjærnås)	30
Figure 5	Electrical Hook-Up (photo by the author)	44
Figure 6	Campsite Gates, Camping Mares (photo by Terje Tjærnås)	55
Figure 7	Campsite Couple (photo by Terje Tjærnås)	66
Figure 8	'Our best time is now' (photo by the author)	71
Figure 9	For Sale (photo by Terje Tjærnås)	83
Figure 10	External Storage, Camping Mares (photo by Terje Tjærnås)	97
Figure 11	Storage Sections (photo by Terje Tjærnås)	100
Figure 12	Awning Interior (photo by Terje Tjærnås)	104
Figure 13	Kitchen Shed (photo by Terje Tjærnås)	108
Figure 14	Rebuilding Caravan Awning (photo by Terje Tjærnås)	115
Figure 15	Campsite Street (photo by the author)	120
Figure 16	Caravan Resident (photo by Terje Tjærnås)	125
Figure 17	Campsite Panorama, Lake Camping (photo by the author)	131
Figure 18	Home on Wheels (photo by Terje Tjærnås)	138
Figure 19	Caravans exhibited in Mediterranean Gardens, Caravan Salon Düsseldorf 2011 (photo by the author)	142
Figure 20	Between Squatting and Gating (photo by Terje Tjærnås)	146

Acknowledgements

First and foremost, this is a book about, but also for, the caravan residents at Camping Mares and Lake Camping. My deepest gratitude goes to you for letting me peek into your drawers and cupboards, for making sure I was always safe, for making room for me on your coach, for sharing your wine, putting up my awning and for teaching me how to properly play bingo. 'Lucy', above all, this book is the result of our friendship. And 'John', 'Clive' and 'Laura', even though you probably would have objected to the pseudonyms, you are deeply missed.

Many other actors in the camping industry and caravanners I have met since the first fieldwork phase in 2010 deserve special thanks for facilitating my work and letting me hang on to them during trade fairs and meetings. The fieldwork that formed the basis of this project would never have been possible if it was not for the generous funding provided by the Swedish Society for Anthropology and Geography (SSAG), Helge Ax:son Johnson Foundation, Stiftelsen Rhodins Minne and the Department of Social Anthropology at Stockholm University.

This book is also a result of the many conversations and support I have had from my wonderful colleagues at the Department of Social Anthropology at Stockholm University over several years. I have relied on all of those who read drafts, as well as listened and commented on my ideas at seminars and presentations. Beppe Karlsson has been an invaluable mentor and friend, reading version after version of this text and delivering the honest comments needed in order to improve it. Anette Nyqvist and Siri Schwabe have both helped immensely in improving this book, carefully reading and commenting critical sections. Christina Garsten, Johan Lindquist and Mark Graham have offered me constructive criticism and advice, for which I am extremely grateful. Helena Wulff first introduced me to the editor at Bloomsbury, and has generously supported my work and strivings. Erik Olsson and Alireza Behtoui deserve thanks for their support and loyalty. Mia Forrest, Jannete Hentati and Hannah Pollack Sarnecki have commented on parts of this text and always been just a phone call away.

At University of Oxford, where I spent some months as a visiting scholar in 2012, Inge Daniels has been a wonderful mentor, feeding me with interesting thoughts around the issues of materiality and the home. Tim Cresswell read and commented on an earlier version of this book, and this text has benefited greatly from the input provided by such a fantastic mobility scholar. My dear friend, and admirable anthropologist, Ruben Andersson, helped me rethink and reframe my ideas before transforming this into a book.

There are countless colleagues, in Sweden and abroad, who have shared their knowledge and given critical input during academic seminars, conferences and conversations. Thanks to the EASA Mobility Network ANTHROMOB, and especially to Noel Salazar. And to Alice Elliot, Roger Norum and Jamie Coates for showing me the value of academic friendship. Allison Formanack and Jeffrey Albanese co-organized with me a session on mobile dwellings at the annual meeting of the American Anthropological Association in 2015, which helped rethink many of the issues in this book. I have also benefited from advice and suggestions provided by Denise Lawrence-Zuñega, Douglas Holmes, Matthew Hull, Michael Hall, Liz Hallam, Krisztina Fehérváry, Jon Mitchell, Timothy Malefyt, Andre Guedes, Karen O'Reilly, Caroline Oliver, Anna Gavanas and many, many others.

Stephen Glennon deserves thanks for patiently improving the language in large parts of this text. I also wish to thank two anonymous reviewers for suggesting important changes, and my editors Jennifer Schmidt and Miriam Cantwell, as well as Lucy Carroll, for all the work they've put into this publication.

Research for – and the writing of – this book coincided with many deeply difficult years in my personal life. I am for always indebted to my friends and family in Norway, Spain, Sweden, Denmark and elsewhere for showing love in moments of illness, death and separation. To Catrine Rumohr who called every day. To Andreas Adegren for being a great father for our daughters, for towing the caravan and for everything in between. My mother's husband Terje Tjærnås has provided an architect's view on the campsite phenomena and accompanied me to Benidorm taking photos for this book. My brother Eirik Høyer Leivestad not only stood by my side through all these years, but has also been my intellectual sparring partner and carefully read and tidied up my language in a range of drafts and texts. Javier Iñiguez Balsalobre followed me through the last phase of writing up this book, and he took me travelling.

Above all, I am grateful to my mother, Valborg Leivestad, who continues to be the pillar of my life, for her infinite attention and unconditional love. Her deep intellectual and personal engagement with my research has been invaluable. When I open the mobility books I took from his shelves, with the same initials always scribbled on the first page, 'Stolen from KGH', I intensively wish my father, Karl Georg Høyer, would also still be around to see the end of this work, and that we could discuss it on the balcony in Sogndal with the tall mountains and the deep Sognefjord as the background scenery.

Finally, I dedicate this book to the two most important persons in my life. My brilliant daughters Ada Leivestad Adegren and Hedvig Leivestad Adegren. And Ada, when you struggle to explain to your friends at school what your mum actually does for a living and why she spends so much time in caravans. Here is your answer.

Caravan and Camping Glossary

Awning Tent-like fabric structure that can be attached to the side of a caravan or motorhome for extra living and storage place.

Awning Carpet Groundsheet in an awning, made porous to avoid damage to underlying grass.

Camping Outdoor recreational activity.

Campsite An area where people can go camping and spend the night in tents, caravans or other mobile dwellings. Campsites are usually divided into a number of pitches and offer a range of facilities. The word in US English is campground.

Caravan A caravan is a trailer for living. It can be towed on public roads provided that it meets the requirements for construction and use of road vehicles. Caravans are also known as *touring caravans*, *trailers* or *vans*. In this book I employ 'caravan' as a generic term that occasionally encompasses other forms of mobile dwellings, such as the motorhome.

Caravanner A person that goes camping with a caravan. Sometimes used exclusively for members of caravan clubs. Throughout this book I use caravanner as a broad term, encompassing also people that live in caravans, but who do not necessarily see themselves as engaging in any form of camping.

Caravanning Usually employed to refer to the activity associated with touring holidays, here however I use caravanning as a term that also encompasses other forms of long-term and less mobile caravan dwelling.

Cassette Toilet Chemical toilet with waste-holding tank that is accessible from outside the caravan. The chemical toilet is self-contained, storing wastewater for periodic emptying.

Chassis Structural framework supporting the caravan construction.

Dinette Seating area, usually convertible to a bed.

Full-timers Used here with reference to people whose caravan is a primary and year-round dwelling.

Hook-up A connection to water, sewage or electricity at a campsite.

Motorhome Self-propelled caravan that offers living accommodation in combination with a vehicle engine. Also known as motorcaravan or camper van.

Mobile Home A form of caravan that is transportable, but cannot be towed on public roads.

Mobile Dwelling Used here as a generic term encompassing different forms of caravans or dwellings on wheels.

MOT Annual test required for motor vehicles.

Pitch Area on a campsite designated for the use of one unit.

Seasonal Pitch Pitch reserved for a whole season.

Recreational Vehicle (RV) Large vehicle designed for recreational use. Usually refers to the US equivalent of motorhomes (which often are bigger than their European counterparts).

Wastewater Water used in the kitchen or bathroom area that needs to be collected in an internal or external tank for periodic disposal at designated campsite emptying stations.

Sources: UK Camping and Caravanning Club 'Glossary of Caravanning Terms', Merriam Webster Dictionary, Wikipedia.

Introduction: Standing Still

Benidorm, Spain 2011: 'You're free. Out in the open. Even though you're inside you're still in the open . . . . You can see everything that's going on,' Lucy explains. It is midday, but John and Lucy are inside with the heater on full power. Yesterday's cool breeze has turned into vigorous gusts of wind that whirl the warm-brown dust on the pitch and threaten to drag along the flapping canvas tent used as a utility shed. Lucy is seated on the pink, slightly faded sofa in the salon, which at night before she goes to the campsite club is converted into her bed. Her short-cut, silver-grey hair stays neatly in place as she gazes out of the large side window, spotting the hill opposite the heavily congested road and the neon signs of Benidorm Palace. She had known it was right as soon as she stepped into it three years ago. It was the small kitchen located in the back, with gas plates and storage, where John could make the toast for breakfast. And it was the bed in the ceiling above the driving compartment of the car that they used to sleep in, but that now accommodates extra bedding and the presents they feel obliged to keep, but cannot possibly fit anywhere else. As the result of lifelong dream of travelling, with a lump sum of Lucy's pension they had paid 13,000 pounds cash for the second-hand British-manufactured motorhome. 'I can't imagine what it would be like to live in a house again. It feels claustrophobic,' Lucy says. 'It sounds silly, the van is so small and the house is big. But it feels claustrophobic. I feel closed in! We're gonna end up real gypsies, us!'

The motorhome has been their full-time dwelling since John and Lucy left northern England, rented out the terrace house they were not able to sell in a slow housing market, and relocated to Spain. Together with hundreds of other northern Europeans they have settled down on Camping Mares[1] in Benidorm, looking for 'the good life' – on wheels that stand still. In John and Lucy's opinion, the campsite is the realization of the community life they no longer find accessible in their house and neighbourhood in the UK, or as John puts it: 'We don't even lock our door when we go out at night.'

In another corner of Europe. Sweden, 2011. On an open, plain field on the outskirts of town it is afternoon and Benny is cutting the lawn. Again. His wife Louise, who is in her forties and works in a kindergarten, is seated in the shade on the wooden veranda the couple has constructed in front of the awning. From the quiet pitch they have a full view over the factory towers of Benny's workplace, just a short bicycle ride away. They live in the caravan at least five months of the year, passing by their apartment a few kilometres away once a week to pick up the post. There are 55 of them who have reserved their pitch for the summer season and Benny's brother owns the caravan next door. Across the small dusty road that separates the rows of caravans, and next to my tiny 78' model rented for the summer of fieldwork, is another caravan hidden behind an impressive awning and an abundance of garden furniture. Since they sold their apartment and moved to live on Lake Camping[2] on a full-time basis, this is Edward and his partner Petra's new home. Here they can still commute to work, while on the campsite encounter other forms of what they term 'freedom' – 'freedom' from the house and its possessions and from neighbourhoods in decay, and 'freedom' in the wheels that are parked behind flowerpots, but that potentially can take them anywhere.

This book starts off from a rather simple paradox, where the mobile dwelling is 'immobilised' and when a home that is potentially mobile can nurture dreams of a life in movement, even when its static wheels are standing still. *Caravans* is an ethnography of the mobile dwelling in present-day Europe, about its transition from a prefabricated leisure vehicle into the domestic sphere as a seasonal or full-time home that is seldom – or never – moved. It traces the caravan in different social settings: from a Spanish campsite inhabited by the British working class, to a Swedish summer campsite where nothing really happens, through trade fairs where caravans are marketed and displayed, and to the historical remnants of the mobile leisure dream. *Caravans* is, as the title suggests, a book about these vehicle-homes, but it is just as much a book about the people that like John and Lucy – in pursuing a different life – have chosen to live in one. It is about their search for 'freedom', for security and for a specific quality of social relationship that John and Lucy agree is only to be found in a campsite context. And it is a book about the implications and consequences of a life on wheels, about the economic fragilities and conservative social control wherein class and social distinctions are reproduced among mini-lanterns, artificial butterflies and fake fireplaces in a changing Europe.

A move towards the mobile dwelling

The European Caravan Federation calculates that more than five millions caravans and motorhomes roll around on European roads.[3] Only in the

European Union (EU), camping and caravanning stands for more than 20 per cent of all tourism accommodation, and in 2015 the leisure vehicle sector reported remarkable sales jumps. But caravans and motorhomes are not only found among holidaying Europeans. Newspapers frequently feature articles of the mobile dwelling as the solution for the future, as housing prices rise and people seek new options with no fixed abode. But while caravans have been part of working-class leisure in Western Europe since the popularization of the car, we know surprisingly little about these tin-boxes on wheels and the people inhabiting them – seasonally or permanently.

The caravan is a 'hybrid' – a comprised dwelling for sleeping, cooking, eating and socializing that is also a vehicle that can be transported and moved (Wallis 1991: 178). Officially registered as private property (vehicles) and not as real estate (houses), caravans and motorhomes escape not only taxing issues, but also the major housing statistics produced on a European level. The alternative homemaking described in this book identifies a category of mobile housing largely invisible in official statistics due to its blurred exposure of leisure and domestic practices. Whereas the temporary character of caravan life has come to be appreciated as an integral part of Europe's tourism landscape, caravans as permanent housing raise difficult questions regarding class and mobility. How then, can we account for the caravan and the campsite's ongoing conversion into full-time and seasonal housing for northern Europeans? What specific interrelations between material qualities and configurations of mobility enable, sustain or constrain this conversion? And how, as it appears, does the camping phenomenon both encapsulate and produce imaginations and experiences of 'the good life'? This book thus takes as its point of departure a particularly ambiguous form of dwelling to examine the intersections of mobility, materiality and class in contemporary Europe.

But does it at all make sense to examine mobility through static caravan dwelling? To answer this question I argue for an analytical shift that turns away from a focus on mobile people towards the dwelling itself. This analytical shift includes the introduction of three interrelated key concepts: *potential mobility*, *withdrawal* and the *present continuous*. As I will explain more thoroughly in the upcoming section, potential mobility refers to mobility in its unfinished or unrealized form, and is expressed in the ways caravanners imagine mobility without actually moving. While caravanners like Lucy and John seldom move their caravans, life on a campsite still implies some form of relocation. The concept of withdrawal treats such caravan relocations as a stepping back from undesirable domestic, local or national contexts and into a more manageable social and material periphery. By using the concept of withdrawal I place the campsite realities of places such as Lake Camping, where Benny is cutting the lawn, and Camping Mares, where Lucy and John are having their tea, within the turbulent political and economic landscape of present-day Europe.

A withdrawal to campsite life is directed by a class-oriented narrative of 'the good life'. As an analytical concept, withdrawal evokes a specific tension between activated agency and notions of passivity, similar to what Vincent Crapanzano, when writing on a different topic, terms 'passive activity' (2010: 40). The term does not hold the same sense of active and largely individualistic geographical mobility that I find connoted with the word 'escape'.[4] Rather, while still referring to a move away from a specific national or housing context, withdrawal identifies a move within the realm of the already known. Withdrawal is not directed towards the utopian future, but is located in the realm of the known and the familiar present. The home on wheels is, as caravanners repeatedly emphasize, a home you take with you, wherever you go.

To understand how processes of withdrawal are embedded in a material form such as the caravan, we need to look closer at how the caravan itself and its material properties are linked to imaginations of mobility, but also to particular moralities of safety, visibility and control. Among the caravanners, the potential for moving one's dwelling resonates with a wider and more complex idea that a potential for spatial mobility prevents a sense of being 'stuck', both physically and socially (cf. Hage 2005, 2009). Caravanners' own references to what they see as a problematic sense of fixity nevertheless reveal ambivalent relations to the nation state, to politics and to what they see as a loss of morality and community in their neighbourhoods, caused – they regard – by economic crisis and immigration. Looking closer at how caravan dwellers articulate their vision of the good life, it is however not located in the future, but rather in the present moment.

Their referral to the good life as happening in the moment (as they are, for instance, sitting outside their caravan drinking a beer) is situated within a specific temporal frame that I understand as the present continuous – as in the grammatical tense, known as the *-ing* form. The present continuous refers to something that is happen-*ing* at the moment of speaking, tak-*ing* place as we speak. The caravan's present continuous thus holds a critical temporal character, wherein the good life is located in the present: in the sitting, talking, drinking and living. It can be read as a timid, and carefully rolling, present. But the present continuous also constitutes a particular relation between past, present and future (cf. Adam 1990, 1995), outlining the ongoing good life as something new, and contrasting it with a previous state or condition, while simultaneously neglecting economic risk and uncertainty. These three concepts, 'potential mobility', 'withdrawal' and 'the present continuous', will reappear throughout the different chapters of the book, tying together people's imaginaries of mobility and the materiality of their caravan homes.

From motility to potential mobility

Mobility has been one of the buzzwords in the social sciences during the past few decades, portrayed as *the* central element of globalization and capitalism. Leading thinkers in the social sciences, from Anthony Giddens to Zygmunt Bauman and John Urry, have all described the movement of people, ideas and materials as constitutive of a contemporary world in flux. What has been termed a 'mobility turn' in the social sciences has taken mobility one step further, forefronting its capacity as an analytical category in and of itself, not only as an object of study (Cresswell 2006; Salazar 2016). This is clearly articulated in the 'new mobilities paradigm' (Hannam, Sheller and Urry 2006; Sheller and Urry 2006; Urry 2007) where mobility is employed as an all-encompassing category referring to everything from walking to complex migration movements. Although it points to the importance of 'immobile' material forms and how they regulate or produce mobility, the 'new mobilities' literature has rightly been criticized for its tendency to reproduce a problematic mobility–immobility binary and for simplifying the complex relationship between mobility and stasis (Glick-Schiller and Salazar 2013).

Mobile dwellings are intimately linked with people's production of dreams and ideas of 'freedom' and 'the good life', but parallel to what we can see as both practices and discourses of mobility is, however, a similarly important idiom of fixity. One of the terms that briefly appears in the 'new mobilities' research paradigm and that aims at bridging a gap between mobility and immobility is the concept of 'motility'. Originally a biological term and referring to the potential to move, motility was first introduced into the interdisciplinary mobility literature by the sociologist Vincent Kaufmann (2002). Kaufmann argues for a need to separate realized mobility from that of its potential, and argues that every human being has a potential for mobility that, depending on aspirations and circumstances, can be realized into movement. Kaufmann's theoretical ideas have mainly stayed within the fields of transport sociology and neighbouring disciplines,[5] and his use of the motility term has encouraged problematic Eurocentric visions of mobility and an approach that too strongly rests on a belief in the individual agent (Leivestad 2016). However, I think that valuable insights can be gained from shifting the focus from a broad category of mobility, to instead dissecting it and pinning down one of its central elements: the potential or possibility to actually move (Cresswell 2010; Leivestad 2016, 2017; Merriman 2014). Potential mobility thus implies an analytical shift from *actuality* to *potentiality*. But in contrast to motility where mobility is seen as a resource that needs to be appropriated, potential mobility captures mobility as an idea that is constantly deferred. Potential mobility is mobility as unfinished or unrealized, and this book shows how it can be expressed as a powerful idea that in practice is constantly deferred, altered or resisted.

Beyond doubt, mobility – and the potential for it – means very little on its own. It needs, as the anthropologist Julie Chu (2010: 15) puts it, to be 'materialised', through both people and words, but also through objects and other material forms. In this book I illustrate how mobility means very different things in different social contexts and how mobility is given meaning and expressed through material objects and people's engagement with them (Adey 2010; Cresswell 2006; see also Lindquist 2009). This means that mobility is not only experienced, but also mediated, by both human and non-human actors (Xiang and Lindquist 2014: 124). To see that mobility is mediated means taking into account how it is both facilitated and hindered by and through material forms, infrastructures and social actors with different degrees of power (see Latour 2005).

Tin-boxes on wheels

Back there in 2011, on an unusually windy Benidorm day, the pensioner Lucy, who had lived all her life in northern England before moving to a campsite in Spain, talks about the 'claustrophobia' of her former house, a house that despise its size, she argues, 'closes her in'. To Lucy, the mobile dwelling represents a contrast to this claustrophobic house. Caravans and motorhomes do not fit in neatly with a common idea of the home as representing something stable and deeply connected to territory, or with what Judith Okely (1983) terms a 'house dwelling ideology'. Historically, in a European context, one can see that the house was built to last, with long-term material, emotional and symbolic investment and strong implications of stability (Birdwell-Pheasant and Lawrence-Zuñega 1999: 13). Twenty years ago, Janet Carsten and Stephen Hugh-Jones framed an important critique against how the house itself as an object of study in general had suffered from neglect within the anthropological discipline, arguing that 'notions of process, cycle and development are commonplace in the analysis of households and domestic groups but, in contrast to the people involved, the buildings are often portrayed as relatively fixed and permanent' (1995: 37; see also Dalakoglou 2010a: 762 on the same point). While we in the last decade have seen a renewed interest in the house and the home perceived of as a changing process in itself[6] (Dalakoglou 2009; Daniels 2010; Miller 2001a), the material particularities of the mobile dwelling have escaped the radar of most researchers.[7]

In *Discovering the Vernacular Landscape*, the landscape writer John Brinckerhoff Jackson (1984) finds an important distinction between two different types of dwelling: those houses that are built to last, and the house that is expected only to last a generation or less (1984: 93). J. B. Jackson links the dwelling's temporality to that of its material structures, such as the temporality of the wood – houses built rapidly with the idea of eventual change (or abandonment), and mobility, such as dwellings that were easy to disassemble when work or land were sought elsewhere (see also Leivestad 2018). The temporary and mobile dwelling, with antecedents in medieval Europe, have, Jackson argues, formed vernacular architectures such as the box house, the prefabricated house, the mobile home and, as it arrived in America by the 1950s, the trailer (1984: 86). The trailer is, Jackson argues, 'the low-cost dwelling for the future – lacking in solidity, lacking in permanence, lacking in charm, but inexpensive, convenient and mobile' (1984: 100). But when Jackson sees the trailer as cheap and temporary when occupied by people looking for that next step to something more permanent and long-lasting, the caravan realities described in this book are far more complicated. Here, a costly motorhome might be a step towards a caravan or the other way around, but in this context caravanners' create a temporal frame wherein 'the good life' is one realized in a mobile dwelling at the campsite.

Hybridity is built into the caravan's walls and wheels, contributing to the appearance of what I term the caravan's 'ambiguous' character that in turn can make it hard to classify and comprehend. Hybridity is also present in the materials caravans are built of, which produce and evoke multiple human interpretations of 'quality', 'stability' and 'weakness' (see also Wallis 1991: 160). However, these same materials are also potentially 'open', for example, an openness actively made use of by caravanners, for instance to expand and transform living space. The transformative potential of the caravan can thus be located in its 'openness' to human interpretations – evoking a variety of conflicting meanings and values. However, as some of the chapters in this book illustrate, the caravan's material structures are particularly vulnerable to sound and envisaged 'threats' to the desired privacy commonly associated with the Western domestic sphere. And when floors rot and pipes start leaking, it shows that the caravan's material properties are also transformable in ways that go beyond the intention of its caravan owners. The caravan's potential is thus not limited to the scope of human intention (Pinney 2005: 256). Chapter 4 in this book, in discussing both the material culture and the material properties of the caravan home, shows the necessity of bridging an otherwise theoretical gap, perhaps most polemically posed in Tim Ingold's *Materials against Materiality*, where he seeks to 'reverse the emphasis, in current studies of material culture, on the materiality of objects as against the properties of materials' (2007: 1).[8] While this book rests heavily on a material culture approach (see Miller 2005), it also raises questions on how to link issues of agency and temporality with that of material properties.

Figure 1 'Permanent' Caravan at Camping Mares (photo by Terje Tjærnås).

A caravan class

About a decade ago, in 2007, *the Guardian* reported caravanning to be the most popular paid-for holiday in Britain.[9] In the article, the manager of the Camping and Caravanning Show argued that 'caravanning is no longer *Carry on Camping*,[10] bad cabarets and tin boxes on wheels'. In 2013, a *Huffington Post* blogger reflected on what he termed the 'caravan holiday resurgence': 'There was a time, in the not so distant past, when most British holidaymakers could think of nothing worse than spending an extended period of time with their family confined to what could only be described as a box on wheels.'[11] What caused these exalted headlines was a notable increase in membership in the UK caravanning clubs and booking on campsites, read as a result of a new popularity of camping and caravanning as an affordable domestic holiday in times of economic crisis.

But as the newspaper features also reveal, the popular attitude towards caravans is an ambivalent matter. As *the Guardian* so smoothly puts it: 'But while caravanning is undoubtedly big business, there is one leap it has yet to make: being seen as cool.'[12] On British television, Jeremy Clarkson and Richard Hammond have made success out of crashing caravans to bits and pieces in the popular programme *Top Gear* – to entertain the many motorists annoyed with the slow-driving caravanners blocking roads in summertime. And in Sweden, during the years from 2010 to 2017, no less than five different docudramas on national Swedish television were broadcasted that showed caravan life wrapped up in sunny, lazy summer days entangled with various forms of conspicuous consumption.[13] Produced from an urban, middle-class media point of view, these series presented caravanning with large doses of irony, but also painted a picture of caravan enthusiasts as overweight, sun-seeking, alcohol-drinking, barbequing people who are overprotective of their property and have bad taste (Leivestad 2018).

In popular portrayals, the caravan is historically linked to unsettled, homeless or travelling people who in some way or another have been stigmatized due to their mobility. In a European setting we can observe that caravans have been objects of both confusion and political and social exclusion. The history of Gypsy-Travellers, for instance, shows how the caravan has been used as a means and an object for government control of mobility and residency of an otherwise stigmatized group (Okely 1983; Taylor 2008). The US parallel, the trailer, evokes similar connotations of the poor working class. Despite such examples, the caravan has had a visible position in the leisure landscape of Europe through large parts of the twentieth and twenty-first centuries. Its history is inseparable from that of industrialization, the development of leisure and public holidays, as well as the expansion of the car and the motorway infrastructure that came in its wake. Although caravans were manufactured and in use in Britain from the 1920s onwards, caravanning had its great breakthrough in the 1950s and 1960s, following the expansion of private car use in Western Europe. It grew to be a mass leisure phenomenon, largely associated with working-class domestic tourism.[14]

While a common saying in the caravan industry and among caravanners states that 'camping people are all kinds of people', this hardly reflects the ethnographic reality. On Camping Mares and Lake Camping, the majority of the residents are white, heterosexual couples, with what one traditionally would term working-class or lower middle-class background, usually with little or no formal education. A short household survey I completed at Camping Mares in 2012, covering sixty caravan units, showed that the majority of the residents at this site came from the northern areas of the UK, and had occupational backgrounds such as manual work, self-employed manual business, retail, shop keeping and healthcare. Among the Swedish caravanners I engaged with, the majority of the men worked in industry or in manual labour, while common occupations among women were healthcare employees or shop assistants. However, as many researchers have pointed out in recent years, it is perhaps necessary to approach social class through more fine-grained categories. In this book there are individuals that easily would fit the British sociologist Mike Savage (2015) categories of the 'new affluent workers' and the 'emergent service workers', whose economic means are relatively generous and their wish to live the good life likewise. Class, however, is more than income and occupation. In order to understand how camping and the caravan has come to be associated with notions of 'un-cool', and why caravan dwellers repeatedly refer to themselves as 'ordinary' or 'common' people, it is useful to see class not as given, but 'in continual production' (Skeggs 2006: 3) through the ways in which we materially live. *Caravans* shows that class, as Lynsey Hanley (2007) so elegantly put it in her book about the British council estate, is 'built into the physical landscape' and continues to divide us through the types of homes we live in.

In and out of the caravan unit

For more than twelve months in total, on and off from 2010 to 2017, this project has taken me through many hours of strolling caravan trade fairs (Leivestad 2017b), meetings with actors in the caravan industry, interviews[15] and conversations with caravan dwellers and home inventories in people's caravans (Leivestad 2017a).[16] In the following chapters I will repeatedly turn to the everyday realities of Camping Mares and Lake Camping; tease out their spatial and social particularities and tell the stories of the people inhabiting them. Throughout this project, these two campsites have however never been treated as pure comparative entities with the goal of producing a symmetrical presentation. Rather, as any reader will note, the sites and their residents occupy very different portions of the text as they sometimes raise and illuminate distinctive discourses.

In the quiet outskirts of town low stone walls and tall hedges prevent any view of Camping Mares from one of the town's northern entrance roads before you actually enter the broad asphalted road that leads up to the reception building. Established in the late 1980s, Camping Mares is owned by a well-known figure in Benidorm's tourist life and the owner of several downtown hotels and properties. Benidorm, known as the birthplace of package tourism, still receives five million visitors a year, and is home to an important British[17] – mainly working-class – diaspora.[18] In the 2016 Channel 5 docudrama *Bargain-Loving Brits in the Sun*, we are told that the key to a cheap and cheerful life in Spain is a caravan at one of the town area's seventeen campsites, some of them with room for up to a thousand caravans and motorhomes (Leivestad 2017c). A few of the protagonists of the Channel 5 series live on Camping Mares whose 750 pitches, divided into a 'touring' and a 'permanent' area, house large British and Dutch populations.

But when standing outside the campsite restaurant looking at a poster announcing a Friday quiz on an early October day in 2010, most of this was still unknown to me. My lonely presence among sunburned Brits bringing along tap beer from the bar counter has not gone unnoticed and I am approached by a friendly looking tall man with glasses and grey hair. 'Are you here alone?' he asks, 'Would you like to join our team?' The man's name is John and this opening phrase is the fumbling start of years of friendship. Lucy is there as well, and so is the Welsh couple Margaret and Gary, who introduced John and Lucy to Camping Mares when the latter couple first came here a few years ago. They still meet every Friday during the winter season to compete in the Camping Mares Quiz. Every time a team gets the highest score, the contestants burst out in a collective 'nobody likes a smartaaaasss'.

My first quiz night on Camping Mares is also a reflection on the turn this project took during the first fieldwork phase. The initial project idea had been to study motorized camping as a leisure phenomenon, and I had spent two months in the summer in the orange-brownish interior of a rented 1970s caravan in a popular tourism area of Sweden, experiencing leaking awnings, heatwaves and car bumps. But as campsite neighbours came and left, I became more interested in those who stayed put in caravans that were not moved. How could a leisure form so associated with mobility express itself in these apparently static ways?

The choice of the national contexts was no coincidence. From a few years as a Norwegian in my neighbouring country I had come to be fascinated with the Swedish obsession with camping and caravans. Not only was it the country in Europe with most caravans per capita, but television drowned in stereotyping series about camping people and their campsite lives. When I on the other hand decided to spend the summer and winter on the Mediterranean coast of Spain, it came from the initial suggestion that many caravan dwellers from northern Europe go south in the winter months. But, life at Camping Mares, a site I had located through googling and talking to an experienced motorhome traveller, came with additional surprises.

There were also the British 'permanents', such as the Welsh couple Gary and Margaret, who lived full-time in a caravan. Like Lucy and John, they had also left the UK with the wish of downsizing and pursuing a different lifestyle and thus sold their house, and invested in a caravan that had already been previously owned and rebuilt on the site during more than ten years. Like the other permanents on the site, Gary and Margaret pay an annual pitch rent of 4,200 Euro that covers services such as water, sewage and cable TV, as well as the use of the campsite's common areas including the outdoor and indoor pool and sanitary buildings. I spent my first winter on Camping Mares over a stretch of four months during the peak of the European financial crisis in 2010–11. From 2012 to 2017, I revisited the site once a year, with stays varying from four days up to one month. In 2011, I also visited John and Lucy in the UK when they were back to clear their former house. On Camping Mares, I lived in one of the rental mobile homes on the site, hardly ever spending a single day or evening alone, attending patio dinners and parties, outings, quizzes, bingo and cabarets.

The experience of campsite fieldwork was radically different when I for four months in 2011 rented a caravan and kept a seasonal pitch at the Swedish Lake Camping, located within commuting distance from my home in Stockholm. Lake Camping is a four-star campsite, run by a leading campsite chain in Sweden. It is situated on municipality ground in a recreational area in the outskirts of a former industrial town of about 150,000 inhabitants with a high percentage of immigrants.[19] While public administration and service today employ most people, the town I in this book have called Lake Town, is marked by the remnants of an expansive industrial town with factory towers that blur the horizon with grey smoke and areas of dense public housing apartments. Once, these were built to cope with the increasing number of inhabitants, and now they stand in deep contrast to the polished apartment buildings transforming the lakeside scenery along the harbour.

At Lake Camping, social life mainly revolved around the pitch and the caravan. Many of my neighbours were working during weekdays, and were not particularly interested in spending their spare time with a new caravan neighbour. My relationship with the neighbours changed gradually however, and this change was provoked by the caravan itself, acting as an important mediator between the technologically knowledgeable (informants) and the technologically unskilled (anthropologist). During my first weekend at Lake

Figure 2 Row of Caravans at Lake Camping (photo by the author).

Camping, when my closest neighbour, a 70-year-old retiree from Lake Town, and Benny watched the fumbling attempts by my partner and me to put up the awning before deciding to cross the lawn and come to our aid. Without many opening phrases, they got on to the job, commanding us to hold poles and explaining along the way how this would best be done. Whereas the lives of the Camping Mares inhabitants had completely turned my thoughts around the phenomenon of the mobile dwelling, the slow-paced Lake Camping came with additional surprises. Also here I found, though on a more limited scale, people who had sold their houses and apartments to live in caravans and motorhomes. Their neighbours, who had not made this apparently drastic move, still relocated to the campsite five months a year, hardly ever passing by their apartments some kilometres away. In the following chapter I will return to the caravans and their inhabitants at Lake Camping and Camping Mares, and interrogate the everyday making of 'a good life' on wheels.

Caravans: An outline

Through a material lens, the book deepens its focus chapter by chapter. Chapter 1, 'Caravans', begins with the caravan as an object, tracing its material properties through its historical development, production, marketing and consumption. This first chapter of the book follows two parallel courses: while tracing the origins of the European leisure caravan and its material development, it also looks at how caravans are designed, manufactured, marketed and sold in today's European caravanning industry. By looking more closely at the caravan in the trade-fair setting, this chapter illuminates how caravans are judged with reference to a national imagery of 'good' and 'bad' quality. Both manufacturers and caravanners evaluate the caravan's material qualities by referring to its potential for moving, but also to its 'house-like' stability. Here, the thinness of walls, the stability of cupboards and the aesthetics of interior surfaces both come to interfere and clash with the material expectations of conventional Western homes.

Chapter 2, 'Camp', moves from the object itself to the campsite infrastructure as a location for both control and conflict. While the previous chapter looked at the caravan's potential mobility and material structures, in this second chapter attention shifts from the materiality of the caravan to the campsite infrastructure. On both Lake Camping and Camping Mares, the electrical hook-up between the campsite and the caravan partly regulates whether the dwelling remains potentially mobile or becomes a static unit. Offering a history of the campsite phenomenon evolving in the United States and Europe from the 1920s onwards, in this chapter I point to links between democratic politics concerning leisure and nature, liberal visions of mobility and the camp as a site of control. This chapter argues that in their deep concern with safety and security both campsite managers and site residents partake in an extensive neighbourhood watch and implement security measures which eventually leads to the transformation of campsites into semi-gated communities.

In Chapter 3, 'Circumstances', attention shifts to the life narratives of caravanners who inhabit the caravans and motorhomes on Lake Camping and Camping Mares. Leaving the campsite as an infrastructural space, this chapter takes as its point of departure the life narratives of caravan dwellers at Lake Camping (Sweden) and Camping Mares (Spain). It shows that despite the geographically dispersed settings, these narratives hold several common themes. Among them is people's withdrawal from the house and the material objects associated with it, as well as their move away from an urban and national context they see as exhibiting problematic aspects of late modern life. The 'good life' aspirations that are revealed when unpacking these narratives stand in contrast to the everyday realities at the two campsites. Seasonal mobility and static campsite life, I show, is actually made possible through the selling of property in a shaky housing market, risky caravan investments, economic insecurity and welfare dependency.

Chapter 4 'Containers' returns to the caravan, but now by exploring its domestic aesthetics. While the last chapter looked at life narratives of campsite dwellers, this chapter centres on caravanners' homemaking processes by tracing the downsizing from a house or apartment to a caravan. It does so by accounting for how former homes are unmade through the divestment and storing of personal belongings. Withdrawing to a caravan usually means downsizing, but for most caravanners life in a mobile unit gradually becomes a project of living-space expansion. The construction of extensions such as sheds, awnings and patios, and the rebuilding of caravan interiors, are usually done on the model of a former home and a 'real house' aesthetics. Yet, these caravan transformations can lead to changes in the material properties of the caravans, eventually causing rot, mould and broken floors. And while caravanners hide wheels and clad their awnings, campsite managers and authorities have their own conceptions of what a temporary and potentially mobile dwelling is and should look like. This chapter thus reveals the clashes that occur in encounters between caravans, caravan dwellers, management and legislation.

Chapter 5, 'Community' discusses how campsite community is shaped in conjunction with an outside political and economic context. This chapter takes a step back out, from the caravan's domestic space, to consider the formation of caravan community. In this chapter I identify how a discourse of community circulates among both British and Swedish caravanners. Caravan dwellers nurture nostalgic visions of village life that communicate elements of caring for one's neighbour, the visibility of street life and the safety connected to small-scale communities. Within the framework of the present continuous as the ongoing good life, caravanners contrast campsite living with their former declining and 'multiculturalist' home neighbourhoods. But needless to say, life inside the gates is far from frictionless. The closeness of pitches and the ways sound travels unhindered through caravan walls cause conflicts which can in turn trigger the reproduction of national and cultural stereotypes, where an unwanted neighbour can be anything from 'Spanish' or 'Traveller' to 'Liverpool fan'. A main argument of this chapter is that campsite communities are, in fact, formed and shaped around a white working-class logic of homogeneity.

Finally, in the concluding Chapter 6, 'Troubling Temporalities', I question the notion of temporality in relation to the mobile dwellings, asking how this way of living can be placed within current debates on home, class and mobility. The concluding chapter broadens the gaze on the mobile dwelling by considering the multiple causes and consequences of a life on wheels, discussing the potential of the mobile dwelling as a housing form that is both flexible and legally troublesome. The previous chapters have all illustrated that when home meets mobility – or at least the potential for it – clashes between human aspirations for change and needs of stability become curiously visible. This final chapter thus picks up on the notion of temporality, discussing how 'the temporal' home is shaped within legal voids that can be advantageous to tax-avoiding caravan owners, but also how mobile dwellings are potentially risky investments. Doing so, I raise the question of what caravan life can tell us about the restructuring of class and sociality in Europe today. If the campsite provides one answer to a pursued good life, found in the sitt*ing*, drink*ing* and chatt*ing* of the present continuous, can caravan withdrawal reveal anything about the relationship between home, mobility and belonging?

1

Caravans: 'These cupboards look like plastic'

When they had travelled slowly forward for some short distance, Nell ventured to steal a look round the caravan and observe it more closely. One half of it – that moiety in which the comfortable proprietress was then seated – was carpeted, and so portioned off at the further end as to accommodate a sleeping-place, constructed after the fashion of a berth on board ship, which was shaded, like the little windows, with fair white curtains, and looked comfortable enough, though by what kind of gymnastic exercise the lady of the caravan ever contrived to get into it, was an unfathomable mystery. The other half served for a kitchen, and was fitted up with a stove whose small chimney passed through the roof. It held also a closet or larder, several chests, a great pitcher of water, and a few cooking utensils and articles of crockery. These latter necessaries hung upon the walls, which, in that portion of the establishment devoted to the lady of the caravan, were ornamented with such gayer and lighter decorations as a triangle and a couple of well-thumbed tambourines. The lady of the caravan sat at one window in all the pride and poetry of the musical instruments, and little Nell and her grandfather sat at the other in all the humility of the kettle and saucepans, while the machine jogged on and shifted the darkening prospect very slowly. At first the two travellers spoke little, and only in whispers, but as they grew more familiar with the place they ventured to converse with greater freedom, and talked about the country through which they were passing, and the different objects presented themselves, until the old man fell asleep: which the lady of the caravan observing, invited Nell to come and sit beside her.

'Well, child', she said, 'how do you like this way of travelling?'

Charles Dickens, The Old Curiosity Shop, 1840

I have sunk down in the grey corner sofa with my feet cramped underneath the fold-up table while Benny and Louise move around. For a moment we are alone inside the caravan that a minute ago was crowded with couples queuing in and out of the narrow door and awkwardly colliding in the passageway between the kitchen section and the double bed. Louise rapidly opens one of the cupboard doors above my head and goes for the next one. Benny lets his fingers slide across the cupboard surfaces saying that the cupboards 'look like plastic'. Louise, who has used her polished nails to almost peel off the top layer of a cupboard door, asks me to touch it: 'Feel this, Hege', she says, 'this is just glued on, and it will eventually loosen'. Benny has found other weak points on the cupboards. He knocks on the doors with clenched fists, revealing a hollow sound. 'You hear that?' he says while bending his ear towards the cupboard section, 'these German models are *bullriga* (noisy)'. Benny and Louise argue that the difference is that their own Swedish caravan model 'feels better'. Benny goes on to explain how the difference lies in the feeling of the material. 'They are also laminate, but feel more solid.' Just to make his point Benny has started walking somewhat theatrically over the floor, bouncing with bent knees from one foot to another while looking at me and exclaiming: 'This floor actually sways!'

Some years have passed since Benny and Louise were my neighbours at Lake Camping, and we have met up for a Saturday walk in dull February weather at the 2015 edition of the annual regional caravanning show in eastern Sweden. While slowly strolling the trade-fair halls (see also Leivestad 2017b), we enter the caravans and motorhomes to look at the new models and small-talk with salesmen and retailers. Before its social and cultural placement as a leisure vehicle or full-time dwelling, the caravan is imagined, planned, designed, marketed, ordered, manufactured, distributed and sold. Benny and Louise's inspection of the caravan at the trade fair illustrate how mobile dwellings are objects of complex evaluations concerning not only design, but also their material properties. In this chapter I identify an ongoing alternation between a material form and social life, and in his influential approach to material culture, building on a Hegelian dialectics, Daniel Miller (2005) has importantly pointed to the processes in which 'things' are socialized. But caravans do more than just mediate or reflect social relations, they are also 'material realities' (Daniels 2010: 20) that can 'extend or limit human powers' (Fehérváry 2013: 7). While inspections such as that performed by Benny and Louise shows how a caravan's qualities are evaluated by human actors, the caravan is also a material object that refuses a smooth classification and conceptualization.

In the following pages this chapter takes a double course: while tracing the origins of the European leisure caravan and its material development, it also looks at how caravans are designed, manufactured, marketed and sold in today's caravanning industry with a particular focus on Sweden. In the trade-fair setting, which are central locations for the marketing and sales of mobile dwellings (see Leivestad 2017b), this chapter illuminates how caravans are judged with reference to a national imagery of 'good' and 'bad' quality. Both manufacturers and caravanners evaluate the caravan's material qualities by referring to its potential mobility, but also to its 'house-like' stability. Here, the thinness of walls, the stability of cupboards and the aesthetics of interior surfaces both come to interfere and clash with the material expectations of conventional Western homes. But the history of the leisure caravan can be traced back to the British Isles, and that is where this chapter will commence.

Leisure longings and military materials

He was probably proud, the Scotsman William Gordon Stables, as he climbed into *The Wanderer* to tour Britain. It was 1886 and Gordon Stables, a retired navy surgeon and writer of adventure stories for boys, had commissioned the building of what later became known as the first recreational caravan (Pressnell 1991; Wilson 1986). As a boy, Gordon Stables had envied the Gypsy children in their family vans, and *The Wanderer*, built by the Bristol Wagon Company after his drawings, was the result of Gordon Stables' dream of his very own 'Land Yacht'. *The Wanderer*'s first expedition to his native Scotland covered more than 1,300 British miles, a journey where Gordon Stables himself sat comfortably observing the scenery and that later resulted in the book *Cruise of the Land Yacht Wanderer, or, Thirteen Hundred Miles in my Caravan* (1886).

With Gordon Stables' enthusiasm, the privileged British leisure classes had discovered the caravan, and so began the tale of the so-called Gentlemen-Gypsies (Pressnell 1991; The Caravan Club 2011; Wilson 1986). Horse-drawn caravans had however existed in the UK for some years already, emerging in the 1820s as a vehicle for travelling showmen (Pressnell 1991). By 1860, such horse-drawn carriages were widely used also among Traveller-Gypsies who, up until then, mainly had travelled with tents. Some years later, in 1904, a *Maison Automobile* was shown in Paris; it was a caravan body mounted on a car, and Europe had probably seen the first example of a motorized caravan (ibid.).[1]

The historical development of the caravan reveals a material connection between military technology and the mobile dwelling. During the First World War there was an extensive use of cars and trailers, and in the UK, the aftermath of the war thus led to the foundation of several caravan manufacturers building on the motor knowledge and surplus materials from wartime (Jenkinson

2001; Pressnell 1991). The early caravans were, in general, pricey and the models tended to draw on the horse-drawn caravan, resulting in the caravans often being massive and hard to tow. During the 1920s and 1930s, production was aimed at a wider range of consumers, with considerable progression in construction techniques. By the 1930s, a new standard caravan model had been born, characterized by its streamlined roof and constructed on a steel chassis and with walls of pressed fibreboard, replacing heavier wooden materials (ibid.).

The Second World War nevertheless brought caravan production to an abrupt stop, at least in the UK, as many manufacturers became part of the war effort, building for instance ambulances. The existing caravans, however, came to play an important role for authorities as temporary accommodation and were also converted into canteens and ambulances (Pressnell 1991: 16). A more simple form of caravan emerged, with chipboard instead of plywood, and with a chassis made of wood instead of steel. In the aftermath of the war, the need for accommodation was desperate, and cheap caravans met this new need for housing in bombed-out towns.[2]

Touring caravan production increased again in the 1950s UK, and the 1950s and 60s were a blooming period for an industry that by now was also well established in other European countries. German companies took over as the dominant industry actors, and the company *Hobby*, established in the 1960s, is today the world-leading manufacturer of caravans. While commercial caravan manufacturing started in the UK and Germany from the 1930s onwards, development in Sweden came much later. In 1948, the first Swedish-manufactured caravan *SMV*, 3.5 metres long and weighing 370 kg, came about as a peculiar compromise between an inventive motor enthusiast and his wife, who did not agree on how to spend their holidays; she wanted a cabin, while he wanted to travel.

The European caravanning industry has not only been affected by wars, but is also susceptible to various economic and political factors. The international package holiday emerging in the 1960s was one specific threat; another was increased taxes, the oil crisis and inflation in the 1970s. The 2008 financial crisis hit the caravan industry hard, and resulted in a great decline in European sales. From 2008 until 2015, the European caravanning industry was facing dropping sales, and huge cuts among manufacturers and the press releases of the European Caravan Federation (EFC) report of an industry in crisis. In January 2013, the EFC reported that the industry was hit particularly hard by the 'sovereign debt crisis'.[3] The vulnerability of the leisure vehicle market was commonly explained in the same manner: 'Leisure is where you make your first cuts.'

While their material history clearly overlaps with that of the caravan, motorhomes reached Scandinavia as late as in the 1970s–80s, whereas in Germany motorhomes had been common for a longer period of time. During the time of my fieldwork representatives of the camping industry would repeatedly proclaim the motorhome to be the camping industry's future. Among industry actors, the motorhome – while often produced by the same manufacturers, sold in the same settings and used on the same campsites – is nevertheless regarded as fundamentally different from its caravan counterpart. As self-propelled caravans, built on a commercial automobile chassis, the motorhome is believed to hold and represent an actual realized mobility, opposed to the mere potential mobility of the caravan, which needs to be towed behind a car. With regard to the campsite settings of Camping Mares and Lake Camping that are dealt with in the coming chapters, I will show that this marked opposition between the caravan and the motorhome in terms of mobility is in practice rather blurred.

Lightweight mobility

'The camping people are strange,' the sales manager Jonas says. 'People have their favourites. To sell a *Cabby* to an old *Kabe* customer would be very difficult.' Walking around the Cabby factory building on a winter day in 2011, the sales manager and I are surrounded by men in blue boiler suits. In 2011 the Swedish manufacturer *Cabby Caravan* was one of the leading companies on the Swedish market with retailers in Norway, Finland, Denmark, Germany and the Benelux countries.[4] Started by a local entrepreneur in the early 1960s and pioneering in the development of insulation methods, the company produced caravans from a factory on the outskirts of a small town in southern Sweden. Of the total 80 employees, some have been there since the factory was first established. Cabby's largest customer group are couples between 50 and 65 years old, with adult children and a stable economic situation. The second group of consumers are families where the parents are aged 35–45. While the latter group is actually the customer profile Cabby aims for, they are hard to catch, not least because of the high price of a spacious caravan with an extra bedroom. Cabby's customer profile reflects a general aspect of a rather pricey northern European caravan market, where the largest group of caravan buyers are post-war baby boomers, now in their sixties, with a stable economic situation that in some cases is a result of profits made from investments in the housing market.

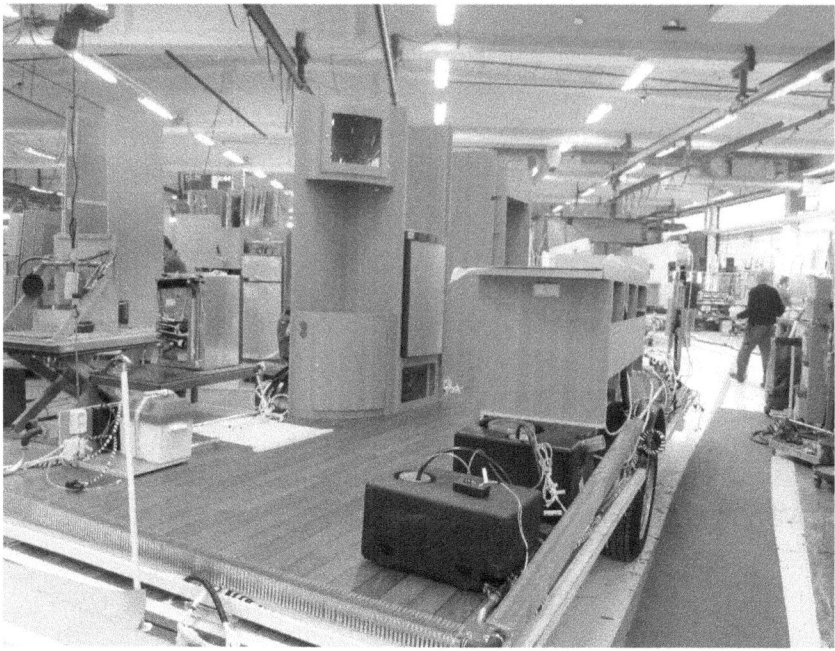

Figure 3 Caravan in the Making (photo by the author).

A caravan spends more or less five days on the production line, where all the different pieces and parts of the caravan are joined and built into a new mobile dwelling. The preparations start earlier though: ordering of materials commences eight weeks before the actual building process, and carpenters needs two weeks to finish their work on one caravan. The habitation area of a caravan is built on top of what is called a chassis, which is a structural frame. Into the 1940s, the chassis were rough steel constructions, but today they are made of lightweight, galvanized material that is integrated with the coach and the floor (Eriksson 2006: 94).[5] The coach construction of a caravan has developed much since the early days, when the walls were often built with masonite. Today one finds that coach-built caravans have body panels that are made up of wooden frames, interior panels are made of plywood, while the exterior consists of aluminium[6] or glass-reinforced fibre – the last of which is a material first introduced in the 1950s. The void between the two body panels is packed with insulation, most often different forms of foam plastic.[7] These developments in caravan technology might at first glance seem irrelevant to the daily practices of caravan living. However, the materials used to build and insulate caravans, and manufacturers' continuous struggle between creating products that are heavy and solid, or light and mobile, interferes with caravan owners' own opinions about the self-sufficiency and the material quality of their mobile dwelling.

Self-sufficient units

In 2011, Cabby Caravan launched new caravan models with bigger bathrooms, evoking 'a spa-feeling', as one of the product developers said, having taken inspiration from bathrooms in boats. As I follow caravanners around at trade fairs looking at new caravan and motorhome models, I witness thorough inspections of both the interior and exterior parts of the leisure vehicles. On one such occasion, inspecting motorhome models with two retired Swedish couples, one of the women is particularly concerned with the bathroom that, in this case, is impressive with shining surfaces and marble-looking sinks. But after minutes of letting hands slip across the materials, bending down to check space and opening and closing doors, the woman finds several weak points. Her main concern is the washing room, where the washbasin is placed outside the door that hides the toilet and the shower. That means you will have to wash yourself in the sight of others, so even if the washbasin is 'nice and everything, you don't want to sit looking at it all the time', she explained.

The early model caravans did not have toilets. Chemical toilets[8] first appeared in the 1960s and still exist in more or less the same form (Eriksson 2006: 136). The cassette toilet is the most popular form of toilet in modern caravans and is a version of the chemical toilet, where the waste-holding tank is accessible from outside the caravan and thus one can remove the tank for emptying without having to transport the whole toilet.[9] Despite a general concern with the bathroom, I was surprised to find how little active caravanners used this space. In most modern motorhomes and caravans, the shower was simply transformed into a space for storage: for clothes or outdoor gear. When travelling and not staying at campsites, the showers would be used, but when staying put at one site there was no reason not to use the facilities provided. Several of the British caravanners on Spanish Camping Mares insisted that a 'proper flush-toilet' was one of the criteria when looking for a caravan to buy on-site. The importance placed on the presence of a bathroom can be linked to how the caravan is approached as a self-sufficient unit. Even if not used, the presence of a toilet allows for the potential of moving the dwelling to a place where facilities are not available. One of my neighbours at Lake Camping, Kim, was the owner of a technologically advanced motorhome. According to him, the motorhome was 'just like living in an apartment' where he could 'manage entirely on my own'. The technical advancement of modern caravans point at the paradoxes of the equipment standardized in the caravan, but never used by the caravanners. Still, a proper toilet, the presence of a shower and advanced cooking facilities are valued by many of the Swedish caravanners, mostly because of the possibilities of self-sufficiency while travelling that such equipment provides.

Kim's neighbours, Kalle and Lena, both with a long caravan history on Lake Camping, no longer take their caravan travelling from the seasonal pitch. When buying their caravan, they were preoccupied with its interior planning consisting of a salon in dark blue at the front, a kitchen and toilet in the middle of the caravan and two separate beds at the very back. Kalle and Lena have had new carpets made professionally for the floor, since the originals were so thick they hardly could feel the floor heating. The awning was new in 2011, hosting a large, plastic cupboard section good for all sorts of weather, an oven, a full-size freezer and fridge, in addition to the fully equipped kitchen part inside the caravan. Kalle, who has technical expertise, has attached an arm to the television so that you can bend it and watch television both in the awning and in bed, installed a loudspeaker system, so you can hear the television sound in the bedroom, and installed lighting in the wardrobe. Kalle has also fastened one of the lamps and a small flower vase to the shelf behind the sofa with a special tape so it does not need to be removed during travelling. Many items in the caravan are fastened in a similar way, enabling a potential mobility. In their former caravan, they needed to secure items with threads and rubber before driving. Even if Kalle and Lena have not taken their caravan away from the seasonal pitch for the last two years, they have made sure to materially prepare the caravan for moving.

The previous examples illustrate how the degree of material equipment in a caravan or motorhome is linked with the caravan dwellers' focus upon self-sufficiency. Caravanners tend to think of the caravan or motorhome as a self-contained unit, even if – as we will see in the upcoming chapter – constantly hooked up with the campsite's electrical infrastructure. Kim, who actually lives full-time on the site, seldom puts himself in situations where the electrical power system of his advanced bus is needed, but the actual possibility of electrical self-production represents a potential of self-containment that is linked to the very idea of a 'free' housing unit. On their part, Kalle and Lena make sure that the interior 'loose' materials of the caravan are secured, enabling potential mobility and thus re-establishing the caravan as a self-contained unit even when 'permanently' hooked up with the campsite infrastructure.[10]

Stabile cupboards and swaying floors

Benny and Louise, with whom I opened this chapter, show how judgements of quality are made with reference to material solidity, expressed in this case through the lack of such and the resulting swaying floors and weak cupboards. Most of the couples and families I follow on trade fairs express similar concerns to that of Benny and Louise referring to the stability embedded in the material. Inside a caravan at a 2010 caravanning trade show, a man in his thirties whom I have spent two days with looking at caravan models, squeezes his somewhat bulky body in between the sofa and the fold-up table, taps on the cupboard doors and turns towards me: 'This material is both thin and bad.' His wife agrees and says she is not fond of the imitation beech colour on the cupboards either: It looks 'plastic and cheap'. 'It is actually plastic', the husband says while carefully walking on the small wooden steps that lead out of the caravan. 'But you can find sorts that look more natural than this ... the looks means a lot; you can't get away from that.'

The couple's sensory inspections of the caravan is mirrored in the practices of a couple in their sixties who at a trade fair explained that their choice of a new motorhome was largely based on how you could 'feel the quality' of the model. A particular critical point was the handles on the cupboards and the importance of them 'feeling stable'. Stability and solidity are here referred to as materials that will not easily break and that are durable. The Swedish couple had also been concerned with the thickness of the inside doors. The model they had bought was the only one that had doors that were four centimetres thick, 'just like home'.

In the latter argument, a link is established between the solid and the home-like, where the value of solidity and stability is perceived as contributing to giving the caravan house-like qualities. Alan Wallis (1991), who has written the history of the American mobile home, points to a parallel discourse concerning the question of thinness. The physical structure of the mobile home, Wallis shows, is one of lightness and thinness (1991: 160). The thinness is not only literal, but also figurative through the borrowing of characteristics from other objects, such as photographed wood laminated on cheaper panelling (ibid.). Caravan inspections at the trade fair reveal a similar attitude to material thinness. While the mentioned couple in their thirties criticizes the cupboards for looking like plastic, and concludes that even if it actually is plastic, one can find versions that 'look much more natural'. Here, the material qualities of the caravan cupboards are evaluated in a double – and partly contradictory – manner. The cupboards are dismissed as 'thin and bad', but the main problem is that they look 'plastic and cheap'. Like Benny and Louise, the couple is very well aware that the material is not wood, but a laminated panelling, but emphasizes that this panelling ideally should appear 'more natural'.

This inspection of material quality also reveals the rather complicated position of plastic as a caravan material. Plastic, as the 'ultimate material of the mass-produced commodity' (Fehérváry 2013: 145), carries negative associations based on its link to affordability and distance from 'nature'. As Fehérváry notes, plastic can also be perceived as a 'cold' material, interfering with vital processes of cooking, decaying and fertilizing (2013: 145). She reminds us that attitudes to plastic are historically changing, showing how in the post-Soviet Hungary a popular focus shifted from regarding plastic's modern durability to questioning its 'unnatural resistance to decomposition' (ibid). There exists an interesting historical link between caravans, the practice of camping and plastic as a material. Writing on the development of car camping in Norway in the 1950s and 1960s, Østby (2014) notes that 'the camping life was formed in conjunction with the breakthrough of plastic as the most important material for outdoor life' (2014: 301). He points to the use of plastic in tents, tables, chairs and cutlery. Among the caravanners at Swedish Lake Camping and Spanish Camping Mares, plastic is a much-used material for outdoor tables and utensils, but also for objects used in the caravan and awning's interior space such as plates, glasses and cutlery. The use of plastic material is often excused or commented upon in relation to practicality and functionality. Such functionality seems related to the potential mobility of the caravan – ceramics are known to break during travelling – but also the potential mobility of the objects themselves, enabling the carrying of cutlery to the main buildings to do the dishes.

In the context of Hungary in the 1960s into the 1970s, Fehérváry (2013) shows how what she terms a socialist modern aesthetic arose with the 'clean, light, and mobile materialities of a future oriented modernism', linked with Western design, but also evoking the socialist values of egalitarianism and civilized society (2013: 4). Her work reminds us of the historical context in which the caravan expansion came to be, in Sweden as part of the 1960s Social Democratic modernity project. But it also points to what in the case of the caravan is a more direct link between the associated light materials and mobility. What becomes apparent in relation to the Swedish caravan, however, is the fact that these 'light materials' nevertheless contradict manufacturers' and caravanners' aspirations of the 'home-like' material stability.

A caravan for all of Europe

Petra and Edward, my neighbours at Lake Camping, who had sold their apartment and moved full-time into a caravan, described their hunt for the right caravan as a difficult process. While they had been holidaying in Volkswagen vans for many years, their knowledge of caravans was close to zero. To Edward it was important to find a caravan that felt 'aesthetically right'. But all the Swedish caravans they looked at reminded Edward of a funeral car: 'Straight lines and so boring.' Petra and Edward agree that it should be an experience when you climb into a caravan. When they finally found a German *Hobby*, entering the caravan gave them a feeling of a yacht. 'Everything is designed. Everything is considered. Constructed. They are planned with style. Just the small window that they have on the door. It is all very inviting', Edward says. In 2011, facing their first winter in the caravan, everyone told them their German caravan would not handle it. 'But we have talked to someone that owns a Hobby and they say it is no problem', Petra says.

Similar national stereotypes regarding a product's design and imagined quality are constantly produced in informal discourse by manufacturers and retailers of camping vehicles. They are often connected to a partly shared and partly contested national imagery of what is considered 'cheap' and 'expensive' or 'good' or 'bad' quality. 'Quality is about choice of material', Jonas, the Cabby sales manager says. 'And quality is more expensive.' According to Jonas, this unique 'quality' lies in the year-round comfort their caravans can provide. While all caravan manufacturers use the same type of furnace, the Swedish manufacturers argue that they have worked better on the ventilation system in the caravan than their European competitors. Aspects of heating, ventilation and energy are of particular technological concerns when building a caravan. A caravan construction consists of relatively large areas of windows compared to the size of the walls. While early caravan models had windows in glass, modern caravan windows are made of plastic double-glazing. It is unavoidable that the large proportion of windows lets a lot of heat out of the caravan, compared to a regular house or apartment where the windows are also better insulated.

Refrigerators, which today are standard in all caravan models, first appeared in British caravans in the 1950s, which was a time of considerable improvement in terms of technical development of brakes and couplings, construction materials and electrical systems (Pressnell 1991: 25). Electricity installation in caravans was still a rare feature however, and most lighting was provided by gas until the 1960s (ibid). Still today, many caravans have gas, more precisely Liquefied Petroleum Gas, as a source of energy to power the fridge and heat water and space when main electricity is not available.[11] Modern caravans have heating both in the walls and the floor. Some caravans have water-led heating, and while this solution is popular among the more expensive Swedish-manufactured caravans, air-led heating is the most common solution on a European level, due to costs and installation labour. Based on such national differences regarding ventilation and heating, Cabby and the other Swedish manufacturers market and distribute their products to Scandinavian customers by playing on an analogy between a harsh, cold climate and the local knowledge of providing heating and ventilation solutions.

Another important differential factor, emphasized by the manufacturers, is what they term 'Nordic design'. A particular 'Swedishness' in terms of interior design is commonly referred to among the manufacturers as *avskalad* (austere), and this quality is closely related to the internationally known Scandinavian design tradition renowned to emphasize 'austerity, functionalism, local materials and quality' (Lundin 2013). 'It has to show that it is Swedish', one sales manager says, arguing that what he refers to as the Nordic style is one with less 'bling-bling': 'I mean, we have light strips as well, but not everywhere!' While Swedish manufacturers worry about the tensions between 'cheap' and 'expensive' looks, a representative of a French manufacturer puts it this way: 'But making a caravan for all of Europe is difficult ... . The Swedish caravans are so dark: that would never work in France. And the typical French caravans would never work in Germany.'

The general absence of British products at the trade fairs was commonly explained with the 'poor quality' of British caravans and motorhomes due to the fact that British people are used to campsites with electricity and showers.[12] Their demands are therefore so low that the manufacturers don't need to do their best and the resulting products are not good enough for the European market, one manufacturer would argue. British caravan dwellers also have a similar image of the 'low quality' British caravans. One of the inhabitants at Camping Mares would emphasize how she liked to live in an old German caravan: 'You can stand on the roof of one of these; you couldn't do that on an English one.' The manufacturers' opinions about the material qualities of caravan products are built on strong national stereotypes that are general and broad in their nature. It is interesting to see that such stereotypes not only concern the national industry's ability to produce 'stable' products, but also stretch into judgements about the practices of the caravan buyers and how these interrelate with production standards.

Colours and cabins

In 2004, the Swedish manufacturer Cabby conducted a large internet survey on design, resulting in a complete change of the wood-imitated interior to a much lighter version. The change turned out to be a great mistake. 'The problem was that it looked cheap. It looked more like a cheap German than an expensive Swede', Cabby's sales manager Jonas says. The sales halved that year, and it has taken them years to come back. In 2007, they had rustic flooring and a dark interior, and sold very well. The Cabby example shows how a wider discourse and tension regarding the quality and design of caravans often revolves around the issue of colour.

In 2012, Cabby changed the wooden colour of the cupboards again after completing a survey among their customer groups. 'Cherry' now became 'Apple', an even darker version of the tree imitation. Jonas agrees that the dark is against all logic, since the space is so limited. But the dark expresses a 'sense of luxury'. When at a trade fair in 2011 I meet the owner of Kabe, the largest caravan manufacturer in Sweden, he is sensitive to what he frames as 'the traditional customers'. They have to be careful with radical changes in the interior, he claims. At the trade fair Kabe has for the first time launched a model with white kitchens. But they have chosen to change only some of the cupboards, not the whole kitchen. The manager laughs about the fact that he read a while ago that 65 per cent of all kitchens sold in Sweden are white. 'But it just doesn't work in a caravan ... . We once made a model with white interior and it just looked dreadful ... . And all these design-looking sofas, they are just not comfortable enough to sit in', he says.

The refusal of the colour white is perhaps surprising, not least seen in relation to the existing trends in the Nordic property market. Writing on the London estate market, Diana Young (2004) discusses whiteness and its ability to produce neutrality, speeding up property exchange and circulation in the

Figure 4 'Wood' Interior (photo by Terje Tjærnås).

market. Among estate agents, Young shows, neutrality is, among other things, thought of as achieving an aimed spaciousness (2004: 8). In the Swedish caravan context however, where white is the dominating colour of the exterior surface, an interior white is addressed as a problem and a hindrance to sales. Whereas whiteness in the property market has the ability to increase value and speed up exchange processes, the example from the Swedish manufacturers points to a different colour logic established in the caravan market. Even if the manufacturer understands darker colours to make the interior space of a caravan look smaller, it is nevertheless thought to provide the mobile dwelling with a luxurious character.

When we strolled the trade fair in 2015, Benny and Louise expressed concern with all the new caravan models launching lighter versions of tree panelling. 'Too much light, it just doesn't work', Benny sighed. Personally they preferred 'cherry', a colour they think expresses luxury and quality. Frowning on the many white cupboards now gradually appearing in the 2015 model caravans, Benny and Louise connected the extensive use of lighter material to the German caravans. 'The Swedish caravans are darker, the manufacturers know how traditional we are', Louise says, as if reflecting the caravan manufacturer's view on 'traditional customers'. A link between dark, sober colours and what is perceived of as Swedish have historical roots in the development of particular aesthetics of Swedish modernity that came into being in the post-war period.[13] As ethnologists Orvar Löfgren and Tom O'Dell have suggested, in the 1950s and 1960s, Swedes confronted international influences with a middle-class definition of good taste 'defined in terms of the functionally subdued and the soberly rational' (O'Dell 2001: 108). Strong colours and large patterns, common in Germany, the United Kingdom or the United States, were associated with vulgarity, whereas the Swedish aesthetic was one of paleness, tranquillity and closeness to nature.

Swedish caravan manufacturers' and Swedish caravans owners' appropriation of a distinctive Nordic style as one of dark colours is however in contrast to the contemporary common features of Nordic interior design, where use of light wood such as birch and white and light colours dominate. This alternative aesthetic version of 'Swedishness' and how it is manifested in caravan colours and design needs however to be seen in relation to a second home or cabin heritage, characteristic of the Nordic societies.[14] Jonas, the Cabby sales manager, explicitly draws a parallel to the Nordic wooden mountain cabin aesthetics when explaining the use of darker colours. 'People seek the cosy factor', Jonas says. 'It is supposed to feel warm and cosy and give warm sentiments. You see that especially among those that do winter camping. It is the cosy feeling you find in a winter cabin.' Benny puts it this way: 'White makes it feel more spacious, right? But the caravan is the *mysfaktor* (cosy factor). It's supposed to feel warm. It's not cosy at all to creep into a white room to go to bed.' In the sales manager Jonas' and the caravanner Benny's reflections, certain types of textiles – wood and colours such as dark wooden tree – are associated with physical warmth (Fehérváry 2013: 8) and affectively resonate with a wider cultural association of the winter cabin's interior warmth.

In the context of the Swedish market and the discourse around colour and textiles, we can see that the caravan is valued as a product operating on the same aesthetic field as the second home or the cabin. Benny and Louise were eager antique buyers, filling their rental apartment in Lake Town with rococo furniture. However, they considered their caravan to be a space unable to accommodate their home aesthetics, apart from a few simpler Persian rugs, not considered of good enough quality for their apartment, but suitable for covering their caravan floor. British caravanners, however, express somewhat contradictory attitudes regarding the aesthetics of home and caravan. Clive and Sarah, one of the couples at Camping Mares, chose green textiles in their British-manufactured motorhome. Clive and Sarah refer to green as one of their favourite colours, and the choice of the motorhome interior reflects their taste of home interior. But upon choosing a model for buying, they were concerned with textiles that would last, or as Clive puts it, 'Many have these modern fabrics and they will go out of fashion. Therefore we went for the traditional.' Even though they lived in the caravan full-time for four years and were not especially careful, Clive is happy the textiles and the furniture do not appear 'worn out'.

In this case we see that the choice of textiles and materials is made with reference to the 'traditional' and materials that will last, with a clear link between aesthetic judgements of the house and the motorhome. The colour white's incompatibility with the caravan is however also brought up as an issue on Camping Mares, for example when one of the site's British couples purchased a so-called Roma caravan with white interiors that Sarah found 'horrible': 'It is all white, you know. All white. And the sofa, it is yellow!' Sarah adds that she actually just painted her kitchen at home white, 'but this is just different'. Sarah continues by saying that her dislike of the white can be explained by her being so used to a 'wood finish'. Her statement resonates with the Swedish caravanners' view on the white as a problematic colour, and the link between a wooden surface and the mobile dwelling.

Trading-up

Limited space puts severe restrictions on how a caravan can be constructed in terms of interior design. The internal spatial planning is however of great concern, reflecting not only aesthetic preferences, but also the considered capability of the caravan to adjust to social settings at the campsite. Many caravan manufacturers make models with a steep bowed front to ensure the best aerodynamics. The steep curve, however, creates a low inner roof in the front of the caravan. A conventional caravan will have the sofa group in the front, and the bed in the rear part of the caravan. The creation of an inner lower roof space in the front, however, makes less room for the conventional placing of the sofa group, and several manufacturers have thus chosen to use this space for the bed. Benny and Louise experienced staying in a caravan with the bed in the front, and found it highly problematic. The requirement of backing the caravan onto the pitch, for security reasons, leaves the front of the caravan facing the road: 'And we were sitting there away from everything, just wondering what was going on.' This example illustrates the conflicts between a manufacturer's interest in making the most of the caravan's interior compartment and the actual placing and use of the caravan in the caravanners' social environment.

Manufacturers' weight restrictions are also critical. The maximum weight allowed on European roads limits the possibilities of both manufacturers and caravanners when dealing with the size of the caravan. EU directives and legislation on motor vehicles and trailers state that a loaded caravan must not exceed the towing ability of the car.[15] The legislative limitations make it hard to keep big caravans within the weight limits, and manufacturers need always to balance on a difficult edge when making changes in the interior or exterior of a caravan. Even so, manufacturers' statistics show that the average length of Swedish caravans is steadily increasing. When we met at a trade fair in 2014, Jonas, the Cabby market manager, pictured the future of the caravan industry as operating with two different categories of travellers: those that move and those that stand still. He imagined the industry having to produce even bigger and heavier models for those that use their caravans full-time or seasonally and transport them directly to the site, thus bypassing the weight limits on towing vehicles.

Swedish caravanners speak of the process of acquiring a new caravan as one of *byta upp sig* (trading-up). Trading-up refers both to size and standard, while a referral to downsizing usually refers just to the actual size or length of the caravan. The acquiring of a bigger and more technically advanced caravan often takes place within a process of trading-in, where the older-model caravan is returned to the retailer for them to sell second-hand, and the couple receives a new model caravan in exchange for the old caravan and (usually) a larger amount of money. Some retailers are sceptical to traded-in products they don't know very well, as they normally operate with two brands. Many traded-in products also impose a great challenge on the manufacturers. Lots of second-hand products stored at the retailers cause a slow turnover. Parallel to dealing with retailers or manufacturers is a huge second-hand market, where caravans and motorhomes are sold and bought by private individuals, using advertisement space in newspapers or caravan magazines, or most commonly, on second-hand internet sites.

Benny and Louise provide an example of how a trading-up process might look. In 2000, they bought a second-hand '89 model German caravan. After four years, they wanted a caravan that was 'bigger and more comfortable', so they ended up buying another second-hand German caravan on the internet and selling their other caravan. The new caravan had possibilities for additional beds and they liked the textiles and fabrics. It was very wide, so at first Benny felt like he was 'towing a whole house'. They experienced some problems with the second caravan – humidity damage and electricity trouble – but had no intention of buying a new one when, in 2010, on their way to IKEA to buy a shelf for the caravan, they ended up having a look at their local retailers. The brief visit ended with a turn-in of their German caravan for a brand new Swedish model. It was nothing they had really planned, but Louise thought it looked nice and it had a central vacuum cleaner (which she now regrets and wants to have removed). They negotiated, got the bigger roof window they wanted and a mosquito net door and bought it.

A common argument among caravanners is that to prevent the caravan from losing economic value, the process of trading-up should be done regularly, around every two or three years. Some couples and families I met at the trade fairs changed caravans every other year, both to prevent the loss of economic value, but also in a continuous hunt for a better model. The processes of exchange and trade-ins also point to the centrality of the caravan's temporal character. Here, value is created through temporality and mobility. This way of creating value in a temporal process of exchange is similar to that of the car, where a speedy and regular exchange is considered a way of maintaining economic value. Benny and Louise, however, doubted that a frequent trade-in process had any economic gain at all, particularly since you get a better price for a caravan when paying directly in cash than with a trade-in product.

Considerations of trade-in and exchange also reflect the estimated lifetime of a caravan. Benny and Louise considered that a caravan should last thirty years, 'if you take care of it'. Taking care of the caravan, they argued, meant making regular check-ups of gas systems and humidity, and if necessary replacing the parts that have become damaged and plastics that don't last. Touring with a caravan necessarily wears it down more easily, and Benny found there to be crucial differences between the national models. 'German caravans have the tendency to look older earlier', he claims. A caravan's death is usually caused by humidity. 'Humidity in a caravan is like rust on a car', Benny argues. Humidity can sometimes be caused from a leak inside the caravan, but commonly it is a consequence of the weathering being worn down from outside, or as Benny puts it: 'Nature takes it.' Benny and Louise's statements show that nature is considered as a threat to the caravan, destabilizing its material qualities and eventually causing decay.

Home-like mobile dwellings

The previous discussions in this chapter point to the ambiguous character of the caravan evoking connections both to 'lightness' of mobility, but also to the solidity and stability different actors tend to associate with the house sphere. The material development of the caravan illuminates the role of different materials and their qualities in the production of products that in the public opinion have been perceived of as either 'solid' or 'weak'. Retelling the story of caravan product development in a variety of booklets and written sources, caravan clubs and enthusiasts emphasize for instance the negative impact the Second World War in particular had on the caravan's materiality. The 'weaker' models built in this period are claimed to have led to the enduring dubious reputation of the caravan, at least in the UK.

These controversies also reveal a material clash: between the lightweight materials believed to facilitate easier and smoother mobility for the caravan, and the heavier weighted materials that alter this easy mobility, but that still are used in production to ensure stability and endurance. However, the agency of materials such as wood, aluminium and plastic can go beyond the intentions and powers of caravan manufacturers and caravan owners. The caravan's material properties and their encounter with weather, with rain, damp and heat, can ontologically change the materials themselves inflicting floors and walls with bulges, leaks and smell.

As European manufacturers struggle to develop more 'solid', but still 'light' and mobile products, the uniform use of materials and designs has led to the development of what I would term a 'conventional caravan'. Industry actors are well aware of this potential challenge, but the reluctance to make drastic changes in exterior or interior is established with reference to a 'traditional customer': one who is sensitive to change.[16] By only looking to their own customers when doing market surveys and making changes in products, the manufacturers seldom make real changes at all, but reproduce the caravan in its conventional form. The example of sensitivity towards colour is particularly interesting, as it shows how caravan aesthetics are separate from the aesthetics of house dwellings. The upcoming chapters show, however, that the ways caravans are inhabited at a campsite may differ considerably from the products manufacturers and retailers construct and caravan buyers initially imagine.

2

Camp: 'You like to be visible'

Kalle and Lena's caravan is parked on a quiet corner pitch protected by the shade from a tall birch tree. While Kalle's brother Benny's caravan is 10 metres away across the lawn, the generous size of the pitch has allowed the couple a separate barbeque area and a table with benches to gather around for afternoon coffee or beer with the neighbours. Kalle who works at the nearby factory and Lena who is a caretaker, have rented a seasonal pitch on Lake Camping for the last twenty years and live on the campsite from May to September. Close to the centre of Lake Town they have a three-bedroom apartment, which is their home for the remainder of the year. While we sit around the spacious awning table decorated with a Swedish midsummer pole in mini version, Kalle shows me old photos from how it all used to be before the rebuilding and improvements, when the site had more vegetation. Lena admits she misses the hedges between the pitches and the tight rows of caravans. The pitches were narrower back then, and the caravans were parked so close, only separated by the low hedges, 'creating a community environment', she explains. Although Kalle and Lena enjoy the standards of the new service building, they miss washing the dishes outside. When the sinks were located outdoors, the men would do the dishes and have a whisky together. 'It was actually much more sociable at the old site', Lena sighs.

The transformations of Lake Camping point to central controversies regarding the spatial planning and infrastructural development of the modern campsite. Historically, the campsite took shape as part of a greater motorized camping expansion, raising issues of free access to nature, working-class leisure and privatization of municipal property. The progress of European camping during the twentieth century carried important influences from American car culture,[1] but in contexts such as Sweden, camping also became part of a larger political and deeply moral project in creating the modern citizen, primarily guiding the working classes in how to spend their leisure time.[2] Camping was something that needed to be taught and learnt as part of living the good life 'correctly' in particular materialized forms. But even today, daily use of the campsite's infrastructural spaces takes place within a moralizing discourse of social and material systems, reproducing particular ideas of an orderly nature that are literally built into the camping phenomenon.

The term *camp* derives from Latin *Campus*, which actually means 'open field, level space'.[3] The camp as a spatial and social formation has gained considerable attention from scholars, read as a sphere of surveillance, discipline and violence.[4] The camp, the ethnologist Orvar Löfgren (1999) argues, is a spatial and social formation typical of the twentieth century, introducing not only summer camps, fitness camps and nudist camps, but also military camps and refugee camps. 'Although these two categories of camp belong to very different spheres, they have elements of a common structure – the idea of large scale, detailed planning and control, self-sufficient communities with clear boundaries' (Löfgren 1999: 256).

The historical threads that converge and materialize in campsites such as Lake Camping and Camping Mares point to the complexity that surrounds the mobile dwelling. While these various histories are brief, divergent and at times unsatisfactory, as explanatory scenarios they raise issues of the moral tensions between politically informed ideologies of collective use of space as well as modernist visions of individualized mobility (cf. Harvey 2011). In these tensions we find a balancing of freedom and control, expressing as such 'utopic ideas of freedom and order' (Hetherington 1997: 12). While the previous chapter looked at the caravan's potential mobility and material qualities, in this chapter attention shifts from the materiality of the caravan to the campsite infrastructure.[5] By briefly outlining some of the historical and current particularities of the campsite phenomenon, in the following pages I discuss how mobile dwellings, through the process of *hooking up*, form conjunctions with the site infrastructure upon which they are parked.

Orderly nature

When the municipality of Swedish Lake Town decided to rebuild Lake Camping in the mid-2000s, it happened out of a general discontent with the present state of the campsite. The campsite housed about sixty full-time residents, in a variety of mobile dwellings. Whereas some of them had moved to the campsite out of their fondness of camping life, others found themselves at the site as a result of a social housing agreement between the municipality and the private campsite owner. In the local media, and among tourists and seasonal caravanners, the site's infrastructure was regarded as run-down and even dangerous. Showers were at times electrically charged, if they happened to work at all. The municipality blamed the campsite owner and released him against his will from the contract. A zoning plan was developed, strictly regulating the use of the site, and 35 million Swedish Crowns[6] were invested in a complete rebuilding. But in 2009, the municipality of Lake Town realized that the newly built site was not generating enough money, and as part of a larger privatization of municipal property, the site was leased to one of the larger camping chains in Sweden.[7]

Gunnar, a Lake Town inhabitant in his forties and site manager, practically grew up on Lake Camping, where his family had a caravan on a seasonal pitch. In 2009 Gunnar was tasked to 'clean up', removing social clients from the site. The following year he introduced even stricter rules when demanding prepayment of overnight stays with a Visa card. Gunnar says it helps him control who is there. It is fair, he believes; it is the same rules that count for everyone: 'The Roma might come and say they only deal with cash, but we don't accept that. Without paying in advance you can also risk people leaving without paying. … In the end we are running a business here. You can say that the homeless have nowhere to go now, but you can't really feel sorry for everyone.' Gunnar now dreams of more new cabins to rent out, boat rentals and maybe helicopter rides, and a conference section with bubble baths and a spa. The seasonal guests are important in order to provide an income; in 2011 they were twenty for the winter season and fifty-six for the summer season. 'But it is important that they don't take over', Gunnar sighs. Quite frankly, Gunnar cannot understand the people who sit out here for six months a year: 'Just sit and talk? I wouldn't have anything to talk about anymore.'

Already in the 1960s, when Lake Camping was first established, European campsites had developed a relatively advanced spectrum of services and camping was starting to move away from the simple to a more resource demanding leisure form. Up until then, campsites were usually a field of land, with a kiosk and some form of toilet facility. While the great expansion of camping in Western Europe in the 1950s and 1960s was linked to car culture and increased leisure for working people, the mass turn to nature soon became a challenge and problem for local and national authorities. Orvar Löfgren (1999) writes about the expansion of unorganized camping taking place in seaside resorts in Sweden in the 1950s, which caused frustration in local communities.

The example from Sweden illustrates how the scepticism from local landowners towards unorganized camping put pressure on local municipalities to establish the first campsites. In the 1960s, local municipalities opened a range of publicly run campsites, aiming at providing inhabitants in need of recreation with a social and affordable choice. In the 1950s and 1960s, many farmers also saw the economic possibilities provided by camping and by the end of the 1950s, a range of campsites were built on the Swedish west coast (Löfgren 1999: 129). Camping guests now found their way to areas that traditionally had been the territory of middle-class cabin owners. In 1960s Sweden, some campsites began to see the tendency of families to return every year and privatize their reserved pitch with fences and gardens – an example of early seasonal caravanners (Löfgren 1999: 130).[8] Löfgren interestingly reads this as a gradual change of the campsite from that of 'transit post for nomads' to 'homes for steady regulars', a change coming as a result of growing working-class affluence making the caravan a less prestigious object (ibid.). This change in use also points to a transformation of the campsite as a place for temporal hook-ups into one of more stable and enduring connections.

While some early northern European campsites were municipally run to provide safe and accessible leisure to the people, camping soon became big business. Today we see a range of private actors in the campsite industry, many of them running sites in privileged coastal locations. In 2011, one of the media buzzwords circulating in the European press was *Glamping*, referring to forms of luxury camping or glamorous camping. One could read about Glamping sites offering overnight stays in tents with chandeliers or a Moroccan interior, and in the Netherlands a whole magazine is dedicated to Glamping or 'nature served on a silver platter', as one Swedish newspaper put it. This example illustrates a still existing tension embedded in the campsite as a controlled space in nature, historically attached to working-class leisure. For actors in the camping industry, this history is viewed as problematic, and one of the measures taken to prevent it has been an increasing commercialization of the sites, now offering a range of accommodation possibilities: cabins, mobile homes and motel sections. Parallel with the technological development of caravans and motorhomes, which, as we saw in the previous chapter, are increasingly becoming bigger, the size and standard of the actual pitch is also changing. Whereas a pitch in the 1970s and 1980s usually would consist of 60–80 square metres, the size of today's caravans demands a pitch size of 100–120 square metres, if taking into account national fire hazard legislation. Most pitches have electrical hook-ups, and for many seasonal caravanners, sewage and water connection has become standard. Some sites even provide a cable TV connection, as well as high-speed internet.

Stars and systems

One of the expressed goals of the Lake Camping rebuilding was the achievement of a campsite that could be rated with four stars by the Swedish national campsite organization SCR. In the era of welfare nationalism, from approximately 1930 to 1980, leisure and domestic tourism became a national integrative project in many parts of Europe, where 'making the modern tourist was part of making the modern citizen' (Löfgren 1999: 271). The car played a fundamental role in this politically charged development. In Sweden for instance, the car had a central part in fulfilling the Social Democracy, part of the promise of a better standard of living.[9] Camping as a mass leisure phenomenon in Scandinavia came into being by ways of peculiar adoptions of an American car culture of 'freedom' and mobility into the Social Democratic project.

The politics of camping, and its relation to nature, is similarly historically evident in the UK. In the post-war period, camping was promoted as offering a meaningful relationship with nature and an answer to the increasing problems of modern civilization (Morris 2003). In both Europe and the United States, correlations were made between family cohesion and the practice of camping (Löfgren 1999: 273). Caravan advertisements featured the modern nuclear family with clothes and camping gear reflecting the fashion of the period. Not only authorities, but also the camping clubs played a central role in producing and promoting an ethos of 'good camping'.[10] Camping organizations not only promoted camping as a leisure phenomenon, many of them also ran campsites and shaped camping practice through the introduction of order, regulation and systems.[11]

Health legislation has played a crucial part in the development and organization of the modern campsite. The health and hygiene hysteria politics visible in both Sweden and the UK from the 1930s until the 1960s was incorporated into the very making and structuring of camping. Campsite organizations implemented systems of classifications and star labelling similar to the ones found in today's camping catalogues, promoting standards of hygiene and sanitation (Østby 2014: 298). Today's systems of classifications that categorize the campsites that are members of national camping organizations appear in marketing material such as camping catalogues, operating with a scale of stars, evaluating a campsite on both their 'hard' and 'soft' values: hygiene, environment, service, recreation and activities. The spatial planning of a site and the regulation of movement, noise and dirt quickly became an object of concern. Already in the 1950s and 1960s, opening hours and the establishment of barriers for entering and leaving the campsite became a way of controlling mobility and of implementing time schedules. Fire hazard legislation informed the placement of the caravan on the pitch, allowing for easy towing and exit and a required distance between different caravans. Sites run by the caravan club would strictly execute the parking of caravans on neat, straight lines. Sites provided particular points for handling garbage and sewage, and how to take care of one's own matters was stated in camping regulations and on printed signs around the site. Tidiness and quietness also became vital parts of the many formal and informal rules, aimed at blending caravanners into 'a moral collective' (Østby 2014: 298).

Lake Camping's current regulations, a one-page printed sheet given to caravanners upon arrival, are common to all the corporations' campsites. Aiming at a range of behaviours and technical arrangements at the site, the regulations explicitly state the rules and norms of good camping behaviour: guests need a camping card to be allowed entry, all payment is done in advance, motor traffic is not allowed between 11.00 pm and 6.00 am, and otherwise only between the gate and your own pitch, pitches are to be kept 'orderly', playing ball on the site is not allowed, and neither is the washing of a car or a caravan. Any break with regulations justifies an eviction from the site at the guest's own expense. Whereas the controlled environment of the campsite is inscribed into formal rules, regulations and signposts, as I will show in the upcoming chapters, a range of informal codes of behaviour form part of the campsite's moral systems.

Another central measure of regulation at the campsite is payment systems. Transnational camping card systems have been developed over the years, providing information about the caravanner and allowing for the industry to partly control mobility on their campsites as well as more precisely direct promotion at their customers. At Lake Camping we see how the payment system and requirement of Scandinavian Camping Cards also have been used to control and regulate the types of camping customers allowed entry to the site and also the implementation of Visa card payment to regulate Roma and Traveller people's access to the site. Another incentive was Lake Camping's demand of one camping card per caravan unit, forcing a registration in the system to be allowed an overnight stay. These and other systems of control show how boundaries are maintained by regulating insiders and outsiders. Certain categories of people are regarded as outsiders to the camping community – not only by site managers, but also by the campsite regulars. As I will show, safety and security are of great concern to many campsite dwellers. They regard their caravans particularly vulnerable to intruders and other dangers, but also see the campsite as a space that allows for a visual and caring internal surveillance that ensures greater security. By now turning to Camping Mares, in the next sections I will discuss in what ways the mobile dwelling is materially connected to the campsite infrastructures.

Hooking up

Located along a Benidorm access road on the grounds of a former orange grove, Camping Mares' spatial structure is similar to that of a small village, where a central street ramifies further into a structure of districts separating areas of permanency and areas with a shifting number of camping units. Compared to other countries in western Europe, Spain's development as a camping nation started at a later stage, and came mainly as a result of a demand for accommodation from the many northern European tourists invading the Spanish coast after the era of Dictator Franco. Spanish campsites were thus developed on models of their European counterparts.[12] Camping Mares' spatial planning resembles a traditional western residential areas, just at a different scale, and its technical infrastructure is exploited to the maximum to ensure cost-effective development. Rationally and effectively built, the site offers water posts centrally placed along the road, and electrical hook-up posts located on each pitch. Since the main spatial function of the site is the actual traffic and parking of cars and caravans, the street network dominates the area. The established 'permanent' area where caravanners such as the Welsh couple Gary and Margaret have their caravan, is localized at the very far end of the site, thereby protecting it from traffic and temporary guests on the remaining area.

At Camping Mares, the site's division into 'permanent' and 'touring' districts strictly informs the ways the mobile dwelling is connected to the campsite. The division suggests two main different modes of connection that contribute to how caravanners constitute their relationship with the site. The term *hook-up*, used among caravanners when referring to the electric connection between a caravan and the campsite infrastructure, can here serve as an analytical entry point to examine the wider connections between the site, the caravans and

Figure 5 Electrical Hook-Up (photo by the author).

their residents. On the permanent area, located at the very far end of the site, electricity cables, water and sewage drains are laid to the edge of the pitch, in one position. Caravanners, if they are not able to do the work themselves, usually employ a local handyman to take care of providing the actual connection between the hook-ups and the caravan. Camping Mares' permanent caravans are usually sold on in a chain of different owners during their lifetime. For most permanent caravanners then, their caravan is already hooked up with the caravan infrastructure in an invisible connection (cf. Lea and Pholeros 2010).

The hook-up makes connections between different components in the system, and in the case of the permanent caravans on Camping Mares, these connections, while at times stabile and invisible, are also perceived of as weak. The weakness of their nature is partly blamed on what the residents see as a qualitative difference between a site infrastructure and that of a regular house neighbourhood. Weakness is associated with what some residents see as a fragile and low capacity of drains and cables, which they also find related to the Spanish campsite owner's reluctance to make larger economic investments in modernizing the site, and the local management's incapacity to take proper care of the existing infrastructure, or as Lucy so frankly put it: 'These Spanish pipes are just rubbish!'

The relatively fixed connection between the permanent caravans and the site infrastructure differs from that found on the site's touring area. On the touring area, electrical hook-up points, similar to those found on Lake Camping, are placed on the inner edge of each pitch. Through the cable that crosses the pitch the connection is utterly visible, and regarded by the caravanners as particularly sensitive because of its direct exposure to nature. Some caravanners express great concern with the electrical connection to their mobile dwellings and are usually loaded with stories of bad connections, when cables become charged in damp grass or fail to work. But the form of the hook-up also regulates site residency in specific ways. The relative fixity of the prolonged connection between the hook-ups and the permanent caravan is one component of these mobile dwellings' actual stasis and fixedness. Here, the caravan's potential mobility is altered through the caravan's infrastructural connection with the site.[13]

Despite their diverging form in terms of regulating residency and mobility at the site, for both 'permanents' as well as seasonal caravanners at Camping Mares' touring area, the hook-up nevertheless produces a visible and regular connection between management and clients. On Camping Mares, full-time permanents, as well as long-term stays on the site's touring area, exclude the costs of electricity. Each pitch, both permanent and touring, is provided with a metre[14] that counts the monthly electricity use. Caravanners will visit the campsite reception on particular days of the month when the site manager Carlos is available to be charged for their monthly use of electricity. With electricity prices rather high in Spain, the use of electricity for, for instance, heating and cooling arrangements, is an object of control and concern among caravanners. One of my informants would once a week bring her portable washing machine to the main electricity outlet outside one of the toilet blocks to do her washing of clothes to avoid increasing her own electricity bill. The electrical hook-up also reveals potential clashes between the numbers provided by the metre and the caravanners' own estimates of electricity use. On several occasions I witnessed how Camping Mares' residents would disagree with a high electricity charge, blaming the counting ability of the metre or equally the management's control of the metre.

Toilet blocks and the mobility of matter

Clive, one of the British motorhome dwellers at Camping Mares would spend most of the day walking around the site talking to people and I would often run into him wandering on the street with an empty bucket or water bottle. When I ask him what he actually does on his walks, Clive grins 'Oh, that's a mystery. Empty the loo and the water. Can go fill a bottle and be away for half'n hour. That's what camping is all about'. On Lake Camping, as well as on the touring area of Camping Mares, pitches do not provide sewage and water hook-ups. Specific points on the campsite are thus dedicated to filling fresh water and caravanners' handling of waste and dirt. Through designated and guided solutions for handling dirt and matter in the site's public areas, performed by physical acts of filling and emptying, the site consists of regular routes followed by the caravanners. These routes of wastewater containers and water buckets are highly gendered, since among the caravanners these tasks are considered 'male', requiring a high degree of physical strength. Through their mobility, bodily matter moves into the semi-public realm of the campsite as semi-visible components.[15] Taking care of one's own matter also represents a different kind of relationship between the caravanner and the campsite, in which the caravanner, at least temporarily, takes responsibility for the removal of bodily matters. The bodily matter's movement from one point to another along the campsite streets thus contributes to a domestication of the campsite's semi-public sphere. Here, the nodal hook-up points, and the movement in between them, are also part of shaping of daily socializing on the site.

A process of domestication however, extends into the very function and workings of the campsite's common toilet blocks, which, in the case of both Lake Camping and Camping Mares, become nexus of social encounters and control. To avoid regular emptying of the caravan or motorhome's wastewater container, on Lake Camping as well as on Camping Mares' touring area, caravan toilets are usually only used for emergency or at night, and as my neighbours nicely put it, 'only for a pee-pee'. Here, the use of campsite-provided sanitary facilities is regarded a practical solution, avoiding extra and unpleasant work. But an extensive use of the site's toilet blocks is more importantly regarded a necessary means of preventing the wearing down of private caravan property.

The last point comes out even more clearly when looking at the practices of Camping Mares 'permanents'. While older-model caravans do not have a proper toilet, most of the residents on Camping Mares own caravan models manufactured in the 1990s or later, which all have furnished bathrooms. However, the permanent hook-up does not prevent the extensive usage of the common toilet and shower blocks. The reasons for avoiding using the toilet, or as some put it, 'no poo-poo in the caravan', are several. One explanation is located in the limited space of the caravan interior, and the risk of undesirable smell; reflecting what anthropologist Brian Moeran points to as the inability of smell to be disassociated from their causes and effects (2007: 156). A problematic link between smell and intimacy comes out in the caravanners' frequent explanation of the limitation of toilet use, as well as indoor cooking, because of the contained space's vulnerability to smell. Another reason why the shower blocks are preferred instead of the private caravan relates to the capacity of the campsite drains and sewage systems. The hook-up between the caravan and the pipes is regarded a potential point where unwanted matter can get stuck and cause problems. The caravan, hooked up with the campsite infrastructure, is thus unable to handle the actual basic necessities involved in full-time site dwelling.

Known among British regulars as the shower or toilet blocks (*baños* among the Spanish), the three sanitary buildings at Camping Mares have different locations on the site, with the building located in the permanent area being the most spacious. The mural building is divided into separate wings for men and women, each section consisting of six shower cabins, with a wall of sinks and mirrors on each side, separating the shower part from that of the eight toilet stalls. During specific hours of the day, usually in the morning and late afternoon, the toilet blocks are particularly busy. Sometimes, queues will be built for the afternoon shower, leaving women with bikinis or only towels wrapped around their bodies waiting in line. In the morning hours, the streets of the site will be frequented by caravanners in morning gowns or towels, carrying their toiletries in a small bag, heading for – or returning from – the toilet block, extending domestic bodies and practices into the public outdoors. For permanent caravanners, visits to the sanitary building are highly routinized procedures, performed at times of the day when queuing is unlikely. Margaret, one of the permanent caravanners on the site, explains that she knows everyone's hours and when they are usually to be found in the shower blocks. 'There is this old lady down here, she is over 80 and lives alone, and if I haven't seen her in the showers, I will go and check if she is ok.' Meetings outside or inside the toilet block are also encounters for the sharing of information and gossip about current events on the site. Thus, the toilet blocks also become locations for social control, where caravanners are familiar with their neighbours' daily visits and a sudden absence might cause concern of illness or unexpected happenings.

At both Lake Camping and Camping Mares moments and periods of disruption with the regular order are looked upon as highly problematic. During busy holiday periods and weekends, the toilet blocks can move from being sites of predictable order to embedding disruptive disorder. On both campsites, we see how a lack of order – of extended socializing, breaks with accepted time frames or spilling and displacement of matter, water or paper – is usually associated with specific types of people that, according to regular caravanners, 'do not know how to behave on a campsite'. On Camping Mares both the 'Spanish', 'Travellers', or young people visiting from the UK are potential disruptive elements, while on Lake Camping, visiting tourists are regarded as more unpredictable than the regulars that are usually known to take better care of the common areas. Whereas order appears built into the very organization and planning of the campsites, identifying potential elements of disruption thus forms part of a highly moralizing discourse of appropriate spatial behaviour. The remaining part of this chapter will engage with what caravanners see as disruptive elements and how a fear of the outside has caused extensive security measures at the campsites.

When the refugees came to Lake Camping

In the wake of what media during 2016 termed a European 'refugee crisis' Lake Camping was suddenly placed in the middle of a heated immigration debate in Sweden. Due to the high demand for temporary refugee shelters, the migration authorities made agreements with campsite owners, hotels and a range of left-behind tourism facilities all over Sweden in order to house refugees during the tourism low season. On a cold winter day in 2016, seventy families, most of them from Syria, were installed in the well-equipped cabins at Lake Camping, located on the central part of the campsite, a one minute walk to the street where Benny and Louise and their neighbours have their caravans parked year-round. The refugees' arrival was the result of a 20 million Swedish Crowns[16] deal between the joint stock company that runs Lake Camping and the migration authorities. But the contract was only seasonal however, and by the end of April the refugees, months after having started their integration process in Lake Town, were moved against their own will to other temporary housing facilities. The situation in other parts of Sweden was similar, and media reported on how investors and entrepreneurs made big business out of housing refugees in campsite cabins and even caravans.

On Lake Camping, the decision of housing refugees was met with protests from many of the regular campsite guests. As the decision was made official, several of the couples that had booked their pitch for the winter season cancelled their booking and got their money back. Sitting in the shade on the wooden veranda outside Benny and Louise's caravan on a sunny day in May 2017, Benny and Kalle recall the reactions both they and their neighbours had. One neighbour had loudly exclaimed, 'If anyone touch anything on my property they will regret they ever came here'. But nothing was touched and nothing happened, the couples admit. Actually they had hardly seen any of refugees, Louise says, just sometimes spotted the children playing outside. Also during the winter of 2017 refugees were housed at the campsite, but this time a lower number.

The situation at Lake Town points to how desperate authorities' need for temporary dwellings in a pressed housing market has led to tensions between old and new campsite dwellers. Some of the conflicts regarding campsites reveal the still existing tension between permanent versus temporary dwellings, and the seasonality of the campsite landscape was already an object of concern in the post-war period. In the case of the UK, families who had been left homeless by the war and were permanent residents at the campsite had to move out of their pitches during holiday seasons to leave room for better paying customers (Wilson 1986: 190).[17] The anxiety of the unknown that led some of the Lake Camping caravanners to leave their seasonal pitches at the announcement of the refugees' arrival was strongly related to a fear of break-ins and protection of private property. And as the next section will show, among caravanners both in Spain and Sweden, one of the central issues discussed in relation to life at the site is security.

Camp and control

At Lake Camping, Benny and Louise had gradually become more and more cautious and aware of the exposure to caravan intruders. In 2012, they experienced a break-in in the awning during the night. And in 2014 a neighbouring couple woke up in the middle of the night, finding a man unknown to them in their awning. Telling him to go away, the man simply tore their caravan door open, 'even though it was locked and all', Louise says. The way the locked door had opened with such ease had scared all the neighbours and led Benny to install double alarms in the awning. Their neighbours Edward and Petra had a camera-based alarm system installed in their caravan and awning.

The material instability and potential mobility of the caravan home is thought of as being particularly exposed or vulnerable to intruders and robberies. Motorhomes and caravanners that have experience of touring and travelling abroad have stories about their cars being broken into and smashed windows, and the arguments for choosing a campsite and not roadside overnight possibilities or so-called free-camping revolve around an imagined or experienced safety and fear of robberies. The fear of intruders however exists also among the caravanners at guarded campsites. A general fear of break-ins, both at Lake Camping and Camping Mares, is articulated in a general scepticism or precaution towards apparent strangers. On one of my return stays on the Spanish campsite I was painfully made aware of this as I attempted to do a short survey on the site by knocking on doors. Five months pregnant and enthusiastically loaded with a bunch of papers in a plastic file I started walking around the site. My appearance at people's pitches caused a variety of reactions. While some were happy to answer the few questions for my survey, others were surprisingly unfriendly and sceptical. Later I am told that a young woman appearing with a plastic file under her arm and questions to ask about residency and mobility had caused many to believe I was a British government officer sent out to map their mobility pattern with the aim of stopping their social benefits. Others however, had more direct reactions to my spontaneous visit. Knocking on the door of a Belgian woman, she eventually brings her retired police neighbour around for support and accuses me of being part of a criminal league that is out to map their mobility pattern only to rob her caravan when she is back in Belgium. When I tried to continue the survey on some of Camping Mares' neighbouring campsites a few days later, I decided to ask for permission in the reception, only to learn that all the campsites in the area, including Camping Mares, have forbidden people to enter and personally contact their guests.

During the winter of 2013, there are several episodes that cause a stir at Camping Mares. Three break-ins take place on the same occasion and one of them in a caravan where an old man is asleep. As one couple retells the story, an 'Eastern European woman' was later arrested on one of the neighbouring campsites: she had been working as a cleaner in all the victims' caravans and given up information to others. Some of my informants living alone, had felt unease. Another informant couple assured me they felt anything but safe since they were on a dead-end road far from any possible escape route. The discovery of holes cut in the fences had nevertheless caused the campsite management to put up more solid fences around the site. 'Well, if they break in here they would probably feel sorry for us and end up leaving us something. They are looking for gold and we could never afford that!' one caravanner laughed.

Lucy says she feels safe at the site and that one needs to feel safe to be happy. Actually, she argues, it is safer at the campsite than in an apartment. 'If you live in an apartment, you can walk in that door and not see anyone for a month. Especially if you live in a corridor apartment. You will only say hello to your next-door neighbour. And if you live in an apartment in a residence that is only used in winter or summer, it will be empty great parts of the year', she adds. Her argument for safety on the campsite is one she shares with many of her neighbours and her concerns reflect the older age of many of the site's residents. Gary and Margaret, for example, emphasize the notion of visibility on the campsite, and its social control, as something that provides safety. 'You like to be visible', Margaret explains. Still, as we can see in the case of Camping Mares, there is simultaneously a discourse of continuous outside threat that raises security issues, and the expectation that the campsite should remove these threats.

Cars, controls and cameras

On Lake Camping, where issues of safety are less prevalent than at Camping Mares, there are no fences around the site, which is accessible both from the passing road, and from the woods that stretch along the lake. Car access to Lake Camping is however regulated by a gate that opens when the driver opens the window and scans an electronic key on the key reader installed on a pole by the gate. The key also needs to be scanned upon leaving the site. This electronic key, coming with the rental of a pitch, also gives access to the toilet buildings, showers and kitchen. The reception building is located after entering the gates, and the access area is observable from CCTV cameras. Campsite residents, such as Benny and Louise, who live at Lake Camping full-time from May to September and also spend weekends at the site during wintertime, find the security insufficient. Benny argues that he would have liked the site to be fenced off to ensure better control of people's mobility.

Camping Mares operates with a similar gate system as that of Lake Camping. During my initial fieldwork in 2010 and 2011, all cars that wish to enter the site need to swipe an electronic card to open the gate, otherwise you have to be let in by the reception staff. Another gate leads out of the campsite and is sometimes kept open during daytime. From the glass windows of the small reception building, located just beside the gate, the man on duty can control all cars and people entering and leaving the site, but there is no explicit control of walking guests. Exception can be made late at night, when the night guard occasionally asks entering persons for ID, but most of the times when we return home late after a quiz night on the nearby road, he is fast asleep in his chair.

Upon arrival, the passport or ID card of all guests is scanned and the registration number of the car taken, as is the full home address and telephone number. On one of my return trips to the site, two years after I last had shown my passport, I was made aware of the data storage system when the reception staff commented on my renewed passport photo. I was also automatically registered with the personal data of the Spanish husband of one of my Norwegian friends and his car as my accompanying guest, since his data was still in the system from a visit two years previous. In 2014, new gates were installed at Camping Mares, with no need to swipe a card, since the opening of the gate now was realized through an automatic registration of the car's plate number. The new system was causing irritation among the permanents at the site, annoyed with how the gate sometimes would not let them in, requiring from them to get out of the car to notify the reception. Other measures have also been implemented to increase caravanners' security. During the summer season, Lake Camping has a security guard making rounds at certain hours of the night. On Camping Mares, security guards also make nightly rounds, but mainly in the busy summer period. The lack of a present guard during the winter season is seen among the British as under-prioritizing the permanent residents at the site.

In 2013, the campsite management put in several new incentives to increase the security at Camping Mares, perhaps as a result of the break-ins that took place in the winter. New and more solid fences were installed around the whole site, as well as increased street lighting. Some were particularly stringently secured. The southern end of Camping Mares borders a poorly asphalted single street road that is used as a shortcut between two of the main Benidorm entrance roads. The road lies along an open field area scattered with abandoned houses, some of them taken over by families that campsite employees refer to as *gitanos* ('gypsies'), a few tied and tired horses and skips of garbage. The area is in deep contrast to the high-rise hotel and apartment buildings that shape the visual landscape of the centre of Benidorm, just some kilometres further down the road. Walking along the exterior road, Camping Mares is hidden behind walls and wire fences. High walls are prohibited by local law, so plants, bamboo and 'looser materials' are used to protect the inside from the outside. At specific points around the edges of the site, the top of the chain-link fences are armed with surveillance cameras.

The Camping Mares owner also runs a bigger campsite in the area with more permanent residents and where cameras were installed a few years back. Now CCTV cameras register movement around all the outer fences of Camping Mares, with five television screens installed inside the tiny reception building. 'It's a campsite, there are always people from outside', one of the receptionists tells me as we engage in a conversation about the new camera surveillance. 'Remember that this is the countryside. … From here to the market there are donkeys, abandoned houses. … Gypsies live there … it doesn't have to be the Gypsies, but they don't help either.' The receptionist, who is from the local area and has worked at the site for the last four years, thinks that what he defines as a general increased insecurity in Benidorm is partly a result of the European economic crisis: 'Today, in Spain, people commit robberies they didn't commit before. Because of the crisis. Benidorm is safe, but even in the market you were safer a few years back than now.' He has several theories on who is actually doing the break-ins. 'People come from abroad … from the East, from Colombia. A lot of them come for work, but there are those that come … and the systems they have … here in Spain we are not familiar with them. The ones that come from Eastern Europe have lived through war and everything.' The receptionist suggests that usually it is groups of 'Romanians' that raid one campsite after another. The receptionist thus shares a common imaginary among the caravan residents where the intruder or outsider is imagined as a 'gypsy' or 'Eastern

European', belonging to a group or league. But, he adds 'if there are robberies, it is hard to know whether they have come from the outside or it is someone from inside, because this is also like a village'.

Unlike the speculation among the British caravanners, the employee suggests that the robberies might also be committed from the inside – if not by a real insider then at least from someone with car access. 'You see, if there is a robbery and they take a television, they have to leave where they entered. They are not going to throw away the TV. It has to be someone with a car that has entered … there are people that come to do manual work … they have it all organised.' Despite the speculation around the ways crimes are committed, the employee doubts that camera surveillance is a solution. 'There is always someone who wants to enter, and can see if caravans are empty or if there is a place with no surveillance. But we can't close ourselves in with high walls and gates with electricity because the law forbids us to.'

Mobile containment

The Camping Mares receptionist's reflections on the security of the site point to several issues regarding the desires and legal possibilities for separating inside from outside through the construction of physical barriers. A growing academic literature on middle-class and upper middle-class gated communities, foremost in the United States and Latin America, shows how exclusion and segregation are materialized through an establishment of walls, gates and guards.[18] In *Behind the Gates* (2003), Setha Low makes the parallel between gated communities and mobile home parks in the US context. She describes how her adopted grandparents at the time of retirement moved into a mobile home park in Californian Orange County: 'Walled on all sides, with concrete lions marking the entrance, it was like a gated community but without the gate' (2003: 199). Low shows how, when the neighbourhood gradually changed into one seen by the elderly as ruled by Asian gangs and with increased crime, an electric gate was added.

A desire to separate inside from outside reveals many similar patterns between my findings at the campsite to those existing in the research on gated communities. This can be recognized in the attempts by the management of Camping Mares to gate the site, but more so through the residents' shared emphasis on safety and security and fear of robberies. Low's reflections on the

Figure 6 Campsite Gates, Camping Mares (photo by Terje Tjærnås).

links between retirement and gating are interesting when seen in relation to the current situation on Camping Mares. On the case of her grandparents' mobile home park, Low argues that the gating provided a 'sense of community' for what she identifies as elderly, white, working-class retirees: providing 'greater safety and psychological security' (2003: 201). Here, the gated community appears as an easy retirement option for retirees who find themselves in a complex period in life with not only worries about security and safety, but also an increased vulnerability in terms of changes in home values and services (ibid.: 218). Yet, she adds, the 'uneasiness' with changes in neighbourhood, and a desire for security and control are shared among all gated community residents, also the younger ones.

Despite the apparent similarities in terms of inside–outside divisions, the legislative, cultural and social components that form and shape the European campsite are historically and currently fundamentally different from that of the North American (and Latin American) gated suburban context. Looking at Camping Mares, I suggest that the campsite provides an example of gating 'from within'. With this I mean that in the processes of shaping permanent housing structures on temporary tourism conditions, a particular form of gating takes place within the leisure park infrastructure. So, in contrast to the planned, and often costly, gated community, we are here witnessing how similar assessments and values of safety and withdrawal create a particular form of phenomenon where the relatively affordable leisure-oriented campsite is transformed into informal – and partly guarded – housing.

In this setting, the spatial production of security is actually provided primarily by an internal valuation of visibility and the proximity of neighbours rather than the measures of security provided by the campsite management. To a lesser degree, but still apparent, this social control over neighbours through visibility is equally highly valued at the materially 'open' Lake Camping, as it is in the materially contained landscape of Camping Mares. The caravan's construction of material thinness and visibility thus produces a perceived safety among its dwellers. Simultaneously, as we have seen in the previous examples, these 'weak' material structures open up for a believed vulnerability to break-ins, for example. An awareness of this material instability nurtures a stronger social control among campsite residents.

Care, in this setting, also takes the form of mutual vigilance, a sensory surveillance, where keeping an eye out for one's neighbour is considered part of a caring community. The potential mobility that shapes the worlds of caravan dwelling also imposes particular tensions regarding the issue of safety. Unlike the rather fixed and material structures of the gated community, the campsite is materially constituted upon notions of openness. This material openness is reflected in how fences around the site are built within the same realm of material instability as those used to form the caravan dwellings. Still, the most apparent reason for the choice of materials that are 'open' and 'weak' has its cause in the legislative restrictions imposed on Camping Mares. More importantly, the campsite is based and economically relies upon a degree of fluctuating mobility.

People's comings and goings through overnight stays within a tourism sector is still an important economic basis, and maintaining insight and openness thus remains a commercial requirement.

Self-sufficiency hooked up

Through various hook-up connections, the mobile dwelling forms part of a wider social and material infrastructure of the campsite. It is interesting to note how a system of hook-ups both work in coalition with, but also alter a caravan self-sufficiency ideology based on the logic of potential mobility. Because of its material weakness and 'thinness', a caravan, we see, is dependent upon a complementary infrastructure to operate as a long-term and full-time dwelling. At the same time, the hook-up infrastructure provided by the campsite management is also regarded as irregular and 'weak', and the caravan's risk of being worn down is thus corrected with an extensive use of the campsite's common buildings that stand out as more fixed and stable. An extensive use of these buildings is seen as a right one should manifest and take advantage of, and among seasonal and full-time caravan dwellers the distinction between the private property on the pitch and the presumed ownership of common areas is rather blurred.

The developments at Lake Camping described earlier in this chapter bring in other aspects of the links between spatial planning and social behaviour, or at least the expectations of a clear correlation between dwellings and places 'designed to construct a collective life' (Humphrey 2005a: 42). The infrastructural rebuilding on Lake Camping had, at least according to its regular seasonal caravanners, a negative impact on the way social life was enabled. Seasonal caravanners' nostalgic memories of the old campsite contain central visions of idealized spatial behaviour that was made less possible as space between caravans increased and kitchen facilities moved indoors. These wistful reflections are also fed with particular historically moulded expectations of the campsite as a location of dense working-class sociality. As we will see in the following chapters, however, such expectations are continuously challenged when the campsite becomes an arena not primarily for leisure and tourism, but for full-time housing.

This account of the recent development on Lake Camping furthermore points to what can be identified as a temporal clash, revealing an anxious relationship between leisure and domesticity. While control of people's mobility has long been a challenge to the nation state, camping history illustrates that the immobile may become equally problematic when the presumed mobile caravans appear as – or are transformed into – static housing. Camping as a leisure phenomenon is built on specific expectations of seasonal activity. When the use of caravans and motorhomes go beyond these expectations associated with the mobile and highly temporal leisure dwelling, they may become problematic. Among working-class or middle-class people that have actively chosen the caravan as an alternative way of living, temporal clashes are articulated through an apprehensive relationship between leisure and domesticity. The following chapters dig into the making of troubling temporalities on and off the campsite, in situations where the caravan at the campsite has passed the asserted timeframe of the leisure landscape and has become part of a greater project of creating 'the good life'.

3

Circumstances: 'Why don't we just sell the house, all our things and leave?'

'We are hoping to win the lottery,' Gary smiles, 'but if we won the lottery we would stay where we are! If we won the lottery we would lead the same life. Just get a bigger caravan.' Margaret, so the story went, was the village girl who had continued school until eighteen and later ran her parents' newsagents. Gary was a miner's son and was only seventeen when he was sent to Hong Kong to dig out dead bodies from a landslide, a military career that would take him around the world for more than twenty years. Margaret was never allowed to attend the Saturday night dances where soldiers like Gary used to go out for night-time splendours on granted leaves. She often imagines how different her life would have looked like if they had only met earlier, but both had failed marriages behind them and several children each when they were in love. After having run Margaret's family business in Wales for a few years after getting married, they decided to apply for jobs in the British Camping and Caravanning Club. Over the course of fourteen years, they ran different campsites around the country, never spending more than three years at the same place. While working 24 hours a day during the summer season, they had the winter off, which allowed them long journeys to Spain. In 2004 they were both made redundant and tried to go back to Wales to get a job. They had kept their house during all these years without actually living in it, but had no luck in getting employment.

One day in 2008, Gary said to Margaret 'Why don't we just sell the house, all our things, and leave?' She thought about it for two days before she said yes. The recession had made things difficult in UK at the time, but in October they finally managed to sell their three-bedroom house with garden. Belongings and furniture were sold and given away and what they decided to keep was loaded into a big yellow Volkswagen van. In December they had to be out. They only had a ferry ticket to Bilbao on Christmas Day, all their belongings in the van and a towing storage room. As they rolled out of Margaret's daughter's driveway, her family waved at them when they drove into the sunrise. A sign on the back of the car said 'Don't worry – be happy.' Without a firm decision about where to go, they drove straight to the south-eastern coast of Spain, to Benidorm and Camping Mares, where they once had attended a caravan rally with the caravanning club in the late 1980s. On the site, which had not changed much in the last twenty years, they found a caravan for sale and an elderly lady ready to go home. The next day they were back with the cash in their pockets. This was on a Wednesday and on Friday she was out. She just packed her clothes into a suitcase and left the two of them with drawers full of things and five televisions to get rid of (Leivestad 2017a).

Chapter 2 showed how motorized camping as a European leisure phenomenon boomed after the Second World War and how campsites throughout the twentieth century developed into spaces created out of concerns related to safety and control. Caravans and campsites form conjunctions, I argued, through particular infrastructural connections that by their very nature challenge clear separations between mobile and static dwelling. In this chapter I turn to the people that inhabit these campsites, people for whom the caravan and the motorhome has become a primary home, or a seasonal extension of an already existing domestic dwelling. What are the reasons behind, and the consequences of, a life on wheels, be that on a full-time or seasonal basis? And how is life in a caravan on a campsite perceived, organized and financed? This chapter looks at both the reasoning around, and the consequences of, a turn to caravan life, identifying the overlaps as well as the disjunctures between aspirations and the actual agency and possibilities to fulfil them.

Margaret and Gary were both in their fifties when they decided to leave the UK and opt for a campsite life in Spain. Too young to receive public pensions, they used savings to fund their new lifestyle. A caravan life was still familiar to them, after having spent more than a decade as campsite managers. Margaret admits her children think they are 'a bit off the wall'. And the grandchildren call them 'grandma and grandpa caravan', compared to 'grandma little house' and 'grandma big house' back in the UK.

Margaret and Gary's move to full-time caravan life is portrayed in a specific narrative form that allows for an analysis of what kinds of fantasies and moral evaluations are involved in a campsite withdrawal. The first part of this chapter thus dissects caravanners' 'coming out' stories, showing how these revolve around narratives of rupture and change, as well as a rather vaguely formulated 'freedom'. Freedom in this context, I will argue, is intimately linked to the notion of potential mobility in which the caravan is perceived of as a home allowing one to 'move better', enabling a life away from 'stuckedness' (Hage 2009, 2005; Sneath et al. 2009). While the caravanners' coming out stories contain central elements of 'freedoms from and freedoms to' (Turner 1982: 36), this chapter points to the adjustments and compromises between what is dreamt of and what is encountered as possible. In the second part of the chapter, I turn to everyday realities as they are played out in two very different campsite contexts and the different economic arrangements that enable lives on wheels.

Claustrophobic houses and abundance of things

Edward, my neighbour at Lake Camping, is a tall man, whose height seems even more apparent when walking his tiny, noisy dog, or appearing next to his short and rather brusque partner Petra. After only a week at the campsite, Edward and Petra had literally built themselves in behind garden furniture and flowerpots, and their four-season awning was far better equipped than a regular apartment living room, with a glassed dinner table, a sofa with a table and a storage section (bought new from IKEA for 1,000 Euro) with photos of the family on display. A synthetic grass carpet lets humidity through in case of spillages, and covers the wooden flooring built underneath the awning. When asked to reflect upon their very recent decision to sell the apartment and move to live in a caravan on a campsite some five kilometres away from their neighbourhood, Petra says, 'There were many reasons. But we didn't have any debts or anything. It's nothing like that!' Edward interrupts:

> We were just tired of things! I was an only child and I inherited things from my mother, my father, my grandmothers and grandfathers, my uncles and aunts. It was just things, things, things. At one point we had three cars, two apartments, one boat and a summer cabin. And all the storage places full. You know, it's like that scene in Batman when one says the one who has most things when he dies wins. And I was very close to winning!

Petra nods in agreement. 'Life shouldn't consist of things. Do we really need all of this, we asked ourselves', Edward continues. 'You know', Petra interrupts, 'we had one bedroom we only passed through to reach the balcony … it had no function … we both like spending time outdoors, feel the fresh air. We both like the camping life.'

In Petra's version of the story it had all been decided one day at home. 'We sat in the sofa in separate corners. He was on the computer and I was watching television. This is just crazy, I said. Why are we sitting here? We might as well live in a caravan!' Petra had a friend who had just come to a similar decision, and her friend's decision to sell the house and move in at a campsite had seemed appealing to Petra: an actual opportunity to get rid of all the 'must dos'. Petra describes the following weeks as being full of doubts. 'Can we really do this, we thought? Have we got room for all the things? Will there be a caravan big enough for us to live in?' But after finding a caravan model they both could agree on, the couple sold their apartment and moved to Lake Camping.

Edward and Petra's story of their decision to become caravan residents is directed by a narrative of how an excess of things became unbearable and brought them to a crisis point. Edward and Petra link their choice of a caravan life into a strong argument on how things tied them down and prevented them from living the life they wanted. Other aspects of Edward and Petra's life have however changed very little in the course of moving. Edward is still driving the car to his job in public administration, and Petra's invalidity benefits ensures her days at home, walking the dog and decorating the caravan awning.

What these examples reflect are expressions of peculiar kinds of materialist critique. The caravanners at Lake Camping and Camping Mares do not place their own consumption or lifestyle within a wider environmental discourse. In this sense, their concerns are located far from the anti-materialist discourses found for instance among the urban well-educated middle class and among some lifestyle migrants. Nevertheless, the reasons for opting for a life on wheels are commonly retold in a narrative of a problematic excess of things. This narrative reflects what seems to be a common theme in popular discourse about domestic life uttered by contemporary Western urban dwellers. How can we understand the caravanners' critique of the consumption patterns associated with a house-led life?

Making recourse to the previous chapter, ideas about the simple life was deeply embedded in the very making of the larger camping project. Caravan and motorhome advertisements still visually place the caravan distanced from urban environments, playing on portrayals of freedom through mobility and closeness to nature. A wider caravan infrastructure in forms of campsites, service and neighbours is literally invisible in caravanning promotion material. In Margaret and Gary's retelling of their choice of moving from the UK, the house is framed as specifically problematic. As Margaret puts it, life in a house tends to 'tie you down in material things'. In the opening passages of the Introduction to this book, Margaret and Gary's friend Lucy also portrays the house as a dwelling that, despite its size, 'closes her in'. The expressed sense of feeling trapped in the house, I argue, should be seen in relation to the different nature of the caravan dwelling that in these narratives features as a viable option.

Downsizing to a caravan is also commonly seen as a withdrawal from practical and time-consuming tasks that come with the maintenance of a house or a larger apartment. In Sweden in particular, caravanners emphasize the easiness of managing the much smaller caravan domestic sphere where, as one caravanner put it, 'Wiping the floor takes me two minutes.' The caravan reduction of scale of domestic work thus forms part of its attractiveness as an alternative housing form (Southerton et al. 2001: 5). When caravanners try to explain what they mean by freedom as part of their caravan narratives, this reduction of housework is seen as a freedom from burdening and time-consuming housework tasks in the former house, which are often allocated to the women. The caravan comes however with its own housework demands and technical tasks that remain highly gendered. In both the Swedish and Spanish campsite context, one can note a general and rather traditional division of tasks, implying that men will collect water, empty toilets and perform the outdoor cooking, whereas the women take care of clothes washing and cleaning (see also Southerton et al. 2001: 5 on the same point). The fact that cooking is mainly enabled or preferred in an outdoor environment has in some cases nevertheless shuffled the responsibility and initiative of cooking to the men. One of the residents at Camping Mares complained she was not even allowed to cook anymore by her husband, who enjoyed standing outside in his kitchen tent, cooking a chilli and 'watching the world go by'.

In the negative portrayals of the house and its possessions lies also a referral to the complex economic arrangements tied up with a house-led reality, stretching from maintenance to taxation issues. Some caravanners see the caravan at a campsite as a withdrawal from such economic obligations, leaving them with a home sphere that is economically easier to handle. Whereas the caravan or motorhome carry other demands, such as road tax and MOT (the annual Ministry of Transport test), many caravanners find these easier to manage and less burdensome than the many bills piling up in the house. To John and Lucy for instance, the motorhome was portrayed as an actual economic improvement of their household economy, allowing them 'freedom to' spend money on leisure and drinks, rather than taxes and bills, as John put it.

From these different angles, the house is portrayed as problematic and seen as owning its residents rather than the other way around. The caravan, however, is seen by the caravanners as a housing option they remain in control of. The shift in housing arrangements is thus also regarded as a reshuffling of agency between the dwelling and its residents, and where the mobile, downsized caravan is one where its human owner remains in control. While freedom from the house thus is found in the mobile dwelling, it does not mean that the caravan dwellers refuse the house in all its forms, they still maintain that living in a house might be a good thing for certain periods over the course of life, when children are younger and there is an apparent need for more space. The caravan thus remains in this setting an alternative, perceived of as better in particular life instances. And whereas caravan narratives can circulate around a critique of the material abundance of modern life, campsite living still reproduces these material arrangements and house aesthetic in downscaled or miniature versions.

'It's our time now'

Whereas Edward, like many of his neighbours at Lake Camping, works full-time and the campsite was chosen out of a possibility to commute to work, the majority of the residents at Camping Mares on the other hand have funded their full-time camping life through public economic systems, in most cases pensions and invalidity benefits. One of these couples is Lucy and John, whose struggle in life is manifested in every inch of their bodies: in the bad knees, the crooked hands and the deep cough. Lucy and John's story is also one of change, but it is a change that has been anticipated for a long time. John and Lucy's plan was never actually to move abroad; it was Camping Mares that opened their eyes up to the possibility. Their dream had rather been one of travelling. 'But not moving', Lucy says, 'just travelling really, just going away.'

A dream of travelling abroad had followed them through the rough years of economic struggle, both left in economic debt by their former partners, the years of raising four children, and later grandchildren, hardly ever able to make ends meet. This dream had taken Lucy through her long days of demanding cleaning and care work for the local government, and it had followed John on his days and nights away from home, behind the steering wheel on the motorway. Confronted with the fact that their choice of a caravan lifestyle had implied leaving their children and grandchildren in the UK, Lucy quite simply put it like this: 'It's our time now. We've worked our whole life to be able to do this.'

Their new life in a motorhome was an achievement chronologically following a final termination of work. They both left school at fifteen; he ended up working for transport companies, while she had various council jobs as a cleaner and care assistant. They met in a bar in 1970, but it was hardly love at first sight. Lucy thought, 'Does he always look as ill as that?', whereas John, who did not appreciate Lucy's snobby appearance, said to his friends, 'I'd like to take her down a peg or two!' Some years later they nevertheless both said 'I do' at the local registry office, followed by a reception in the working men's club. In 2010, Lucy had retired a few years earlier, and John a year after her. They had always wanted to do something like caravanning, but John had seen so many caravans on the road and found them to be 'dangerous things'. A motorhome seemed safer. They had a lump sum from Lucy's pension and the van was bought in January 2008. Deciding that they wanted to travel abroad with it, 'Spain was the main destination ... because of the weather, and pricewise.' Their only experience from travelling abroad had been a few charter holidays. Holidays in England were just odd times with the kids and then mainly holiday camps when they could afford it. With the debts they were left with, it was seldom. 'But we got there, didn't we. It took a while, but we got there', John says.

During the first few years, Lucy and John toured Spain and Portugal in the motorhome. But travelling was expensive, and on Camping Mares they found stable weather and friends to return to. Return visits to the UK were only needed in summertime, first of all to do the MOT[1] on the motorhome, but in 2012 they bought a permanent caravan on site, funded by a loan. The rent on the campsite is paid with the incoming rent they get from their house in Lancashire, which is stuck in a slow housing market. Lucy and John's story of their way to caravan life consists of more elements of economic instability than those presented by the majority of their friends and acquaintances at Camping Mares. What many of them share though is the way caravan life is funded by pensions, and perceived as an alternative retirement option. When embarking on their first motorhome journey, Lucy and John were still in good health. The decision to opt for a caravan lifestyle can in other cases be closely linked to severe illness or other life-changing events. As such, these narratives stress the importance of specific events that act as stationary markers where time is punctuated (Adam 1990: 99; Guyer 2007). Among the residents I met at Camping Mares, the survival of cancer is a common experience. Such experiences of grave, and often life-threatening, illness make many decide to take the step to travel and go abroad before it is too late.

While in his fifties, John and Lucy's friend Clive fell seriously ill with a difficult and rare type of cancer. In 2011, in his mid-sixties, slim, grey-haired

Figure 7 Campsite Couple (photo by Terje Tjærnås).

and tanned, with a murderous sense of humour, a broad Geordie accent and a toothy smile, he often recalls how the illness took away his black hair and beard, his big muscles and his physical strength. But it did not take away Clive's life. 'There are only 27 like me in England,' he would say, sometimes showing an impressive scar crossing his stomach. 'Now I wake up every morning, look at the sun and say "cheers", referring both to his enjoyment of life and his love of alcohol. Clive had been working for the same employer for forty years, working his way up from a young apprenticeship to manager. He worked long days, every day of the week, hardly seeing his children growing up. Trying to return to work after recuperating from the cancer, his joy and engagement was gone. Clive left, but with a solid private pension to live on. Sarah, more than ten years younger than him, had not even turned fifty when she decided to leave her job and enjoy life together with her husband while she still had him around. After having spent twenty years caravanning in England with the children during holidays and weekends, they bought a motorhome and went abroad. In addition to six months at Camping Mares, they also go travelling in other European countries before they return home only for a few weeks in the summer. Clive and Sarah kept their house in the UK, and are now spending their savings to lead this life, 'The house will be the only thing that will be left for the children, so they can fight over that.' The awareness of the fragility of life made Clive and Sarah fulfil the travelling plans they had nurtured through many working years in the UK.

Lucy and John's decision to try motorhome life as a retirement option, and Clive's turn to full-time camping after severe illness, point to how a caravan lifestyle is commonly opted for at a certain point in life. Retirement and pensions not only financially enable ways of permanent leisure: a withdrawal from working life usually overlaps with a decrease in family engagement in terms of economically providing for children. To Lucy and John, retirement opened up a realm of possibilities for physically withdrawing from a working-class Lancashire environment that had been their everyday reality for more than sixty years.

8 × 8 metres of freedom … from what exactly?

Based on caravanners' obsession with a reference to what they term 'freedom', it is possible to argue that the camping dwelling's historical link with leisure practice, deeply grounded in the capitalist industrialized division between 'work' and 'non-work', continues to inform the way it also is perceived as a housing or alternative dwelling option. It is a separation of work and leisure that is based on an old industrial model, and that stands in contrast to the aspects of flexibility that have come to characterize the new economy.[2] Whereas a clear structuralist division between work and leisure is no longer considered academically valid (see Coleman and Kohn 2007: 10–12), the link between leisure and freedom and what such a connection represents for caravanners remains important. As part of a specific temporal framing – a *present continuous*, full-time and seasonal caravanners at Camping Mares and Lake Camping frequently re-establish a sharp contrast between work and leisure, wherein 'work is represented as drudgery', containing 'little intrinsic satisfaction' (Clarke and Critcher 1985: 2). Inasmuch as the campsites are transformed into places for long-term or full-time housing, they still remain or are transformed into, as we will see in the last part of this chapter, places of particularly class-based leisure modalities.

J. B. Jackson makes a useful attempt at placing the caravan within a discourse of freedom that is not necessarily based on a leisure–work opposition. He argues that the significance of the temporary mobile dwelling also lies in 'the freedom from burdensome emotional ties with the environment, freedom from communal responsibilities, freedom from the tyranny of the traditional home and its possessions; the freedom from belonging to a tight knit social order; and above all, the freedom to move to somewhere else' (1984: 101). Jackson thus resonates along the lines of many of the discourses that are raised in the caravan narratives of the caravanners at Camping Mares and Lake Camping; the perceived freedom lying in the withdrawal from family ties and obligation and from the 'tyranny' of the conventional house and the possessions 'owning their owner'. He importantly adds though a central element of freedom: that of the possibility to move provided by the mobile dwelling's *potential mobility*. What Jackson terms the 'freedom to move somewhere else' resonates with caravanners' own reference to the possibilities enabled by the mobile dwelling. The potential of the wheels makes them feel free, as they enable one to move 'whenever one wants'.

Caravanners' perception of 'freedom' as intimately related with the ability to move places the caravan within a larger historical and moral framework of leisure and modernity, wherein its wheels play a fundamental role. In caravan and motorhome advertisements that appear in newspapers and caravan magazines, 'freedom' is less attached to the unknown than to the familiar landscape. The caravan or motorhome not only produces mobility through its wheels, but provides certain forms of security, safety, comfort and familiarity by also being a home. As such, the unfamiliarity of the road needs always to be balanced by the familiarity of the home on wheels that is safely parked. This is not to understate the observation that a possibility for geographical mobility feeds an imaginary of a wider mobility potential, in the words of Ghassan Hage, 'a sense that one is going somewhere' (2009: 97). Freedom in this sense is related to a withdrawal from what Hage, with reference to an existential immobility, calls 'stuckedness', into a sphere where one 'moves better' (see also Humphrey 2005b).

Caravanners' narrative accounts of withdrawal, embedding 'freedom from' and 'freedom to', entail a move into the present continuous, a spatiotemporal location wherein the stories of change are retold. A caravan everyday is here understood in contrast to the house-lived reality found in the past. A present continuous is thus a temporal location. Still, the present continuous contains adjustments between what was envisioned, and that which came to be. So, where this first part of the chapter recomposed retrospective narratives of change, I am now turning to these adjustments by tuning in on the organization and experiences of everyday life at the campsites.

'People like us, we are the same everywhere'

It is Midsummer Eve at Lake Camping. Benny, Louise, Kalle and Lena are throwing a midsummer party on the lawn just across the road that separates our caravan row from theirs. From our unsteady camping chairs that came with the rental caravan, my partner, daughter and I can from a distance watch and hear the thrilled voices, increasingly louder as the evening advances. While we light the barbeque at 5.00 p.m., all our neighbours seem to start at 6.00 p.m., and having finished the food before the others have even started, we spend the rest of the night watching the neighbours partying, visiting the playground, buying ice cream at the restaurant and sitting down to watch again. Some months later, I learn that Benny had wanted to ask us to join the party, but feared that we might want to spend the evening alone since we did not make the first move. Occasionally someone passes our caravan on their way to the toilet. My tiny '78 model is parked at a strategic spot, in the middle of a potential crossing path for the row of caravans opposite the road to reach the service buildings and shower blocks without having to take a longer route by following the road.

Now, as the midsummer evening evolves, I meet Louise, accompanied by a man around thirty, asking if we have had a good night. Louise's friend is drunk, leaning towards me as he says, 'I heard you are writing a thesis … well I'll tell you something now.' He and his wife used to be seasonal caravanners on this road, for two years. But since his son did not like it very much they decided to leave it. 'But when we came here today, I actually started to cry. And me, a builder, I should be a hard man, but I just … .' He throws his arms around Louise, rambling on about how much he has missed everyone. 'We are all like a big family', he sobs theatrically, recalling the events yesterday when his car broke down when they were towing the caravan back home from the west coast. It cost him 8,000 Swedish Crowns[3] to get it back. Those were the happy times when he had the caravan here and could just go out every weekend with no hassle, he sighs.

This Midsummer Eve of 2011, spent close to, but not really together with, my caravan neighbours, raises several issues of how social life and seasonal mobility plays out at Lake Camping. Louise's drunken friend misses what for most neighbours at Lake Camping is an important part of how life is constituted: the seasonal mobilities between an apartment and the caravan, or in other cases, one mobile dwelling that is moved between the campsite and work. Whereas the first part of this chapter presented narratives of change, where life at a campsite is placed in opposition to the imagined and experienced downsides of modern, urban life, the reality of Lake Camping tells another story. It is a story of how ideals of sociality are constantly being negotiated against a backdrop of tensions between maintenance of privacy and the collective discourses of a caravan community.

Some weeks after the midsummer celebration, I find myself more included in the neighbouring sociality of Lake Camping. One evening, I make my way across the lawn with a bag-in-box wine chosen for its appropriate name, *Chill Out*, and a plastic wine glass, to the wooden table and benches in front of Kalle and Lena's caravan. The sticky heat of the July day has given way to a chilly breeze and the need to put on fleece jackets over summer t-shirts, and trousers over sunburned bare legs. Louise's daughter and her boyfriend, both in their twenties, have stopped by to have a chat before going into town. This is the second year they have a seasonal caravan at Lake Camping and they enjoy it so much they are already talking about selling their apartment near the centre of Lake Town and moving to the campsite on a full-time basis. Louise tells them she has been sneaking around in their caravan looking for something. 'Oh, did you find the dildo?' her son-in-law exclaims, to the great amusement of the little crowd.

Kim, who owns an American motorhome at the end of the road, and his partner have joined us around the table. Kim's partner has brought the guitar, playing familiar tunes that Louise sings along to. Kim works shifts for a small transport company he runs in the area, and while his partner has got an apartment in town, Kim lives all year round in two different mobile dwellings. The summer season is spent in the twelve-metre long motorhome at the campsite, where he has had a pitch for the last thirteen years, and the winters in a caravan on an industrial area outside his workplace. Kim has been importing American motorhomes to Sweden for several years, but he is fed up with the authorities, who he thinks work against him. 'They complain about the brakes and environmental concerns. But that is just rubbish. It's because they don't want these cars brought into the country', he argues. 'When you first have one of these, you never want to have an apartment', Kim says. The others nod in agreement, telling me I should have a proper look at Kim's bus: with the white interior and mirrors in the ceiling it is truly impressive. 'So, Hege, how do you find the camping life?' Benny asks as the conversation continues. I hesitate, saying that I probably would have enjoyed it more if I had a more modern caravan. Louise is amazed I have been around for so long just for this project. Kim cannot believe it is really necessary to spend all this time camping by myself, but Louise

Circumstances: 'Why don't we just sell the house, all our things and leave?'   71

Figure 8 'Our best time is now' (photo by the author).

assures him it is because I want to do a good job. And as I try to explain that the most important thing for me at the moment is to talk as much as possible with caravanners and do in-depth interviews, Louise interrupts: 'We camping people. People like us, we are the same everywhere!'

Seasonal lives

Benny and Louise first laid eyes on each other at another Lake Camping party on Midsummer Eve fifteen years ago, where they were both visiting family and friends. Benny has just turned fifty and Louise is still in her mid-forties, and they both have grown-up children from earlier relationships and several grandchildren. In the year 2000, having decided they did not want to sit in their apartment all summer, they started looking for a summer cabin to buy. The initial idea was to find a cabin close to town, preferably within bicycle distance. And Benny finally found a suitable option. But a visit to the bank deflated him; he could certainly afford to buy the cabin, but their private economy did not allow for any changes or additional work on it.

Benny went home and lay on the sofa in a bad mood. Later that day, Benny told his future wife Louise that they were going to look at a caravan. After three hours at their local retailers, they were owners of their first mobile dwelling. None of them had actually fancied the idea of having a caravan. Louise's father owned one, but she thought it was cramped and very complicated. Just the idea of having to walk over to the service buildings to take a shower seemed tiring to her: 'We are comfortable and lazy as human beings … but there you go. We can change.' Benny did not really want a caravan either, mainly because he wanted something that everyone else did not have, and it happened that his brother Kalle already had a caravan on Lake Camping (see also Leivestad 2018). The summer of 2011 is their eleventh on Lake Camping. Their apartment of 90 square metres and four rooms and kitchen is located seven minutes away by car. In the winter, Louise can walk to her workplace at a local kindergarten, while Benny has a shorter way to his factory job in summertime, celebrating his twentieth work anniversary for the same employer.

Gradually they have started to move out to the campsite earlier and earlier in the summer. 'Soon we will start living here before we move out', Benny laughs. The first years they stayed in the apartment during the week and moved into the caravan only for weekend and holidays, but now this is the fourth year that they have stayed full-time at the site throughout the summer until the end of September. In the last three summer seasons, they have only spent one single night in the apartment – they were getting up early in the morning to go on a boat cruise. Twice a week Louise passes the apartment to pick up the post and water the flowers. On a normal working day, Benny starts at 5.40, leaving early. Louise leaves a little later at 5.50, starting work at 6.30. Returning to the site in the early afternoon, Benny sometimes 'gets an attack' and feels he needs to do something, and cuts the grass even though it is not necessary. But usually he will just lie down in the shade for a nap. 'This is our place for recreation. We are here to rest. If we want to cut the grass or do something, we do it, and if we don't, we don't. That is what is so nice about all of this. You don't have to do anything. And you are outside all the time without having to go anywhere.' Every day from across the road I see Benny and Louise sit about outside their caravan, doing some gardening work or hanging out, eating and drinking with their neighbours and family. In this case, the neighbours are also family. In the caravan behind them live Benny's brother and his wife, Kalle and Lena, while the other next door neighbours are Louise's daughter and son-in-law.

Lena's history of caravanning began in the late 1980s when she met Kalle, who had bought his first caravan as early as the late 1970s, when commencing work as a travelling electrical installer. During their first trip in the caravan, heading for southern Sweden, the rain was just pouring down. Kalle told Lena to go inside the caravan, brought her a blanket and some alcohol. Lena recalls looking out at a family with small children trying to cook outside in the rain and she thought, 'I will never go tenting again.' 'Well, they have chosen it', Kalle chuckled, 'If they have any problems we will help them, if not, they are ok.' When Kalle was working as an installer he lived in the caravan twelve months a year, but caravan life is very different when you share it with someone. It was the early 1990s when they first came to Lake Camping and now, more than twenty years later, they still spend the whole summer season here. Since the late 1980s they have lived in a rental apartment with three rooms close to the centre of Lake Town. It was hard to find a parking space for the caravan in the area, so becoming a seasonal caravanner close to home solved many problems. They normally move out by the end of April and stay until the last day of September. The moving out process is a long one, removing all the furniture and items they have transported to the campsite to equip the caravan and the awning requires weeks of busy work. Kalle and Lena like their apartment in winter, but they would not like to live there year-round. The summers become extremely hot and they have a glassed balcony.

An everyday caravan reality is portrayed in deep contrast to the life that Benny and Louise, Kalle and Lena, lead in their apartments only few kilometres away.[4] Benny and Louise and Kalle and Lena's stories show that rather than conceptualized as a second home, the caravan is positioned as the main dwelling in periods of the year. The seasonal mobility is constitutive for life at Lake Camping and this seasonality raises issues of the interactions between forms of dwelling and social organization and spatial behaviour (Lawrence and Low 1990: 460). Marcel Mauss and Beuchat's (1979) classic essay on the Eskimo makes for an interesting comparison. With strong holistic ambitions, Mauss sets out to ethnographically demonstrate the role of the built environment with regard to social adaptation and integration. Mauss describes a twofold seasonal morphology of the Eskimo, where periods of living in close proximity are alternated with periods that people live apart in isolation. Mauss' argument is useful as far as it describes how seasonal dwelling links with social density. For the Eskimo, the winters are the periods of dense social interaction and where group consciousness arises, whereas the summer is a period where these social bonds are loosened.

Mauss' argument offers a way of entrance into understanding a relationship between the social and seasonal organization of life among Lake Camping caravanners and the alternation between different forms of dwelling. In the Lake Town context, seasonal caravanners like Benny and Louise spend a set number of summer months every year living full-time in a caravan, whereas the wintertime dwelling is an apartment in town. The apartment is considered uncomfortable and hot in summertime, but such factors are far from alone in explaining why they move to the field some kilometres away. As we saw in the opening caravan narratives, the caravan dwelling is regarded as offering a fundamentally different entrance to senses of freedom from specific obligations, some of them tied up with the house dwelling itself. At the same time, the social density, to use Mauss' terminology, at the campsite opens up for other forms of social relationships in what I call a *realm of visibility* that includes important notions of seeing and being seen. When Louise tells me, 'We camping people are the same everywhere', she also reaffirms a sense of group belonging that takes shape during a seasonal period of the year, based on engagement with a particular mobile dwelling. The expectations of what forms of social relationships are shaped within the dense camping context are however often out of sync with how caravanners actually find life at Lake Camping.

'This place isn't quiet. It's dead!'

A stony road turning left after the reception building and stretching on to the main field of Lake Camping goes under the name *säsongarnas väg* (Season's road), and is home to about seventeen of the seasonal caravan units. Throughout the year, this road is the site's busiest area, including in wintertime when couples like Benny and Louise come out in the evenings and weekends. The initial troubles I had in hooking up and establishing relations at Lake Camping in many ways reflect a way of sociality that is characteristic for the site and does not only deal with scepticism towards a nosy anthropologist. The sleepy atmosphere at the campsite was also confirmed by Louise who says, 'This place isn't quiet, it's dead.' The apparent lack of a collective sociality is largely due to the fact that most of the seasonal guests have their primary home or workplace very close to the campsite, between three and ten kilometres away. Living at the campsite thus means no real isolation from family or friends, and is merely an alternative mode of accommodation. What seems to be an apparent lack of a collective, social orientation does not mean that other qualities of social relationships are not longed for.

In Chapter 2, I showed how Kalle and Lena link the lack of an active social life at the campsite to a nostalgic vision of its past. Lena misses the 'primitive', when they only had two toilets and summer showers. It was not so nice, but definitely more sociable, 'and midsummer is not the same anymore either', she sighs. They used to have sinks for doing the dishes outside the building and everyone would gather and talk. The men would smoke and drink whisky and wait for their dinner to be ready. And as seasonal caravanners they feel under-prioritized by the campsite management. Nothing is arranged for them, no parties or gatherings. But they still like to be here and have people all around them, mainly their family neighbours, 'And if it is too much we just go into our own caravan … that is the best, that you can just go into your own if you want to and you don't push yourself upon anyone if they have gone off to sit by themselves.' Kalle and Lena's expectations of organized leisure are reflected in Benny and Louise's view of a campsite in change. They argue that the social activities and possibilities for a collective leisure life have decreased as the campsite went from municipal management into the hands of a private corporation. This materialized nostalgia reflects a mode of linking, as we saw in Chapter 2, the campsite infrastructure to the actual possibilities for socializing.

Other campsite regulars, however, express contentment with the situation. Ulla and Kristian, both in their mid-fifties, who occupy one of the American motorhomes at the site, moved to the campsite in autumn 2009, finding Lake Camping to be one of the few that were actually open all year round. The first winter there were five or six caravans on the site full-time, last year there were four. 'But we don't have much contact with them. We have our friends and don't need to go out hunting for new ones', Ulla says firmly. 'We like to drink at our speed, and then the others can drink at theirs.' Even in the summer season, their acquaintance with the neighbours is sporadic. They do hang out with their closest neighbours Benny and Louise, and Kim and his partner. 'But we work a lot', Ulla says, 'and it is just nice to come home and be alone … and some of them out here are family as well, and they are so tight. It probably would have been different if we were here all the time.' But they both agree the campsite is quite alright. 'We know how it works and how the people here work.'

At Lake Camping, people move to live in closer proximity to others than the housing situation they are otherwise used to in houses and apartments. But beyond the apparent narratives of a caring community and collectivity, one realizes that the neighbouring everyday of Lake Camping is one where such ideals to a large degree are problematized. Whereas Kalle and Lena express a strong nostalgia towards a lost community at the campsite, coming as a result of the modernization changes, Ulla and Kristian clearly have no wish to engage in a similar form of building of neighbour relationships. To them, camping life is mainly a housing option – one that increases their sense of what they believe is freedom, experienced through the mobility offered by their American motorhome. Despite these colliding ideals of sociality, all caravan dwellers at Lake Camping continue to reproduce an image of a 'classless' camping community, where people meet on equal terms and 'where we are all the same'. Embedded in such a discourse is also an expectation of control and predictability. Ulla puts it nicely when saying that she knows how 'it [the campsite] works and how people work'. She affirms a general observation of how the structure, order and visibility at the site are assumed to produce a particular form of management of space among its residents. This management extends to the relationship with one's neighbours, with whom one might not want to spend a lot of time, but would like to have enough knowledge about for handling in terms of securing one's own privacy.

'Caravans have wheels, they are supposed to roll'

In the narratives of change presented in the first part of the chapter, mobility figures as one of the key elements in why a caravan lifestyle is opted for. In this context, the idea of mobility is intimately linked to how freedom is perceived and understood: as the freedom to move whenever one wants to. 'The freedom is important', Lena says. 'You don't feel trapped … and you do in an apartment.' Caravan mobility however, takes on ambivalent expressions in the daily practices of the residents at Lake Camping. Lena and Kalle used to travel frequently in their caravan the first years after they met, touring large parts of Sweden. Kalle keeps log documents on his computer, revealing how they have parked at 112 different places since 1987, two per year. Kalle has it all meticulously registered, with dates, prices and comments, as well as GPS coordinates. One year they travelled 3,000 kilometres, but over the last two years however, the caravan has not been removed from the pitch. Their awning is fully equipped with a dining table, gas oven, fridge and freezer and if they were to travel somewhere they would need to take most of it down, transport it home or store it with their neighbours. 'But', Lena rapidly adds, 'we have everything we need in the caravan so we could take off tomorrow if we wanted to.' Kalle's log documentation reflects a form of mobility fetishism in which caravan life is evaluated in terms of crossing of geographical distance and numbers of overnight stops. In their current campsite living, however, a potential mobility is rather manifested through a material preparedness to move, which simultaneously is prevented by the domestic transformation of their awning into a fully furnished living room.

Ulla and Kristian, on the other hand, who live in the American motorhome, think that travelling is what they most appreciate about their full-time camping life: 'Just go whenever we want to.' Whereas Lena and Kalle would need to pack up their awning and store away their things, Ulla and Kristian can simply close the doors and drive off. The generous size of the car does not scare any of them off. Kristian used to drive school buses on snowy narrow roads. In wintertime their mobility is however more limited, mostly due to the salted roads that the couple believe to destroy the motorhome by provoking rust. While more limited in their touring, they still park the motorhome outside their workplace during workweeks: 'This is our home and we take it with us!' Ulla says she could never have a caravan on a seasonal pitch like their neighbours. 'Caravans have wheels, they are supposed to roll!'

Ulla's latter comment is crucial to understanding the way mobility is related to in the context of Lake Camping. The expectation that caravans are supposed to move because they have wheels is also implicitly present in Lena's assurance that they can take off 'whenever they want to'. Even if their caravan has not been moved in the last two years, Lena and Kalle show great concern in reassuring themselves that they can move. The mobility they refer to is not only in terms of travel, but also the fact that the moveable dwelling allows them to change pitch and neighbours if necessary. Among many caravanners, mobility makes sense in other ways than in its realized form (Leivestad 2016). Lena's assurance that they can move is one way of countering what can be understood as expectations of mobility, but it is also a clear reference to mobility as potential.

The operational element of this potential mobility lies in the wheels that can move, but also in the other aspects of the moveable dwelling as a transportable home. Lena for instance mentions the fact that 'they have everything they need' in the caravan, and that this self-sufficiency allows for them to take off whenever they want to. Among the caravan dwellers of Lake Camping, central meanings of what is considered to be a caravan life circulate around this rather unspecified mobility potential. The importance of this potential is constitutive for caravanning as a practice, and goes beyond a simple employment of mobility as getting from A to B. A potential mobility is recognizable in similar forms, also among caravan dwellers that have realized very different forms of mobility from the residents at Lake Camping. On Camping Mares in Spain, British caravanners seasonally or permanently relocate to start a new life elsewhere. The following sections deal with these (im)mobilities and how they can be understood in terms of visions and adjustments of a withdrawal to the good life.

Seasonal mobility and permanent caravans

Camping Mares' spatial and social landscape is constituted around annual periods of mobility and immobility – of standing still and moving. Particularly among the motorhomers, seasonal mobility is part of a temporal organization of the year. While geographical mobility is appreciated in terms of freedom, of discovering new areas and of seeing new places, the continuity of this movement is challenged by the need to hook-up. This immobility expressed through spending a longer period of time at the same campsite is a way of keeping an active social life, of meeting the same friends year after year and of giving the camping life a sense of mundane daily routine. Clive and Sarah would explain how the lives they lead when staying at Camping Mares and when travelling are very different. At Camping Mares, they go out with friends every day, Sarah goes to the gym and they watch television. Travelling, on the other hand, is rather about the two of them meeting new people on the road, with no regular activities and no television. In the evenings they play scrabble and when they want to see something else, they move on. While life at Camping Mares thus is coloured by its sense of routine and mundane regularity, the periods of travelling and touring with the motorhome open up for the discovery of new places, the unplanned and the impulsive. Sarah told me how much she really appreciated the different seasons. 'I really like it here. But it is nice going as well. There are so many places we still want to see. And we like meeting new people.'

But even for the motorhomers, staying at a campsite is still considered the only possible way to remain secure, and to maintain social relationships. While some motorhomers had experience of so-called free-camping while touring Europe, this was a form of camping they had all stopped doing. One couple that used their caravan as a main dwelling put it this way: 'When we were going out, one of us would always stay in the van because of the burglaries. When it is your home you are more cautious. But if we can't even do anything, what's the point?' For this couple, like many others, the solution had come in going abroad long-term and staying at the same campsite for several months.

Spending six to nine months every year on Camping Mares gives 'the winter people' a specific relationship to place, both to the campsite, its people and to Benidorm and the Costa Blanca. Several of my informants describe how they first saw the skyscrapers of the BeniYork skyline and thought, 'Oh, never Benidorm', but ended up returning anyway. Peter tells me about his and his wife Laura's first meeting with Benidorm many years back when they still were working. He had some time off his job in the construction business and they wanted to go for a holiday to southern Europe. It was still March and the only thing on offer was Benidorm. Peter did not really want to go, but Laura convinced him and it 'was just as bad as I thought it would be'. Many years later, touring with the motorhome, they returned to Benidorm and now they are spending their fourth winter on Camping Mares.

In this seasonal mobility that is repeated year after year, Benidorm grows from being the rather distasteful holiday town offering a pleasant climate, to a place of affection and enjoyment, and to a place where bonds are established and maintained. In the instability that comes with living in the motorhome and travelling, Camping Mares also evolves into a place where stability is offered and where friendships are maintained year after year. Benidorm nevertheless differs from many of the destinations that host large groups of lifestyle migrants and expatriate communities. Peter's comment on his initial dislike of the Spanish holiday town points to the ambivalence towards Benidorm itself, which through its expansive skyscraper architecture and position in the working-class holiday imaginary distances itself from the idyll of the Mediterranean that others might search for.[5]

As Salazar and Zhang (2013) note, seasonality, whether in tourism or migration, is attributed both to climatic and institutional factors. Seasonal mobility is constitutive of life on the campsite. Likewise, the seasonal mobility is to a large part regulated by the rules and regulations of Camping Mares. To be able to get the pitch you have booked the previous season, you need to be present at Camping Mares by 1 October. This system makes most of the so-called 'winter people' that come from the northern and central parts of Europe to spend the winter months arrive at Camping Mares by the first day of October. The low season prices stretch from October until April, with the exception of Easter, which is considered high season and normally fills the campsite with Spanish tourists.

When the low season moves towards its end and springtime is approaching at the end of March and beginning of April, most of the winter people start packing up. While some head straight home to the UK, the Netherlands or Scandinavia, others, like Sarah and Clive, travel for some months in Europe before they go to the UK to spend the summer.

The length of stay is also regulated according to the prices of the campsite and Camping Mares operates with different prices according to the length of stay. For one night, the price surpasses 24 Euro for a motorhome and two adults, even in the low season. Between 15 and 30 days, the price lowers to 20 Euro, while more than 90 days allow a price of 14 Euro a night. Most winter caravanners at Camping Mares plan their stay so as to ensure a good price for the pitch, usually implying a stay of 180 days or more, allowing them the lowest rate of 13 Euro a night. By operating with the different price systems, the campsite ensures a stable income during the low season, while it simultaneously contributes to a regulation of the camping guests' seasonal mobility. Among Camping Mares regulars, economic reasons are often given for why standing still is preferred to moving. Though Laura and Peter express great enjoyment in travelling with their motorhome, they realize they cannot move as much as they want, simply because it is too expensive. The couple is not alone in this form of reasoning. One British caravanner said that even though they come every year, he and his wife never used to stay such a long time at Camping Mares. When the four months now were coming towards an end, they were eager to move on and go back. But, he told me, 'My wife won't realize this, but staying still here and getting the best rate is the only way we can afford this life.'

Stuck with the house

From autumn 2010 to spring 2011, Lucy and John's motorhome is parked on the touring area of Benidorm's Camping Mares. Their house in the north-west of the UK is up for slow sale. It has been rented out for several years, the incoming rent covering their pitch fee on Camping Mares. The rapid sale they planned for when buying the motorhome in 2008 has however not been possible due to a slow housing market brought about by the European recession. In June 2011, Lucy and John pick me up at a windy John Lennon airport in Liverpool. They are back for the summer to 'get things sorted out', as they put it. As I find myself sitting in a small car leaving the airport along the roads that John knows so well, they reveal that they have sold the motorhome and bought one of the permanent caravans at Camping Mares. Lucy and John are thrilled about their new home waiting in Spain, but the past month in the UK has turned out to be a hassle with paperwork and finances. Having borrowed the money to buy the permanent caravan from friends at the campsite, they wanted to take a loan of 15,000 pounds on the house, which would be paid off as soon as they sold it. But their bank for the last thirty years, where they had a joint account, would not allow them a loan. John is still furious. He cannot believe how the bank would just dismiss them.

As they retold the story, Lucy and John finally got in contact with a man named Roy, who had overheard them having problems at the bank. He has helped them find a mortgage dealer that has agreed to give them the mortgage. The agreement lets them pay £45 a month until the house is sold and they can pay it back. To get the mortgage, Lucy and John have to show they have been living in the house, on their particular address – a task difficult to fulfil since they have had their post sent to their youngest son's address while living in the motorhome. Roy has asked them to go to the bank to get sent the papers from the last months with the right address on them. 'Roy has been absolutely fabulous', they repeatedly exclaim while informing me about the past events. Lucy and John were worried Roy required a commission, but he gets paid by the mortgage broker he said, so no worries. As I arrive, in the middle of June, they hope to get it all sorted out quickly. The idea is to take care of the house rental by themselves from now on. The real estate agents required large sums of money for handling it, and Lucy thinks the process of getting the house sold has been too long.

The rental had proved itself to be more complicated than they had thought. Lucy and John had initially dropped the rent for the former tenants on the agreement that they would take care of any occurring problems. Moving back in however, Lucy and John discovered that everything was far from in order. Their tenants had just disappeared, even with plenty of post lying around. Lucy and John are aware they could have sold the house straight away, but only for 60,000 pounds to an estate dealer. They have decided however they want to sell it to someone who 'really needs it'. Considering also that they have already dropped the price from 90,000 to 80,000 pounds, an immediate sale would be a bad deal. Before my visit, they encountered what they think are the ideal tenants – a couple with a child. As John puts it: 'This house is perfect for them since they have their family living close'. The new plan is to let the couple rent the house for a year, dropping the rent to £300 a month so that the family can save up to a mortgage and eventually buy the house.

It was friends from Camping Mares who lent them the money to buy the permanent caravan – otherwise Lucy and John could not have afforded it. Their friends have told them not to stress about paying back, asking them not to get in debts. But John does not feel comfortable having borrowed money from friends and would rather have a mortgage at a bank or at a dealer's. During my days in Lancashire, I follow John and Lucy's worrying mornings opening the post, discovering that they have yet again received the wrong document from the bank, and the frustration in waiting for yet another postal delivery. I follow them to their local bank in the centre of town with a furious and swearing Lucy and a sighing John. In the flashy offices of HSBC, we are told to wait for 20 minutes, with John impatiently and repeatedly exiting the main entrance to get some air on the busy shopping street. Finally, we are told that the bank needs to send the papers by post, which will take another three to five bank days. John and Lucy are exhausted and frustrated, and fear that the process is moving so slowly that they will not get their mortgage approved. 'We are asking for 15,000 pounds and we don't think that is a lot of money.' John says over and over again, 'We have been customers for 30 years and never been in the red.' Lucy and John's situation reveal how the withdrawal to a caravan nevertheless may entail a continuous 'stuckedness' in the economic relations of the house. When buying the permanent caravan on Camping Mares, they use money they have bound up in a house that has proven difficult to sell, but take the risk by borrowing money from friends, a private loan they feel uncomfortable keeping.

Lucy and John's economic situation is more precarious than that of many of their neighbours at Camping Mares. But my visit to Lancashire illuminates the often risky and unsteady economics involved in financing a home on wheels. Whereas houses are rented out, low incomes are seldom enough to secure the purchase of a motorhome or caravan and the campsite life in Spain. The sale of their house in northeast England was the only way Lucy and John's friends at the site, Laura and Peter, could afford to travel in the motorhome. Peter wanted to sell the house immediately, even though they would only get 70,000 pounds for it. Finally they got 111,000 pounds after having it rented out for a year. The motorhome, however, was bought before the house was sold, and they secured it with a deposit and had to get it on hire purchase and max out their credit cards. 'The van cost us 18,000 pounds, which was a lot of money for us, and afterwards we thought "oh, what have we done?"'

Circumstances: 'Why don't we just sell the house, all our things and leave?'   83

Figure 9 For Sale (photo by Terje Tjærnås).

Even at the Swedish Lake Camping, there are similar stories of economic precariousness in the financing of a life on wheels. Ulla and Kristian, who owned one of the big American motorhomes on the site, revealed that the motorhome would have cost more than 500,000 US dollars if they had bought it new. Finally, after a long and complicated purchase process with returning visits to the second-hand dealer in Germany who had the motorhome on sale for 150,000 Euro, they managed to bargain it to about half the price. They had some savings from selling their house, but the rest had to be financed with a bank loan with very high interest rates. With two steady incomes however, Ulla and Kristian's situation of debt was less risky than that of the senior caravanners in Spain. Their example points again to the economic and legal framework wherein the caravan is placed. Both in Sweden and the UK, like cars, caravans are considered private property and not real estate, causing them to be placed under different financing possibilities than those of a house or an apartment. The loans taken by John and Lucy, Peter and Laura, as well as by Ulla and Kristian all carried high interest rates, making the purchase of a mobile dwelling an often costly affair. The manner of risk-taking described above is tied up with the notion of present continuous, that a referral to the 'good life' here and now instates an 'enforced presentism' (Guyer 2007: 410). Through a certain negation of forward-looking, the present continuous neglects risks and uncertain elements involved in the financing of a full-time caravan life, deferring problems for later.

Owning on rented ground

The debt and loans carried by the camping home relate to the wider development of property ownership in Britain and Sweden. Among the Swedish caravanners at Lake Camping, emphasis is put on the importance of owning, not renting, the caravan or motorhome. The Social Democratic era of Swedish politics was based on the idea of affordable housing for the people through the establishment of tenancy rights. During the 2000s however, one saw a steady decrease in tenancy rights in Sweden, now converted into apartments on private ownership models. The Swedish census from 2012 showed that half of the population lived in a privately owned residence. The Swedish campsite organizations' own statistics reveal that a majority of active Swedish caravanners also live in houses. Some of the residents of Lake Camping, such as Benny and Louise, however, live in tenancy right apartments in the centre of Lake Town. When I visit them at the campsite in 2017, Benny and Louise have just moved into a smaller apartment in the same building, as a result of the many renovations that had increased the rents considerably and forced many of their neighbours to move.

All caravanners on Camping Mares and Lake Camping own their caravan or motorhome. While the pitch rent of the campsite easily surpasses the rent of a spacious apartment in downtown Benidorm, Margaret and Gary emphasize that there is a fundamental difference between owning their caravan, instead of what they see as renting others' property. That the ground upon which their caravan is parked and their sheds are built is rented off the campsite, whose management remains in full control over its future development, is seldom questioned. Camping Mares residents repeatedly defend their choice of a caravan life, opposed to one in an apartment in the town of Benidorm by reference to 'community' and 'freedom'.

But a clear linkage is also established between notions of freedom and the ownership of property (Dolan 1999). In the case of Britain, John Dolan (1999) sees the link between freedom and ownership as part and result of the Thatcher regime from 1979 to 1990, when the political project was one of transforming Britain into a property-owning democracy. This is also the period when several of my informants on Camping Mares had been able to buy their first house, often former local authority homes (Dolan 1999: 63). This rise of the individual at the expense of the collective that was initiated during the Thatcher era and that bears resonance in a continuing priority of property ownership informs the caravanners' emphasis upon self-sufficiency and ownership right to their caravan home. In that sense, their perception of freedom reflects classical liberal theories found for instance in John Locke's idea of the social contract, in which freedom and liberty really is found in the owning of property.

But the selling and buying of property at Camping Mares furthermore points to complex economic consequences of the economic recession, particularly apparent at the time of my fieldwork from 2010 and onwards. Caravans that had been bought for 30,000 Euro in the early and mid-2000s were in 2010–14 desperately sold at as little as a tenth of the price. Carry and Roland, a couple in their late thirties and friends of Clive and Sarah, had bought a permanent caravan at one of the neighbouring sites of Camping Mares in 2010. The caravan and all sheds and installations on the patio cost them 3,000 Euro. The annual pitch rent of 4,200 Euro also had to be paid up front. In addition, they had to pay a changeover fee to the site of 3,000 Euro, in cash with no receipts. The changeover fee is meant as a compensation for the fact that all property is supposed to be removed from the pitch when you move. It is in reality possible to move all property onto another pitch, but Roland calculates that would cost them 2,000 pounds and hours of work. Roland is highly critical of the changeover fee, arguing it was both a cause for people to move and a reason they could not sell. The way changes in ownership are regulated in an informal market at Camping Mares thus contributes to a high degree of immobility through a changeover fee that becomes an obstacle for sales. A locally contained campsite property market that relies largely on payments in cash however, is also largely inclusive, since buyers and sellers can avoid formal economic channels in the shape of banks and agents.

Crisis caravanning

Whereas some Camping Mares residents manage quite well economically, others struggle to maintain life in a motorhome and caravan. A couple I interviewed during my last weeks at Camping Mares had endless stories from their life as pub managers. Of all the hard work and long days, about the interesting people they met and the parties they had, but also about the recession that struck their part of England in the early 1990s, which made them close down and go back to part-time working, and handling years of illness. So from managing quite well economically, they are now aged seventy receiving a very low pension. Too low to live on, they admit, and soon their savings will be finished and they will have to stop going abroad. The private pensions they had saved for were cashed out when the recession hit them. A 2008 financial crisis and the increasingly weaker pound had made life in Spain more expensive, and they would check the exchange rate every week to ensure they got every decimal on their side when getting the Euro they needed for the pitch rent and alcohol.

Caravanners' stories about their own economic struggles are deeply embedded in a larger discourse on the financial crisis that at the time of my fieldwork was peaking in the UK, Ireland and southern Europe. In times of what Thompson (2013) refers to as 'growing darkness and uncertainty', Margaret and Gary's move is an example of how a relocation from the UK may partly be due to what they term the recession. The impacts of the recession, especially in the UK, had consequences that also resulted in contrary processes. When I first came to Benidorm in the autumn of 2010, walking the streets of Camping Mares and the neighbouring campsites, I was struck by all the signs saying *se vende* (for sale). For a price as low as 5,000 pounds, one could buy a permanent caravan on the site. Camping residents would reveal the prices had fallen quickly over the last year and that just a few years ago you would have to pay at least 20,000–30,000 pounds for a permanent on the site. The many caravans up for sale were taken as a sign of the difficult economic state many of the British caravanners found themselves in at the time of my fieldwork. In 2011, *the Guardian* headlined an article *The Pain in Spain*, focusing on the many expats caught in *la crisis*, stuck with property they were not able to sell.

On Camping Mares, *la crisis* had mainly struck the people that still kept a house or a flat at home and kept a 'permanent' caravan in Spain as a holiday home or lived there only through the winter season. Some, like John and Lucy, also experienced the problems of a slow British housing market, preventing access to money for extra spending or for buying a permanent caravan at the site. The residents that had spent several years on Camping Mares complained about how empty the campsite was in the autumn of 2010. Both the campsite staff and the caravanners themselves saw the recession in Britain as the cause for why many caravanners and motorhomes had stopped coming.

The troubling times were also highly present in Spain, a country on the brink of economic collapse during the autumn of 2010. The difficulties in the tourism sector and the high level of unemployment were particularly visible in the tourist destination of Benidorm. The couple running the restaurant on Camping Mares found themselves in the middle of a difficult period. With dozens of bars and restaurants closing down in the area, they still managed to survive on regular campsite customers. But from having run the restaurant with several employees – a cook, a cleaner and someone to help in the bar – the couple now had to do everything themselves, only with the help of their teenage daughter. With opening hours from 8.30 in the morning to past midnight, there was not much time to look after their eight-year-old son, and years had passed since they last had a whole day off. The caravanners' stories of change and progress are thus clearly positioned within an unstable economic context that affects both the country they have left and the one they have arrived to. As such, the withdrawal that takes shape in the caravan narrative necessarily carries with it economically unstable elements. Sometimes the negotiation of such instabilities is carried out at a level of ensuring the best exchange rates, whereas in other cases they can quite abruptly put a stop to the life on wheels that one has worked hard to construct.

In the context of Camping Mares, it is sometimes possible to view the caravan mobilities as part of a larger process or circuit of migration. Ronny, the quiz organizer, for instance, used to live in a caravan at Camping Mares. He eventually moved on to buy a house in the area as a registered citizen of Benidorm, only coming to the campsite to run the quiz or have a meal. Ronny's story points to a rather common arrangement among the British in Benidorm. They start off with a caravan, and end up buying an apartment or a house. It is a test to see if you like it, and buying a caravan for 20,000 pounds is considerably cheaper than buying an apartment. In such migration processes, the caravan is positioned as a highly temporal dwelling: affordable, but not suitable as a permanent solution. For most of the British caravanners on Camping Mares, however, a 'permanent' caravan at the site is envisioned as an accomplishment – as the last stop. Gary and Margaret's opinion that they would only buy a larger caravan, but not leave the campsite if they won the lottery, is one they share with many neighbours. To Margaret and Gary, it is the social life and what they articulate as the safety of the campsite that are valued as the most important. Even though they know that they could rent an apartment in Benidorm for less money than the annual rent of the campsite, this was never an option. 'If you live in an apartment you close the door and you don't talk to anyone', Gary explains.

Withdrawal and continuity

The analogy (see Strathern 1992) presented in this chapter, between the short-distance mobility of the caravanners in Sweden and the transnational caravan migrations of the British on the Costa Blanca, in many ways tells a common story in terms of narratives of change and withdrawal: from the urban, from 'the things' and, to a more varying degree, a perceived 'community'. Caravanners' own narratives entail clear expectations of a reinvention of self, assumed possible to achieve through relocation to a dwelling that is associated with potential mobility. The narratives point in different directions: to a discontent with current life situations, but also to long-standing aspirations to travel or, as in the case of Camping Mares residents, moving abroad. But whereas a move from a house or an apartment to a caravan is recounted in terms of 'freedom' and 'liberation', it is simultaneously perceived by others as a downward mobility, which points back to the caravan's ambivalent position as a main dwelling.

In caravanners' mobility narratives, freedom features as mobility, or rather, the potential of it. Downsizing to a smaller and moveable domestic sphere is considered an act of liberation. Whereas some motorhome owners still find the financial means and interest to travel with their motorhome in a quest to see new places and maintain what they regard to be a mobile lifestyle, mobility is challenged by a need to stand still. Petrol costs and campsite fees are examples of such institutional factors that strongly regulate the mobility of caravan and motorhome dwellers. In this chapter we have thus seen that the fantasies or plans of travelling, of living in a dwelling that is moveable, soon are adjusted through practices that involve stationary home building at the campsites. Long-term dwelling is also associated with certain qualities of social relationship, of maintaining social bonds and building neighbour relations.

In contrast to the domestic, close to home relocation of the Lake Town caravan dwellers, the Camping Mares caravan migration posits central questions of the economic and political context in which their acts of withdrawal are taking place. Uncertainty, it seems, is an outcome of the current political and economic situation in most of Europe (cf. Bauman 2007). For the working-class British, a decision to sell houses to live in a motorhome or caravan abroad partly comes as a reaction to this uncertainty, of a lack of progression in life or lack of economic stability. When talking about the unmaking of their former homes, caravanners that have taken the active choice of moving into a caravan refer to the house as an evil, carrying elements of 'stuckedness' and interfering with their chances of living life to the full. Framed as holding other qualities than those of a house, the caravan's potential mobility thus extends its potential for moving geographically into a much wider potential. To use Hage's term; its *sense of possibility* is located in its perceived potential for offering a qualitatively different life. Nevertheless, as we have seen in the case of Lucy and John, the insecure and risky economic choices embedded in the purchase of a caravan or motorhome can prevent the total unmaking of the former house. Many full-time caravanners remain entangled 'in "the market" in profoundly disabling ways' (Chu 2010: 168) because they are stuck in economic arrangements, insecurity and transactions resembling the ones they sought to withdraw from in the first place. The next chapter will again return to the interior and exterior of the caravan interrogating how the formation of a 'permanent' mobile dwelling take place through particular negotiations with temporality.

4

Containers: 'You won't even see there's a caravan in there'

Sitting on the sofa made of a fluffy rug, Helen who is in her forties and established as a full-time resident at Camping Mares since a few years back admits that she really had no experience of living in a caravan apart from that her father back in Yorkshire used to build them. 'He put them together. And when people buy one now, the first things they do is to take them apart. Take it all out. He should have seen,' she smiles. Helen says her caravan and the awning were very basic when she moved in. After ripping out the original kitchen and sitting groups, Helen has made the caravan skeleton into a bedroom with a double bed and with an adjoining boudoir with a room for makeup and clothes. By use of three layers of paint and antique lacquer to paint the fitted cupboards she is continuously working to fulfil her dream of a camping home in what she calls 'antique retro' style; the awning fully furnished with an inherited stag's head on the wall, a fake fireplace,[1] and various antiques bought at local markets.

Helen's caravan is an example of how the prefabricated mobile dwelling is continuously transformed into a static housing entity. Whereas the previous chapter reinstated the caravanners' own narratives of change and rupture and teased out the adjustments and clashes between the aspirational stories and life on a campsite, this chapter returns to the interiors and the exteriors of the caravan home. While the 'conventional' European home often is characterized by its physical solidity and fixedness, the caravan and its embedded potential mobility questions the static representation of the house dwelling (Birdwell-Pheasant and Lawrence-Zuñega 1999: 9). At the same time however, as discussed in the previous chapter, many caravanners gradually turn their caravans and motorhomes into dwellings for full-time and geographically fixed housing – into mobile dwellings that seldom or never move. In this chapter I will, by looking primarily at Camping Mares, examine the material processes wherein such 'static' or 'permanent' caravans, like that owned by Helen, are shaped. Through building and refurnishing, 'permanent' caravan homes take form in a continuous negotiation with particular logics of temporality. In this chapter, I describe how what we can call 'conventional' house aesthetics are reinvented at the campsite – a reinvention that also implies a concealment of the caravan's mobile properties. But, as I will explain, the temporal character of the caravan, enabled through its potential mobility, is simultaneously the actual basis for long-term 'fixed' dwelling.

The processes of withdrawal in a caravan home needs to be seen in relation to the unmaking of other kinds and variations of domestic property. Such unmaking, involving the move from an often spacious domestic sphere to the limited space of the mobile dwelling, raises issues both of emotional and material downsizings. Through storing, disposal and renewal, downsizing bears evidence of both social and material rupture and continuity. The unmaking of a house or apartment is not a clear-cut process. Rather, as I have shown in the previous chapter, it contains complex economic elements that can result in the caravanners' 'stuckedness' in variations of economic transactions and debt that are parts of the economic systems they seem to seek to withdraw from in the first place. When Lucy and John bought the motorhome with the idea of turning it into their full-time mobile dwelling, they did not foresee how their terraced house would eventually bind them to loans with high interest rates and the difficulties of managing a situation of double housing.

For the purpose of the framing of this chapter, I have turned to a much-used metaphor – namely that of the container. Its material similarities with the caravan are obvious: through their relative uniformity and potential mobility, containers and caravans are designed to store and transport smoothly.[2] The container is however more than a mere ethnographical analogy. Identified in the work of both Lakoff (1987) and Johnson (1987) as a bodily experienced 'image schema', the container is also a powerful concept metaphor that carries problematic notions of holism. The container suggests a boundary, separating interior from exterior, one can however also think of containers in forms of openings and movements from inside to outside.[3]

Such discourses of space, boundaries and movement relate to a wide range of literature of the anthropology of home and domestic spheres that deals with the creation of domestic boundaries and inside–outside divisions. Domestic boundaries have commonly been read in terms of private versus public spheres, the most influential example being Bourdieu's (1990) analysis of the Kabyle house. Readings of the house and the dwelling, through the metaphor of the container, may easily bring us into a similar structuralist analysis. But domestic boundaries are not fixed, but rather fluid and an object of constant negotiation, a point that leads towards an understanding of the container (or here – the caravan) not as a fixed entity, but as a process.

Unmaking homes

In 2008, Gary and Margaret went through the long process of getting rid of the furniture and belongings that filled their two-storey house in Wales. They had both inherited furniture from their families, lots of it antique, and their collection had once been the focus of attention in the BBC television show *Cash in the Attic*.[4] Margaret describes how they, upon moving from the house, had family and friends coming over, putting post-it notes on the things they wanted: 'I felt like I had died.' Arriving in Benidorm with a van full of things they had decided to keep, it then took them weeks to clean up after the British lady whose caravan they had bought. Furniture and belongings were cleaned out and driven to the gate of the campsite. When returning to the gate with a new load, most of it was already gone, and Margaret can still recognize some of their old furniture when walking around on the site. Margaret and Gary's arrival at Camping Mares shows how the campsite's infrastructural nodes, such as the toilet blocks, have become places for an organized circulation of objects. What is commonly known as 'The Camping Mares shelf' illustrates this, where residents or visitors can leave objects they do not want. Only if not taken before 5.00 pm does the campsite maintenance remove them. Margaret and Gary's old belongings and patio furniture have continued their life on other patios, and on returning visits to the campsite I have seen one of my old dresses come wandering down the road.

The material and emotional making of homes on wheels implies at the same time an unmaking of previously owned houses or apartments. A central part of the unmaking of former homes involves decisions of what material objects to bring along to a more physically limited domestic sphere. Like most of their neighbours, Gary and Margaret's 'permanent' caravan is one filled with various objects brought from the UK and from the house they sold, but also of possessions bought in Benidorm and furniture from the previous owner. Buying one of the permanent caravans at Camping Mares is thus seldom a blank-sheet beginning, and often implies an inheritance of previous owners' furniture, belongings and home aesthetics. When residents at Camping Mares, like Gary and Margaret, have moved from a house to a mobile dwelling, their own possessions are in some cases disposed of, but also recycled through mediums of charity shops, auctions, bazaars or by being passed on to family and friends.

In the following passage I will briefly go through how processes of divestment, disposal and storing are connected to the shaping of life in a caravan and the unmaking of a former (or still existing home). These descriptions, of how objects are disposed, given away and related to when downsizing to a caravan, indicate aspects of change and rupture, but are also related to creating a life in the present continuous (see Marcoux 2001a, 2001b). In the stories that follow, the relationship between the house and the caravan remains a contradictory one, where an anticipated break with the former home is seldom fully accomplished.

Divestment and disposal

Many full-time caravan dwellers experience a move from spacious houses into a spatially smaller domestic sphere. Among caravanners in Sweden and Spain, one can see that the disposal or divestment of objects is often expressed as a relief, largely embedded in the anti-material discourse narrative (see also Gregson and Beale 2004; Gregson et al. 2007). For others, however, the selling, giving away, disposal and storing are deeply emotional burdens. Laura and Peter, both around seventy, live in their motorhome on a full-time basis, most of the year on Camping Mares. Laura and Peter got married when they were eighteen and twenty years old respectively, and started their life together in different flats and for periods with their mothers in their native village in the northeast of England. When a house they rented was demolished, Laura and Peter were given a council house with three bedrooms that they at a later stage were able to buy. In the mid-1980s, however, the children had moved out, they had experienced a break-in and Laura wanted to move. So they ended up in a two-bedroom semi-detached house close to the village centre, which they lived in until they, upon retirement, decided to buy a caravan and leave the UK.

Eight years ago they did not know what a motorhome was. 'Well that's a bit of a lie', Peter says. At home they would pass a place by the local airport called 'Homy Motorhomes'. 'I saw them and thought, oh these funny caravanning things.' At first they wanted to buy a flat. They had not really been to Spain much, but Greece, where they liked to go on holidays, was too cold in the winter. When they started looking for what was up for sale, they soon discovered that it would be too expensive. Peter and Laura bought the motorhome in 2003 and sold the house in 2005, doing some travelling when the house was rented out. At first they thought about buying a caravan. They never thought of motorhomes because they had never really seen them. 'It is like with anything else, once you get one, you see them all the time', Peter smiles. They had a Renault Mégane car, but the caravan dealer said they could not tow anything with that car. Realizing they would need to get a new car and a caravan, Peter thought about the motorhomes they had seen by the airport. They drove over and ended up buying a small van. Neither of them had ever driven anything bigger than a car before. When finally selling the house, they left furniture with the woman who bought it, and gave a lot of belongings away.

Laura and Peter's story shows how the process of downsizing through material divestment is not instant, but stretched over a long period of time and shaped by the couple's mobility pattern. 'We have thrown clothes all over Europe. We just ask; have you worn this the last 6 months?' When moving, Laura made a small photo album out of the boxes and boxes overflowing with photographs. One box was put together and given to her daughter, but the rest of the photos were brought to a container of recycling in the centre of their village. 'It was very difficult', they admit.

Clearly, in the context of Camping Mares, downsizing is perceived as a necessary step towards what I call the present continuous. The caravanners' ideas of the good life are strongly connected to arguments about an excess of things. While the caravanners recognize the emotional burden of leaving their inherited things and possessions, they simultaneously employ a moralizing materialist critique as part of a larger argument around their own discovery of the good life in a 'mobile' lifestyle. For most of the caravan dwellers at Camping Mares, the good life is also made possible at a particular stage in life, where the unmaking of a home rather should be understood in terms of change and rupture than a stabilizing process of reworking memories and relationships.

Issues of rupture are particularly crucial when dealing with acts of disposal. When reflecting upon their move from the house, John and Lucy repeatedly refer to their possessions as having little value, either to themselves or their family. In their motorhome wardrobe there are few clothes on the hangers. John is mostly concerned with comfort and Lucy claims she has to 'tear the clothes off him' when they are dirty. When working full-time in the UK, the couple both had uniforms or work clothes, and they only brought warm clothing for wintertime and what they term to be 'comfortable camping clothes' in lighter material to the campsite. Clearing the house in the UK and moving into the motorhome, they dispatched most of their belongings to charity stores.

'What matters is the people', says Lucy as a comment upon how she, like Peter and Laura, threw bags of family photos in the bin when moving from their house into a motorhome. When sorting through the photos, they separated the ones that would interest the children and gave some to each of them, but they threw away all the photos from their own youth. 'You keep them in your head, you remember them', Lucy explains. 'And you don't want people laughing at you', John grins. No photos were brought with them in the motorhome. 'We don't have room for all of them anyway', Lucy says, when referring to her grandchildren. 'There are sixteen of them; it would be unfair to have just some of them. Some vans have shelves, but here you would have to stick them everywhere.' In the case of Lucy and John, the absence of photographs come as a consequence – and embedded part of – the process of downsizing to the motorhome. Lucy excuses or explains the lack of family photos with the size of the caravan. Here, the construction and planning of their motorhome is seen as not giving room for the display of family photos. The example of Lucy and John suggests that we can also read this sorting of objects as part of the making of a caravan life in the present continuous, creating a home with a particular temporal character – not directed particularly towards maintaining continuity into the future, but to adjustment to an immediate present.

Disposal of personal objects and possessions have similar expressions among the permanent residents at Swedish Lake Camping. Petra and Edward, my neighbours who in 2011 had recently moved into a caravan on a permanent basis, had sent many of their belongings to bazaars and auctions. Only a small table, covered with candles and ornaments, is brought from the apartment they sold. 'I don't miss all the stuff', Petra says, 'When we were out travelling I never missed home and all the stuff', recalling her huge wardrobes that were never empty and the shelves with things and clothing. There were drawers they had not opened in years and three spacious IKEA bags full of just curtains. 'Why do you have that? To change curtains all the time?' Edward agrees, adding: 'Are we the ones that own the things, or do they own us? It is very hard and a lot of work to own that much.' Edward here clearly recognizes the agency of the things themselves, indicating that they can 'own him': they are beyond his control, and force him to socially deal with them in a particular manner. The act of disposal

Figure 10 External Storage, Camping Mares (photo by Terje Tjærnås).

for Edward is thus the intention to get back in control by actually 'breaking' with his possessions through an act of downsizing.

Storage

Whereas acts of disposal of possessions occupy a rather central position in caravanners' narratives of moving, the actual homebuilding on the campsite by large contradicts the materialist critique they connect these acts to in the first place. I will show later in the chapter that a conventional house aesthetic informs the ways 'mobile' caravans become 'static'. When possessions that do not fit in the new mobile dwelling are not disposed of or passed on because they are deemed necessary or of sentimental value, an attempt is made to store them. Insights into the strategies for storing are central to an understanding of the actual problems many caravanners encounter when downsizing to a smaller living unit. Storing is usually enabled in the interiors of the caravan or motorhome itself, but also in awnings or in separate storage sheds. The caravan's spatial construction is one that visibly and materially separates areas for storage: closets, cupboards and wardrobes. Caravanners' preoccupation with storing is a common object of discussion and of great concern when choosing a model to buy. During the caravan trade fair inspections, evaluations of internal and external storage took up considerable time and effort and were often a determining factor for which model to buy. Among caravan and motorhome manufacturers, the possibility for adding storage space needed however to be valued against the needed space for sofas, tables, beds and kitchen counters. Among full-time and seasonal caravanners, the actual prefabricated caravan or motorhome is usually unable to accommodate the range of housing gear and possessions that caravanners find necessary for maintaining a full-time caravan life.

By means of comparison, the anthropologist Inge Daniels (2010) shows how, since the 1960s, the number of possessions making their way into the relatively small dwelling of the contemporary Japanese house has increased steadily, leading Japanese middle-class couples and families to invent a variety of storage strategies. On Camping Mares, Lucy and John have also invented various systems of storage in their small motorhome. In the bottom of the wardrobe one finds Lucy's *Super King* cigarettes (smuggled in from Gibraltar from one of the British permanents at the site). Important paperwork – insurance papers, pensions and bills – is kept in a pink box in one of the cupboards facing the kitchen in the back. In comparison to newer motorhome models, Lucy and John's motorhome has no outdoor compartments and the couple needs to rely on the interior storage. Sofa seats can be lifted, covering umbrellas, thick jackets and tools, and that which does not fit into the compartments and cupboards is stored on the ceiling bed that is not used for sleeping. Presents given by friends and neighbours at the site can sometimes constitute a problem, as they feel obliged to keep items they lack room for in the limited space.

Likening the Japanese home with that of a container, Daniels (2010) argues that in contrast to the UK dwelling that usually lasts over time and with a steady movement of people moving in and out, the contemporary Japanese homes 'hold a particular group of inhabitants who during one generation fill the space with their possessions' (2010: 150). The surplus of objects involves the addition of storage space, but Daniels shows, after four decades the limits are reached and the building is destroyed (ibid). The Japanese case poses an interesting parallel to the caravan, whose temporal character is visible in its function as home to a limited part of a family in a new life phase. In the case of Camping Mares, external storage in the form of sheds and boxes is commonly constructed, because the space of the caravan itself is viewed as too limited to actually enable full-time dwelling. Some of the permanents on Camping Mares cover their pitch area with a number of plastic storage sections bought at a local hardware store to enable the storing of objects regarded necessary for full-time living. Caravanners that do non-contracted work on the site are particularly in need of external storage facilities – for cooking, food preservation or tools.

But storing personal belongings also requires more mobile arrangements that cross national borders. In the case of Lucy and John, they still have winter clothes in the wardrobe of their neighbour in the UK. When moving into the motorhome, Laura and Peter, on the other hand, decided to keep some ornaments and things, packed away in boxes in their daughter's loft. On recurring visits back to the UK, they however slowly cleared it out, keeping only a few nice dresses and the only suit and overcoat Peter has ever owned. The suit now travels up and down the UK for funerals and weddings on Peter and Laura's return visits. This relates to how the move from the house to a motorhome or caravan, and later in the mobile dwelling from the UK to Spain, is embedded with notions of insecurity related to both finances and health. Whereas daily life in a present continuous involves a neglect of economic insecurities, family and own health are seen as the only possible reasons for why caravan life could possibly come to an end. Storing certain objects thus becomes a way of securing future options if changes need to be made. Peter's travelling suit and overcoat also provide an interesting example of how certain belongings – even if left behind – gain mobile patterns of their own, separate from that of the couple in the mobile dwelling.

The problem of minimizing and downsizing that the caravanners face when having decided to move from a house or a large apartment is in retrospect often framed as a positive change, where the new life on wheels is experienced as liberated from the material constraints of daily house-led life. For seniors like Laura and Peter, and many of their campsite neighbours that have quit work prior to fully paid retirement, caravans play an important part also in what can be approached as a changed household structure. The new life is lived in couples, physically detached from family obligations encountered in the UK, but is also in many cases based around a household unit that no longer is one of production, but merely consumption. The material form of the caravan and the motorhome enables a certain form of daily life, and puts constraints on others (for instance related to the issue of space) that are closely related to the couple as primarily a consumption unit.

Figure 11 Storage Sections (photo by Terje Tjærnås).

What is a 'real home'?

When parents, family or friends opt for a full-time caravan life, clashes occur in expectations towards the material form and qualities of a 'home'. This ambiguous relationship to 'home' is frequently a topic of conversation, especially among couples that live full-time in motorhomes and spend some months every year in the UK. Peter and Laura emphasize the fact that the motorhome is now their home, wherever they park it: 'We can bring our home wherever we want to.' When visiting their family in the UK, Peter and Laura will seldom spend the night inside their children's house, even though one of the daughters even has a spare bedroom only for their use. 'But we like to stay in the van,' Laura says. 'We don't like staying in the house ... we feel like this is our house and it is wonderful to get here again. It is like when you have been away and you think it is so nice to be back again and back in your own bed.' Margaret, on the other hand, laughs about how her family thought 'they were nuts', when she and Gary preferred to sleep in the van on the driveway when visiting children and grandchildren in the UK.

While a central part of such stories shows the importance of maintaining independence and intimacy even when visiting family members, it also reveals tensions between the family's expectations of a 'proper' home sphere, and what the mobile dwelling has become for the couple in question. Petra's children did not support her and her husband Edward's move to a caravan at Lake Camping, even if it entailed a geographical distance of only some kilometres. The caravan couple's own attitude to a 'proper' home is obviously one that also has changed throughout their life. As the coming out stories in Chapter 3 show, some of them had little or no relation to mobile dwellings before getting the idea of 'going away' or 'travelling'. For the seniors at Camping Mares for instance, full-time caravan dwelling is thus an option that appears at quite a late stage in their life course.

The resistance of family and friends to caravans and motorhomes as full-time dwellings reflect the ambiguous position the caravan holds in contemporary Western societies. In some instances, a negatively loaded 'gypsy' analogy is near to hand. Lucy and John told me that their son back in the UK had had the impression 'we were living like gypsies'. As their son had visited the site however, he was impressed with the pool and the 'resort-like feeling'. Sarah's granddaughter, with whom I coincided on a visit to Camping Mares in 2012, told me that her friends in her UK school thought her grandmother was 'some kind of gypsy' since she was living on a campsite in Spain, reflecting again the stigma attached to the caravan and its public association to a negatively perceived 'gypsy lifestyle'. In the next section I will show how extensions of living space hold elements of conventional 'real home' aesthetics, while simultaneously securing potential mobility through logics of temporality.

Fake fireplaces and 'real home' aesthetics

Much effort, time and money are put into transforming the caravan and the awning into what is referred to as a 'real home', a process that can take years. At

Camping Mares, caravanners like Gary and Margaret had bought their caravans on-site and fully furnished. A couple in their thirties that I ran into during my early stages of fieldwork had been able to directly move into their caravan at the site, without the need of work, or purchases. The previous owners had left everything, including the bed sheets. On my second visit to their awning, the couple had put their first private belongings on display: two family photos. 'Little by little we will try to make it more our style', they said.

Karen and Tim, on the other hand, a couple in their sixties, had slowly moved from keeping the caravan as a holiday home to relocating to Camping Mares on a full-time basis. Their awning was a pastel experience, including a fireplace decorated with white rocks and candles, and an almost intimidating presence of artificial butterflies. The caravan was bought in a year when the prices on Camping Mares were very high. Only managing with some money from Tim's redundancy, they nevertheless spent 10,000 pounds on 'doing it up'. 'Wasn't it nice?' I ask. 'Oh, yes', Karen says. 'I fell in love with the way it was, it was beautiful, but everyone wants to put their own stamp on it.' Their inspiration mainly came from looking around at other caravanners' arrangements at the site and a gradual learning of where to buy materials.

Expanding one's living space beyond the caravan exterior walls is an active project that includes the balancing of establishing permanent versus temporary building structures. The expanding of living space on the pitch reveals how temporary structures of living stretch towards those of permanency while simultaneously protecting the potential mobility of the mobile dwelling. Campsites, like Camping Mares and Lake Camping, display particular caravan aesthetics that manifest how boundaries between interior and exterior, temporary and permanent, as well as private and public are fluid and constantly negotiated. Among the dwelling practices of full-time and seasonal caravanners, not only the external changes to, but also the interior design of the mobile home is similarly challenged, maintaining important aspects of mobile self-sufficiency, while at the same time managing modifications of the standardized interior, providing the caravan with a house-like character.

Some of the more heavy work in Karen and Tim's caravan required skilled expertise, and rebuilding caravans and sheds has become one of the main niches for non-contracted work at the campsite. On the permanent pitches of Camping Mares, water pipes and drainage are laid to the pitch, in one position, as well as one plug for electricity. It is the caravanners' responsibility to employ a handyman and install drains or wires from the pitch into the caravan. Many of the younger male residents at Camping Mares have experience with carpentry or electricity work and take on cheap building jobs for their neighbours at the site, advertising their services by word of mouth (Leivestad 2017c).[5] Many of the site's younger, male residents have thus been able to extend their working engagement into the very site itself. It often happens that the work is poorly – or slowly – done, leading to enormous amounts of frustration on the part of the caravan owner.

The possibilities of buying cheap caravans and redoing them, however, also open up for various forms of property investments within an informally organized market (cf. Castells and Portes 1989; Hart 1973). A central part of the informal economy that takes shape on Camping Mares circulates around the caravans, in the forms of subrentals, refurnishing, building, investments and sales. The property market that has developed thus exists as an informal parallel to the regulated property market many caravanners have withdrawn from. When prices were dropping on the site, some of its permanent residents made profits out of buying up cheap and worn-down property and redoing it. One of Lucy's neighbours, a retired builder, had bought several caravans on the site and sold them on at a profit. When experiencing problems with the owners of a caravan on his street, Lucy's neighbour offered to buy it off them and refurnished the awning before selling it on, thereby also choosing who he wanted as his street neighbour. Helen is an example of how the self-contained campsite has provided a niche for financing her life in Benidorm (see Appel 2012). She has specialized in sewing caravan heavens, layers of fabrics – usually white – to cover the ceiling of the awning. Helen has a small business card and takes orders from Camping Mares residents and from neighbouring campsites. In 2011 she had also, together with her neighbour and boyfriend, bought two worn-out caravans on the site, which they were moving to an empty pitch, redoing and putting up for sale (see also Leivestad 2017c).

In the case of Karen and Tim's caravan home, and Helen's antique retro fulfilment, one finds how the redoing, furnishing and decoration of caravan homes often are done on the model of a former or ideal home. Karen wanted the fake fireplace, evoking the one she left behind in the house they sold in the UK. At the same time, the aesthetics of these caravan homes carry material elements commonly found in conventional holiday homes, with the display of local 'Spanish' objects and souvenirs, such as ceramics. What is most significant however is the use of materials such as plastic, laminate and synthetic fabrics – a use that has both economic and aesthetic reasons. Whereas Gary and

Figure 12 Awning Interior (photo by Terje Tjærnås).

Margaret buy furniture and decoration at the IKEA near Alicante, the many local Benidorm businesses run by Chinese migrants, also called 'Chinese shops' or €1 markets, are popular places for obtaining products for decoration and furnishing. Judy Attfield (1999: 81) suggests the use of synthetics and plastic materials in British council state home decoration to evoke a 'popular contemporary'. In a similar vein we can see the caravan aesthetics, by its use of particular forms of ephemeral materials, holding an aesthetic ideal of transition and temporality. The use of materials that are easily changed, moved or transferred is part of a wider construction of the temporary dwelling and its owner's negotiation of illegal permanence that will be discussed later in this chapter.

'Don't go knockin' if the caravan's rockin''

In the context of the caravan as a contained domestic sphere, structural explanations on the use of space are near at hand. The separation of zones of cooking and sleeping, motivated by an explicit discourse of interior and exterior related to smell, odours and humidity, are kept in regulated domestic areas. But these divisions of space are also related to forms of human practice in an intimacy with the outdoors. My neighbours at Lake Camping, Petra and Edward, were concerned with how a specific material in their awning carpet absorbs humidity, and how ventilation openings are meticulously kept open in order to maintain an indoor life in the outdoors. Benny and Louise, in the caravan on the opposite side of the road, emphasize that no matter how comfortable their camping routines are, this life is still 'primitive'. Louise loves to hear how the rain hammers on the caravan roof, and would much rather sit inside in her caravan during bad weather than in her town apartment. While such boundaries between the outdoors and indoors are reworked and adapted to, there are ways substances travel on a campsite that might cause problems and necessitate measures. Sound, noise and smell travel smoothly along the tight rows of caravans, and sneak almost unhindered through thin caravan walls. The open fields of Lake Camping or the closeness of pitches on Camping Mares can allow for sometimes unfettered view into domestic life. One campsite resident laughingly repeated the common saying that you 'don't go knockin'' if the caravan's rockin'', and emphasized the fact that she would never approach a friend's caravan if the door was locked. 'That means they could be up to anything', she said, revealing how a locked door could be an indicator of sexual encounters.

Writing on Dayak longhouses on Borneo, Christine Helliwell (1996) offers an example for comparison. She sets out to critique earlier ethnography in the area, where portrayals of the Borneo longhouse have tended to put a strong belief in the 'private' character of the inner section of the Dayak longhouse apartment (1996: 137). Her ethnography convincingly shows however that the material nature of the partition that separates one apartment from another is one characterized by permeability, made up by pieces of bark and similar materials, leaving gaps for movement in both directions (ibid.: 137–8). This example illustrates well how sound and light flow easily through a leaking boundary and the very material character of these boundaries – 'their flimsiness and permeability' (ibid.: 139).

On the permanent area of Camping Mares however, insight and maintenance of privacy are carefully regulated. On the roads of the campsite, one side of the street has patios facing the road, whereas on the other the awnings and patios are in the back. Lucy and John's new permanent caravan that they bought in 2011 is of the first kind, fitting well with Lucy's self-ascribed nosiness. The tiled patio is located in front of the glassed awning that completely hides the caravan. On plastic chairs in the shadow of a parasol, Lucy and John sit reading while small-talking with neighbours passing on the road and receiving spontaneous visitors from people all over the campsite. One British woman living on her own with the caravan facing the back, on the other hand, tells me that she 'likes her privacy', lived out on the spacious patio with no insight from neighbours and views towards the Benidorm hills. The building of physical barriers is one way of maintaining such privacy. Small gates, hedges and barriers made of wood and bamboo are used to separate one's pitch from others and to establish one's residential identity as owner-occupier in a hybrid leisure–residential space (Dolan 1999: 67).

But more importantly, the awning also serves as a medium of separation, hiding, but also protecting the caravan – the bedroom – from visual exposure. The caravan is parked on the edge of the pitch, and small blocked windows obstruct the view. Inge Daniels (2008) importantly notes that this creation of domestic boundaries is too often associated with what is read as a need for privacy. In the case of contemporary Japanese homes, while displaying a large number of physical barriers, Daniels argues that this should not lead to the conclusion that the Japanese home is particularly private. One of the points she makes is that one must not only look at the creation of physical barriers, but at embodied, everyday practices (2009: 126). Inside–outside boundaries are not clear-cut, but need to be seen as fluid and continuously re-created (2009: 134). In the case of caravan dwellers in Sweden and Spain, inside–outside boundaries are particularly fluid, as they create intimate relations with weather and the outdoors through living behind thin walls and temporary building structures. As also noted by Daniels, the small plot of land – in this case the pitch – with little room for exterior space, also affects how the dwelling itself is used to create physical boundaries. The caravan's permeability however leaves many of these attempts unsuccessful – not hindering, but rather allowing for insights and sound flows.

Sound, in this context, is viewed among the caravanners as particularly troublesome. The sensory openness of a site, where spatial planning and material 'thinness' allows for insight and the easy travel of sound, is seen as providing safety and a positively valued internal surveillance, and it is also the basis upon which moral conflicts around social order arise. Most critical is the issue of experienced noise. Among the British caravanners at the site, issues and problems of noise will often go along the lines of national stereotyping. One of the Norwegian couples at the site caused Peter to eventually report them to reception for having the television on too loud inside their motorhome. What Peter regarded as 'noise' was also reinforced by the fact that he did not understand the television language. Quarrelling among couples or family members with loud voices often cause reactions among the full-time residents at the site. Not being able to accommodate your tone of voice illustrated a lack of experience with the caravan materiality, and lack of concern for your neighbours (cf. MacDougall 1999). One British resident that had lived on Camping Mares for ten years put it this way when reflecting on the recent changes on the site: 'There are too many people from Liverpool, they don't know how to behave in a caravan. A caravan is your home, but you also need to think of your neighbours, in terms of shouting and traffic.' 'Noise' in shape of loud sound and voices thus breaks with the established national codes of behaviour that caravanners regard as part of 'good caravanning', and also feed into regional portrayals of indecent caravanners.

Concealed caravans

Expanding the domestic space to the outside patio is a way of earning more living space, but also to close out smells and humidity. Thus, while kitchens are placed in sheds on the patio, the toilets in the caravans are seldom used, except for a pee during the night. At Camping Mares, most awnings attached to the permanent caravans are insulated with wooden cladding and have double-glazed sliding doors or windows in the front. Gary has himself laid the tiled flooring in the awning and the original caravan door has been changed in favour of a wooden one. Even the wheels of the caravan, the wheels that are crucial for its potential mobility, are concealed behind wooden cladding and caravan skirts. These material arrangements prevent wind from passing underneath the caravan, but also attributes to the changing of a caravan's physical properties – from one of mobility to one indicating stasis and permanence.

Seen from inside the awning, the caravan itself is usually hidden behind big curtains. The awning is covered by white fabric heavens, while the floors are tiled. In Helen's caravan, the caravan heaven expands on the sides of the exterior caravan wall, hiding its original structure and shape. Karen and Tim, on the other hand, have two large printed curtains that hide the caravan door 'so you won't even see there is a caravan in there', Karen smiles when showing me around, 'we have made the caravan the bedroom while the living room is out here', she adds, referring to the furnished awning. Also Helen points out that 'the caravan is really a bedroom, that is all it is' (Leivestad 2017c).

Figure 13 Kitchen Shed (photo by Terje Tjærnås).

These material changes point to how the caravan home is separated into different spheres, evoking separations of the classical backstage and frontstage and where the difference between outdoor and indoor is of great importance (Birdwell-Pheasant and Lawrence-Zúñiga 1999: 4). Although most caravans are fully self-contained with original kitchens, most permanents at Camping Mares have removed their interior kitchens, leaving the interior caravan space purely as a bedroom that usually is hidden from view. While the caravan is kept as the intimate space for the couple, the awning and outdoor patio is where you eat, watch television and have guests. The awning thus appears as the all-purpose living room (Attfield 1999: 74) and through the extensions of the caravan, the caravanners largely reproduce domestic patterns of spatial structure and division. On Lake Camping there are similar separations between the different spaces of the caravan home. The awning remains the most important space, where daily social life and socializing takes place. In Sweden however, there are stronger legal restrictions regarding the built structures on campsites, meaning the indoor living space is more restricted to the caravan and the awning. As long as weather permits it, outdoor barbequing remains a popular way of preparing food.

On the Spanish campsite, cooking and food preparation are usually done in a separate kitchen shed. The kitchen might, in some caravan units, be placed within the awning, but as Karen thoroughly explained to me, the best thing is to have a separate kitchen shed to avoid the smell and the fire risk. The motorhomers on Camping Mares' touring area also installed separate kitchen tents outdoors to avoid the smell. 'You wouldn't like to cook in your bedroom either, would you?' one informant smiled to me. On the campsite then, particular attention is paid to smell. As Moeran has suggested, smell has 'situated meanings' (2007: 165). Smell as it occurs as an outcome of cooking, through damp and frying odours, is in this setting viewed as negatively loaded and something to be avoided in interior caravan areas.

Not made of bricks and mortar

On Lake Camping, seasonal and full-time caravanners take great care to prevent humidity and maintain an indoor environment within the awning tent structure. Wooden flooring is a common arrangement, covered with synthetic grass and specialized awning carpets that are designed to handle the damp and humidity. On Camping Mares' touring area, caravanners also cover the ground in their awning with different layers of materials that are used to keep humidity out. The top layer is usually an awning carpet that lets humidity through if necessary.

But on Camping Mares' permanent area, humidity appears as a rather surprising, but nonetheless troubling, outcome of what I have described as the concealing of caravans. When I returned to the site in spring 2015, problems had occurred in several of my informants' awnings. Lucy's family had first discovered the bulges in her bathroom floor. An inspection by Lucy's builder neighbour revealed a pipe leak, and the whole toilet interior would have to be renovated. What Lucy did not know was that the pipe leak inside the caravan had transported water out of the caravan and underneath the entire awning wooden flooring. Now, humidity had revealed itself through a bulky awning floor and an intense smell of mildew. Lucy asked her neighbour to take on the job of digging up the floor, tearing down the fabrics covering the awning, and putting new panelling in floors and awning walls. Since Lucy had bought her permanent caravan on-site, fully furnished, no one knew what would be hidden underneath the awning floor. After a day of work, an intimidating smell of rot filled what was left of the awning structure, bringing to light the wet and rotten wooden pallets that had been supporting the awning floor.

Several of Lucy's neighbours were also experiencing problems with bulky and swaying floors, and one resident suggested that the awning structures in general could not handle more than fifteen years: 'You realise these aren't made of bricks and mortar.' The problem, as she saw it, was the heat and the containment of the interior space, pointing to the problem of using a prefabricated caravan as a full-time home in an environment it is not built to cope with. The decay produced by humidity at Camping Mares also shows how the transformation of the mobile dwelling into full-time housing through a concealment of caravan features have material consequences that go way beyond the intentions of the caravan owners. Here, water and heat contribute to changing the properties of the materials that have been used to advance a more conventional home aesthetic with solid flooring and 'proper' walls. The tent structure does not provide the same ventilation channels that a house-built structure would, and the use of cheap materials not designed and intended to support a floor, such as the pallets, contribute to a rather rapid decay of the domestic sphere. How these materials come into play with further ideas about the 'temporary' or 'permanent' home is a question I will return to in a moment.

What is a temporary dwelling?

By extending the domestic living space and continuously building to improve the living standard of the caravans, caravan residents like Gary and Margaret contribute to physically immobilizing the mobile dwelling. The changes made, however, are easily changeable (and normally within what is a reasonable economic investment) and such experienced ease in changing one's living space makes the mobile dwelling potentially mobile in another sense. Despite their nickname 'permanent', the fact that these caravans are not permanent, but hold possibilities for moving, changing and leaving, makes up an important part of what we can argue is their potential mobility.

The caravan adjusts to, bends and challenges notions of temporality. Building practices at Camping Mares are performed in processes of transforming the temporary structures of the caravan dwelling into a more permanent kind. But caravans also shape and form temporal, shifting and contained landscapes. Campsites are regulated under national, regional and local legislation. Such legislation is not only concerned with issues of safety and nature protection, but also hold particular conceptions of what the temporary should be and should look like.

The company that owns Lake Camping has formulated a long list of regulations that concern the use of the campsite, stating clearly that all their establishments are directed towards tourists, meaning that it is prohibited to use the campsite for full-time residency, or 'other kind of temporary accommodation that is not aimed at tourism'. Through the regulations, the company also states that no one is allowed to register the campsite as their place of residence, but, upon agreement, post can be sent to the reception. The daily manager of Lake Camping solves these apparent legal issues by making his full-time guests sign separate summer and winter season contracts, and residents like Kristian and Ulla are registered at their family's address, while having their post sent to reception. While municipal legislation and the local area plan of Lake Town regulates the placing of touring and permanent caravans at Lake Camping, it does not regulate building installations such as wooden terraces. Within the campsite regulations, however, there are also directions concerning the private material constructions of the site. No fences are allowed, and while fabric wind protections are permitted, they have to be placed at least 1.5 metres away from the road or the neighbouring pitch. The enclosure of pitches is prohibited and so is the planting of flowers and bushes in the ground, as well as the building of floors and verandas outside the awning. Wooden flooring is allowed, but it must be removed by the end of the contract. Most of the regulations are however not strictly followed. From 2011 to 2017, on regular visits to the campsite, I watched how some of the seasonal caravanners' pitches had transformed into large wooden verandas, with decorative walls, barbeque areas and flowerbeds. Benny and Louise had built a wooden veranda outside the awning, and admitted that the management seemed to allow them as regulars to break with some of the site regulations. 'We try and have as little to do with them as we can', Benny smiled.

The material building practices of the residential caravanners at Camping Mares are seldom consistent with the campsite's own regulations, or the Valencian legislature that informs them. Every January, the residents at Camping Mares are given a ten-page contract to sign. And although the last article states that the contract has been translated into other languages, this is not the case. While she has carefully signed every single page of the contract, Lucy admits she has no clue what it actually says. The contract is protected by Spanish civil law, *Código civil*, and its content has a continuous referral to the regulations of the Valencian government concerning regional tourist camps.[6] Stated in the contract are the regulations for the use of the pitches on the site and the site's facilities, such as how many persons the pitch fee covers, the parking of a car in such a way that it does not block the way for a potential fire brigade, and the payment of the annual rent.[7] The more interesting part of the contract however is found in an article which states that 'the renter is not allowed to sub-let the pitch'. Though clearly in disagreement with the contract, and among the residents a well-known illegal activity, the sub-letting of caravans is a central part of the site's informal economy. Keys are left with a number of contact persons who often control the sub-letting of caravans for friends and neighbours.

But during the winter of 2017, the manager Carlos decided it was time for retirement and a new manager was appointed. Gary and Margaret, Lucy and all the other permanent residents at Camping Mares were called to a meeting where the new plans for the campsite were announced. Here they were told that all private renting out of caravans would be sanctioned. Gary thought it was fair 'in the end they are running a business. And actually it's the way it has always been.' But the news that the possibility of renting out would disappear, 'freaked' people out, Gary says. Eventually, some of the permanents on the site sold their caravans and left, including Lucy's handyman neighbour and his wife.

Article 4.4 in the regulations of the Valencian government deals more importantly with how a notion of the temporary is protected through prohibiting certain material installations. It reads that it is prohibited to install elements that do not correspond with the temporal, proper and habitual stay on campsites, or that threaten the touristic image of the establishment.[8] More concretely, it is added in the article that the installation on pitches of floors, fences, washing rooms, white goods or 'any other element that through its fixation transmits an image of "permanence" at the campsite' is not allowed.

In general, all the regulations and restrictions concerning the material installations of the campsite revolve around a temporary structure that resonates with the practice of the hook-up. Gary and Margaret, for instance, have laid their tiles without cement and nails to prevent the nature of a permanent tiling. Cement also stops the water from coming through, which is a problem at the site. Building regulations demand that structures must be capable of being removed within hours. Many of the owners of permanent caravans have so-called 'benillars'; an awning structure with wooden cladding in the canvas that is screwed to the floor. The campsite manager has allowed the already established benillars to exist, but does not allow for any new ones to be put up. The awnings are not supposed to be concreted to the ground, and neither are the sheds. Wooden fences are not allowed, and though most awnings have wooden cladding, this is normally screwed on so you easily can take it down again (Leivestad 2017c).

Valencian authorities occasionally perform checks on the campsites. When a check is coming up, the campsite manager will make sure to put up an announcement so people will have the opportunity to take away anything that could be considered permanent. Gary recalls how on one such control, a neighbour would take down a fence, and then simply put it back up again when the authority's representatives have disappeared from the site. Many permanent residents have sheds with inside bathrooms and showers that contradict the temporary structure regulations, but as long as one closes the sheds, inspectors will not know what is inside and are only allowed to enter with a warrant. The location of the pitch is however not without importance, and it is worse for those, like Gary and Margaret, who have a caravan facing the main road. Their neighbour across the road, who also holds a corner pitch, had in 2013 just put up a new red shed. It came in a flat pack and is now a fully equipped bedroom. Referring to the fact that there were already a few of the same model around the site, they refused to take it down. As Gary and the others agreed, they would never like to have stayed on the other campsite run by the Camping Mares owner: 'It's way too regimental with no sheds allowed or anything.'

Others hurry to silently build their illegal sheds, arguing that 'as long as it is up, he [the manager] won't ask to take it down again'. During fieldwork in 2013, Lucy and John's neighbours across the road were working from day to night, with help from their handyman neighbour, to build a new extension. Located on the part of the road where the caravan prevents a view of the private patio, from the road one could only hear the constant hammering. The British couple in their fifties were happy to show me the ongoing project, but would not let me photograph it as 'we are not really allowed to do this you know. It is not allowed. Better that the campsite doesn't know about it', the man literally whispered. I entered the backside patio to see a large extension built of chipboard with solid structure and proper doors coming to life. 'It is not allowed, and we don't want to upset them. But we thought that as long as it is already up, they can't do much about it', the man smiled. Information about the illegality of permanent building structures is part of the silent knowledge shared among the campsite residents.

National, regional and local legislation and regulations – both in Sweden and Spain – are clearly preoccupied with how to maintain the touristic image of campsites and to avoid any risk of a shantytown appearance. This can be related back to the historical controversies of the campsite as a contested place located in a conjuncture of permanent housing and temporary leisure life. It is well worth noting how the regulations of Lake Camping and Camping Mares aim at protecting a touristic image through regulating and maintaining 'the temporary'. Through a written abandonment of 'permanent structures' and material objects that embed notions of permanency, the campsite is imagined as a mobile space – as one constituted of people and materialities passing through, but not staying on.

From mobility to fixity

Establishing a full-time caravan home is based in the unmaking of an already existing domestic form. I have shown in this chapter that unmaking takes place in a process of downsizing through divestment, disposal and storing of material possessions that do not fit in a spatially limited domestic sphere. Whereas downsizing can be emotionally burdensome, it is often referred to as a relief and a central aspect of *withdrawal*, liberating the caravanners from the material house order that they feel has taken control over them. At Camping Mares and Lake Camping, conventional aesthetic ideals of domesticity inform the caravanners' constructions of extensions, patios and barriers. Regulations and national legislation, however, affect and structure what kinds of materials are prohibited on a campsite intended for touristic activity. Whereas planning, legislation and directives imagine the temporariness of the campsite and its residents in certain ways, the practices of both the campsite managers and the caravan dwellers tell other stories of the relationship between 'the temporary' and 'the permanent'. Here a potential mobility is built into notions of temporality through concealed wheels and structures that can be easily dismantled. Such temporary structures of permanence co-exist with more stable and fixed building arrangements that alter the very idea of the campsite's temporariness.

In the case of Lake Camping, we can see that even if the company that owns the campsite prohibits full-time residency at the site, such permanency is made possible by the help of the daily manager's double season contracts, and the practical ways of avoiding the problem of registered residency. On Camping Mares, the semi-illegal permanence of the mobile dwelling is made possible by the management of the campsite that clearly is economically benefiting from their full-time residents. One issue that becomes prevalent is how residents in these semi-mobile places also find themselves in legal grey zones. Just as the mobile dwellings are legally supposed to be temporarily parked, its owners are also expected to be temporary residents.

I find it useful at this point to return to J. B. Jackson (1984) and the vernacular, where he puts forward an understanding of the moveable dwelling as characterized by the temporary, of realized mobility and impermanence. In the campsite setting however, the self-contained caravan and its relational exteriors produce landscapes where temporality and fixity seem mutually dependent. Whereas the potentially mobile features of a mobile dwelling are concealed and even altered by caravanners, these same mobile qualities are simultaneously actual requirements for the caravan's fixed immobility. Mobility, in this setting, is a requirement for stasis, as the mobile features of a mobile dwelling are necessary elements in enabling the caravan or motorhome to actually stay put.

In his account of the American mobile home, Wallis (1991) notes that just as the mobile home is a hybrid of vehicle and dwelling, the mobile home *land* is also one that holds a hybrid character. As Wallis shows, this hybrid character is evident both among the land's residents and how a site is institutionally

Figure 14 Rebuilding Caravan Awning (photo by Terje Tjærnås).

categorized. In the case of Lake Camping and Camping Mares, despite being legally regulated as tourist campsites, we see that they both appear and exist as hybrid spaces: as tourism destinations, country retreats, transient overnight stops and residential neighbourhoods. In the next chapter, I will explore how this hybrid vernacular space resonates with ideas, longings for – and practices of – particular forms of community.

5

Community: 'We have found here what we can't find at home anymore'

It is late August 2013, the hot and sticky end of summer. Dark clouds are hesitantly waiting over the mountains of the sierra, threatening to explode, only then to pass unnoticeably on. British holidaymakers are still absorbing the last bits of summer sun on Benidorm's beaches, while Spanish families are enjoying their last weeks of holiday before school starts in the second week of September. On Camping Mares' touring area, the pitches are empty, waiting for the hordes of winter-birds to arrive in mid-late September. All that is left is the red-brown dusty earth, the iron installations for shade curtains and the hedges and trees separating one pitch from another. 'Está flojito' ('it is slow'), the receptionist says, 'But we are not surprised, it is always the same at this time of the year.' The permanent area, however, is bursting with activity. Visiting children and grandchildren have taken over the caravans, spending their summer holiday in their parents' and grandparents' homes. The year-round permanents have moved into the shade, leading their regular rhythm, though less active than in the winter months when more friends are around. Sarah has had her family visiting for more than a month, all sleeping inside the caravan and awning. Margaret and Gary have put their chairs outside on the patio facing the awning and TV so they can spend every minute of the day outdoors.

For others, summer has brought along unpleasant surprises. A huge tumour has been discovered in John's body, unsettling the ground for both him and Lucy. He has rapidly lost weight and his otherwise cheerful face is dragged and grey. Following the decision to register for residency in Spain, he is able to receive the medical help he needs in Benidorm, and at the time of my visit he has started his first chemotherapy sessions. As we sit in the shade outside their awning, it is quieter than usual. Lucy and John are not alone, though. There is a steady movement of neighbours passing by. One brings cakes, another brings painkillers left over from their daughter who succumbed to cancer a few years ago, another brings strong painkillers he got on prescription, and another is offering lifts to the hospital and to take them shopping. 'It is everybody for everybody', Lucy says. The news of John's illness has reached England, and newly returning residents are stopping to express their worry. 'It is just like a little village you know', Lucy says. She is positive they would never find the same comfort of friends in England as they do here. 'At home you would lock yourself up. Here you sit outside and everyone passes by', John says.

Lucy and John's reflections on the mutual care found in their campsite village introduce several aspects of how specific understandings of community[1] are imagined, aspired for and practised among contemporary European caravan dwellers. Among the British caravanners at Camping Mares, the campsite emerges as the fundamental expression of a desire for village life that is considered to be lost or inaccessible in their home towns and (temporarily) abandoned neighbourhoods. In Sweden and Lake Camping, notions of good neighbourhood are, on the other hand, practised and valued through the technical and materialized skills and knowledge caravanning requires, where a reciprocal sharing and helping out become crucial parameters for how a particular form of community is understood.[2] While idealized forms of sociality at Lake Camping might seem less of a reality than what we find played out at Camping Mares, the caravanners at these two places still share many ideas about that which is longed for and that which is left behind.

Whereas the previous chapter focused on the material homemaking processes of creating homes on wheels, this chapter turns to how these same material structures and practices produce and nurture nostalgic narratives and aspirations of community based on expressed ideals of care, safety and visibility. Here, the spatial organization of the campsite, in balancing temporariness and permanence, the private and the public, also enables and facilitates certain forms of sociality that come to be connected with these same ideas of community life. John's observation of how sitting outdoors contributes to forms of care is important, as it raises central issues of the regulation of – and use of – space, and how this is linked to ideas about sociality. John's illness on Camping Mares brings forward questions of how care is found and practised among people that have moved and relocated abroad, but it also raises central issues of how a portrayed 'village' is imagined and understood with reference to a nostalgic portrayal of 'the good life' reinstated in the present continuous.

In scrutinizing such imaginations of the ideal caravan village, one needs also to look closer at that which is believed not to fit into the caravan community. Along with this I will argue that caravan (im)mobilities are acts of withdrawal, from aspects of contemporary late modern life related to national politics and the multicultural society that among the caravanners are symptoms of undesirable change and moral breakdowns. Understandings of the good life in a present continuous at the campsite are thus constructed in a repeated referral to an imagined good past and a problematic contemporary.

Neighbourhood lost and found

Let me spool even further back, to a chilly and windy June 2011 when a terraced brick house is in a state of transition. The living room floor is covered in boxes filled with Lucy and John's belongings, while one of the bedrooms upstairs is blocked with boxes belonging to the family that is going to rent the house until they can afford a mortgage and buy it. John tells me about the phases of redoing the house. On the walls there are posters they once put up, and broken wallpaper reveals layers of periods in their family life. From the leather couch in the dark living room, heavy with cigarette smoke, John shows me how he once built the fireplace himself with help from his granddaughter. Even the kitchen extension is John's own work. But now they cannot wait to move. 'We have had our time here … the children growing up here and everything. But it is time to move on … . It's our time now,' Lucy says. While we are watching another episode of the game show *The Weakest Link,* she admits that it does not feel good to be back. They 'feel trapped' since all they do is to sit inside, smoking, reading the *Daily Mirror* and the local newspaper and watching television.

Lucy and John bought the house for 10,000 pounds in the early 1980s. 'This neighbourhood used to be a good one, but not anymore', John sighs. 'Welcome to the slum', they say about the old worker's area with mostly terraced houses made for the workers in the cotton mills, once the big industry in Lancashire. 'It was a very good neighbourhood where people looked after each other. You didn't even have to lock your door … . Much like Camping Mares actually', Lucy says. 'But it has just gone down. It is worse every year we come back', they sigh. 'You only buy what you can afford,' John tells me, 'I would probably also like a big house in a nice neighbourhood if I had the money for it.' Lucy and John complain about the garbage that fills the streets and the 'immigrants taking over', people fighting

Figure 15 Campsite Street (photo by the author).

outside and the need to watch your car. We walk through deserted quiet alleys, looking at shops that are closed down. They used to have thirteen pubs on their nearby avenue, but the smoking ban struck hard and now there are only two left. The shops in the area used to be run by 'Indians and Pakistanis', but are mostly taken over by 'Polish and Eastern European'.

In the nights during my visit, we go out to the local working men's clubs to have a beer and play bingo. John knows the guard at the entrance and I am allowed in even though it is members only. In huge locales with carpeted floors and dark wooden furniture, John and Lucy used to come on Fridays, Saturdays and Sundays for the bingo. They know most of the people around: young girls working behind the counter and elderly women and men coming for their daily bingo session. John even used to be in the committee of one of the clubs and was in charge of the bingo. While we drink our beer, neighbours will stop and ask Lucy and John when they are leaving. The rumours of them moving abroad have spread. They tell me about a couple that rarely go out anymore, even though they used to be out all the time. John says it again, what he mentioned so many times in Benidorm: with their pensions they would not have been able to keep up a good life here, or even keep the house with all the taxes and expenses. Lucy and John's return visit to their Lancashire neighbourhood, between the TV shows, the abandoned pubs and the perceived insecurity, points to both continuity and rupture between the house-led life that many caravanners have withdrawn from, or dream of leaving, and the various relationships and connections they establish through relocation on campsites.

Death in the awning

Some years later, August 2014 is, as usual, humid and warm. Camping Mares is busy with holidaymakers displaying sun blisters and burned backs, the nights noisy with enthusiastic revelling from the pool parties organized by the campsite, and the weekly music shows in the restaurant. Not even the roads of Camping Mares are quiet, since children and teenagers have embarked on the many mobility scooters available for rent in Benidorm, and now use them for transport to the pool and into town. But inside John and Lucy's caravan, it is dark. The air conditioner installed on one of the awning inner walls pumps cool air into the room that has been rearranged to make room for the double sofa bed, covered with extra mattresses and clean, white sheets. John is dying. He has not had a proper meal since Christmas and I have rushed from Sweden to say goodbye. But as Lucy quietly says to me, 'How do you say goodbye to someone who is still there?'

The funeral is already arranged, prepared by Lucy and a Costa Blanca-based British funeral agent. Paying in advance has given them a considerable discount, so now Lucy's funeral, hopefully many years to come, has been pre-paid as well. John has insisted on taking part in the planning and choosing the last song: *Johnny Be Good*. Lucy has already seen this happening to many of her friends on Camping Mares, and John is not the first of my informants that passes away at an early age. In summer 2011, just after my fieldwork at Camping Mares, Clive passes away abruptly from a sudden and aggressive cancer. Sarah, then in her early fifties, finally decides to sell both the house in the UK and the motorhome, and buy a permanent caravan on Camping Mares. She is active, attending walking groups and Spanish classes, and has found a new friend in a campsite widow, which makes her feel less lonely among the site's many couples.

Life at Camping Mares is for many of its elderly residents closely connected to issues of illness and age and the need for, expectation of and demand for the care that comes along with it. As John is spending his last days in the awning, Laura and Peter are back at Camping Mares from a longer stay in the UK. They have left the motorhome in the UK, and bought a caravan on the site that is now parked in the touring area. Their stay in the UK is the result of Peter's sudden heart problems. He was miraculously saved at one of the local hospitals in Benidorm, but, still registered as resident in the UK, Peter was not entitled to health care in Spain and had to go back to get an appointment for follow-ups at the doctors. Being abroad for such long periods has put Peter far down on the priority list, so after months of waiting for the doctor's appointment they decided they might as well be waiting in the caravan in Spain. Peter and Laura's story illustrate how health appears as a rooted structure in this context and can in matters of life and death become a hindrance to mobility. A few months after John's last days in the awning, Laura is also diagnosed with cancer and passes away after a short illness some weeks before Christmas, leaving her husband of fifty years alone in their newly bought caravan parked on Camping Mares.

John and Lucy, on the other hand, registered their residency in Spain after they made the final move to Camping Mares. This has allowed John the necessary treatment from the Spanish health system, where a translator is available at medical visits. But going in and out of various hospitals in the area for months has taken its toll and John no longer wants to live. Their family has been around for holidays and to say goodbye, it is what Lucy calls 'the extended family' that takes their car out shopping, drives them to the hospital, brings medication, food and gifts and keeps them company. This is the social network that allows Lucy to stay on in the caravan even when John is gone. 'I will not be alone', she says. Lucy here refers to her Camping Mares friends through an idiom of kinship (Bell and Coleman 1999: 7; Oliver 2007: 135), where the conceptualization of friends as extended family not only reflects a geographic distance from one's kin, but also a belief in the campsite as producing these kinds of close relations.

But it is not only the care of the extended family that is believed to make life possible on one's own. Such belief in a caring community is also manifested in the material practices and spatial organization of the campsite. In the previous chapters, I have ventured the idea of the caravan as a self-sufficient unit, and much of the social organization of Camping Mares rests on the same aspects of self-sufficiency. Camping Mares' formal and informal service infrastructure enables a life to be led within the gates of the campsite. Apart from the services provided by the campsite such as laundry, restaurant, pool and a grocery shop, as well as weekly visits by a nurse in exchange for an extra fee, there is a wide range of informal services available at the site, offered by those who also attempt to make a living out of it (Leivestad 2017c).

Lucy and John's neighbour, who used to be a hairdresser in the UK, bakes cakes that she takes around and sells to neighbours from whom she also receives orders. Others again make extra income on offering lifts to and from the airport; 40 Euro is cheaper than taking the taxi. What we see developing is an informal economy of care, located mainly within the campsite gates. This care economy stretches into a wide range of domains – from cooking to building – that facilitates life on the site. Thus, both the informal care and the wider range of services provided by local businesses at Camping Mares contribute to the possibilities of continued life at the campsite even in times of death and illness. Just a few weeks after my final visit, on a sunny morning, John dies in the caravan awning. I follow the funeral in a Benidorm crematory via frequent Facebook messages from Margaret. *Johnny Be Good* is the last song.

Village nostalgia

Reciprocity as an essential part of a life on wheels relates closely to how the campsite is paralleled repeatedly with that of the small village. This 'village ideal' is most strongly apparent at Camping Mares, where many live during large parts of the year in the permanent area and where a nostalgic vision of sociality in part resonates with images of rural England at a past time (Andrews 2011: 107). Helen, who is in her early forties and has lived full-time at the site for four years, says that life at Camping Mares is 'really like living in a small village': 'You can be sure that if there is something you are curious about, someone will tell you before you have the chance to ask.' Friendship and networks are mainly formed through establishing relations with neighbours. In the permanent area, networks are formed among neighbours on the same street, while in the touring area, the proximity of the pitches allows for new friendships to be made. Lucy and John first got to know Peter and Laura when their motorhomes were parked next to each other in the touring area of Camping Mares. Later, Laura and Peter moved to a pitch next to Clive and Sarah, who on their part met Carol and Ben the first time they stayed on Camping Mares after recognizing a familiar dialect from northern England. Some, however, have extended their networks by socializing in the club, where the broad common tables allow for interactions with strangers when many people are present. This is where Lucy and John first were introduced to Margaret and Gary after forming a team for the Friday quiz.

This spatial planning – where physical daily mobility is channelled along a main crossing road, passing the common building and toilet blocks – contribute to the feeling of community sociality among the residents. In *The Dialectics of Shopping*, Daniel Miller (2001c) sees the importance of local shops in relation to an ideal of street life in British ideology. Miller uses the soap opera or the sitcom as an example, showing that while in the United States these are often centred around the home or the workplace as central loci of sociality, in the British version one can add 'the ideal of street life based around pubs and shops that remain paramount sites for the imagination of sociality and community' (ibid.: 67). Miller finds support for this observation in historical material, arguing that the street has been a hub for sociality in British society, an idea of street community we still find reproduced in soap operas such as *Coronation Street*[3] and *EastEnders*.[4]

On the touring area of Camping Mares, there is a wider network of smaller roads, whereas the permanent area consists of single streets departing from the main road, several of them dead-end. The neighbours seated outside, where their patios are facing the road, observe residents and visitors' comings and goings. In the opening vignette of this chapter, John and Lucy show that the outdoor life and the passing of people is one of the central elements in what they understand to be a caring neighbourhood. Due to this spatial planning, daily mobility – entering and departing the campsite, in between neighbours and toilet buildings – takes place within a specific realm of visibility. Neighbours meet in the street where news and gossip[5] are shared. Gossip can related to neighbours' economic behaviour or family relations, thereby asserting values and defining community standards (White 2000: 58). Temporary hook-ups with neighbours in the street and the site's communal areas also allows for rumours to circulate.[6] Rumours can at times deal with the infrastructural changes observable on the site and the intentions of the management with whom direct communication often is sparse, not least due to language issues. 'Poised between an explanation and an assertion' (ibid.), such rumours are located in a void between a personal need for predictability, and the sometimes unexpected changes on the site performed by a management that the caravanners have very little knowledge about.

Apart from the street, there are also other localities in the campsite village that are – or are at least expected to be – a centre of the social life at the site. In the next section I will describe the controversies around the use of the campsite 'club' that point to the positioning of the local club as a central location for socializing, and that this location is viewed not as a local commercial enterprise but rather as a public good of the site's – preferably British – residents. This village ideal articulated on Camping Mares is in many ways contrasted with the everyday reality of the Swedish Lake Camping. Here, the relationship between seasonal guests is generally limited to that between the closest neighbours on the street and kin. Lena, Kalle, Benny and Louise will sometimes go together to the campsite restaurant located by the gate to have a treat with a meal and a beer. On a few occasions during the summer season, there will be entertainment for guests by a troubadour or comedian that they attend for a good night out. The restaurant however, is not viewed as a central place for socializing. Social life is rather, as many researchers studying the Nordic countries have pointed to, centred on the private home – a sphere that in the campsite context is located around the awning and the outdoor pitch area. Benny and Louise regard the lack of a nice common building, with decent food and good music in the weekends, to be the result of the recent privatization of the campsite, which is now serving for short-term tourist demand in summer rather than caring for its local inhabitants.

Figure 16 Caravan Resident (photo by Terje Tjærnås).

Bingo tensions

When John dies in the caravan awning, it is been four years since we on my second day on fieldwork got to know each other at the Friday quiz. The quiz is one of the social gatherings that for many British caravanners at Camping Mares make part of a weekly schedule of social activities. Taking place within a frame of what at first glance might seem like a state of permanent leisure, John and Lucy had created their new life at Camping Mares keeping busy attending weekly activities such as bingo, quiz and cabarets, all of which play central parts in an ongoing reconstruction of British national identity through consumption – not only of British food and drinks, but also through forms of leisure associated with the English working-class north.[7] For the British population on Camping Mares, the campsite and their caravan neighbours have become the most important nodal point of reference in their new everyday life, thus largely cutting the campsite residents off, not only from Spanish culture and politics, but also partly from the wider British and international populations in the area[8]. Life at Camping Mares is nevertheless one where the expression of a European community on wheels is far from frictionless.

The weekly activities arranged in the campsite restaurant are all placed within a frame of reference to British culture. Manuel and his wife keep the restaurant open seven days a week, all year round, from 8.30 in the morning until late at night. During the winter season, Manuel's best customers are what he refers to as *los ingléses* (the English), who attend the restaurant on a near daily basis for their pints, bingo, Friday British quiz, cabaret entertainment, Premier League matches and Sunday roast dinner, cooked by one of the British residents at the site. For the Sunday cabarets, Manuel hires in one of the local British performers operating in Benidorm to play a familiar repertoire of classic hits from the 1950s to the 1970s, making Lucy and John, Margaret and Gary and the others sing and dance to 'Bobby's Girl', 'Daydream Believer' and 'Delilah'. 'The English want their beer, and we don't want to go far for it', as Gary puts it.

Among the British regulars at Camping Mares, the campsite restaurant is simply referred to as *the Club* with reference to the British working men's club,[9] where many of the site's caravanners have spent a considerable amount of time when living in the UK. The working men's club first saw light as part of the leisure developments in the industrialized UK of the 1880s, as one of the few working-class self-organized activities. Their greatest expansion, as centres of entertainment and cooperatives for beer purchase, came in the interwar years, offering real competition to the traditional pub as foci of working men's leisure (Clarke and Critcher 1985: 68–75). Lucy and John were regulars at their local working men's club, where John also sat on the board, whereas Clive would always go into his club on the way back from work to have a beer and 'get the tension out' before going home to his wife and children.

A reference to the working men's club is made on several levels. The campsite restaurant's spatial organization, with its open spaces, simple wooden furniture and long tables, pool tables and televisions with sport entertainment, evokes a material similarity with the northern English working men's club, so does also the fact that many of its guests have their regular seats. The nightly entertainment, requested and partly organized by the site's British residents, also resembles the weekend entertainment at working men's club, with bingo, raffles and live music cabaret. Manuel's management of the restaurant, his bad temper, and the national tension concerning the use of the place was, however, the subject of many conflicts during my fieldwork at Camping Mares. On return visits to the campsite, some new conflict always seemed to have emerged, often revolving around Manuel's quarrels with specific individuals, the increase of beer prices (which at the time still were low; a pint cost €1.50 in 2010 and in 2017), or Manuel's supposed preference of Spanish customers, which eventually lead to many of the regulars seeking the bars outside the campsite for their football matches and beers. On my annual visits to the site from 2012 to 2017, the management of the restaurant was causing increasing annoyance among many of the permanents at the site.

Drinking beer on the restaurant terrace in August 2013, neighbours of John and Lucy, a Liverpool couple in their mid-forties who are semi-retired and renting out their house at home to live at Camping Mares, complain loudly about lack of activities at the club. Observations that Manuel, the restaurant manager, rather caters for Spanish customers than the British have not gone by unnoticed. The woman puts it this way: 'I understand he has to please the Spanish, but it is *our* club!' A year later, irritation with Manuel has gone even further. Gary and Margaret argue that Manuel is a 'bad businessman', causing the British residents to go to the bars on one of the nearby streets instead of coming to the club. 'We like our pint', Gary says, arguing that the restaurant's income is mainly secured through the British residents. Gary and Margaret think that there are not enough activities going on for the residents at the site, only in summer when Spanish families are visiting. Even the Sunday roast dinners have been removed during summertime. A British resident in his early thirties who owns one of the permanents on the site has complained to the owner of the campsite, asking them to remove Manuel from the restaurant based on his own estimates of an annual 4,000 GBP personal spending on drinks for family and friends, and the wish to spend it on the campsite.

The comment of being 'our club' touches upon a crucial point that deals with the regular caravanners' relationship with the spatial and social environment of Camping Mares. The club is acting here as a fixed point of reference. The emphasis on the club as a local meeting point clearly also carries links to aspects of British working-class sociality. Some of the conflicts surrounding the club however have a clear national character, reflecting the difficulties involved in the European camping community. After the British, the other dominant group at Camping Mares are of Dutch nationality. In 2010, a large group of Dutch pensioners had started playing cards three days a week, occupying a large part of the restaurant. Many of the British regulars were not happy, complaining 'the Dutch' would only sit and drink a cup of coffee and the bottled water they had brought with them, whereas they at least were supporting the restaurant financially with their consumption of alcohol.

Annoyed with what they saw as a noisy British dominance, during the quizzes and the bingo nights, a group of Dutch pensioners prepared a counterattack, deliberately making noise during the British activities. During my first visit to Camping Mares, there was also a growing conflict surrounding the international bingo on Saturdays. The Belgian that had run it for several years experienced a decline in British attendance, due to the fact that most of the British preferred to go to the British (and cheaper) quiz on Mondays. The Belgian and his companion who owned the bingo machine thus reacted by refusing to lend it out to the British bingo organizers. Eventually, the Belgian and his wife decided to sell their caravan at Camping Mares to live on a site in Belgium; they disliked the way the site was developing 'with all these tattooed young people from Liverpool'. The conflicts point to a critical way in which national categorizations are made and maintained in an environment where people live in close proximity to each other and share facilities, not only for daily necessities, but also for organizing daily socializing. The 'classed' ways leisure activities were becoming organized in the campsite restaurant clashed with some residents' view of a decent campsite community.

With regard to British working-class charter tourists in Spain, Hazel Andrews (2011) argues that in tourists' acts of consumption one can witness an ongoing construction of British identity that is rooted in an imagined past, and reinforced in the presence of other nationalities. The episodes from the campsite bingo furthermore underline the reproduction of a north–south English divide, in which specific features of northern English sociality is reproduced and reinforced.[10] However, as we see in the Belgian couple's discontent with the changing camping environment, an increasing regional presence of people from the Liverpool area is also regarded to be a risk for established relations between caravanners on the site.

Noisy neighbours

On Camping Mares, where individuals from several different nationalities share the campsite facilities, conceptions of how social order is practised and maintained vary, and repeatedly become the object of both tension and conflict. It is therefore necessary to emphasize that the experienced 'community' described at the beginning of this chapter is in general constituted around national categorizations and boundaries (see also Nóvoa 2014). For Lucy, John, Margaret, Gary and their neighbours, community is created around a rather loosely defined term: 'British', an identification that is reinforced and established in a continuous contrast to other nationalities at the site, and where 'imaginings of what it means to be British can be lived out and constituted in a very particular way' (Andrews 2011: 229). On a winter day in 2011, a police car and an ambulance were called to the touring area of Camping Mares. A British retiree, who for months and months had complained about his Dutch neighbour's beating of carpets in early morning hours, had had enough and punched him in the face. The episode was referred to as a conflict arising on the grounds of national tensions, where the 'British' stood against 'The Dutch', illustrating how sense of 'Britishness' in this context is reinforced in the presence of and meetings with other nationalities (Andrews 2011: 65). Read this way, the 'threat' of the Dutch in the camping context is thus seen as undermining British sociality, resonating with what they see as a much larger threat against British identity in general associated with the problems of the nation they have left behind. This is a nation they see as suffering from a danger imposed from external forces such as immigrants and asylum seekers. Whereas episodes of violence are obviously less common, caravanners repeatedly comment that what they see as 'cultural conflicts' at the site often end with complaints and reports to the campsite reception, which is believed to be the final instance of power, maintaining and keeping social order.

Most of the conflicts regarding sound are located on the pitch itself, where the physical proximity of neighbours and a constant potential mobility constitute the everyday. Articulated frustration, anger and even growing conflicts thus arise because of the qualities of the material constitution of the site, particularly on the touring area, where mobility challenges an ideal of stability and predictability. Disagreements often tend to revolve around ideas of temporality regarding daily and basic practices of eating, sleeping and socializing. Camping Mares, whose reputation among caravanners in the area of being an international hub that brings together different nationalities, poses a certain problematic around how such international neighbourhoods are lived in practice, particularly regarding issues of social order. Particularly difficult is the problem of dealing with unexpected neighbours. The system of booking pitches in advance for the next winter season illustrates what can be regarded as Camping Mares caravanners' wish for – and need for – predictability. This point leads back to the question of how potential mobility in this context both is framed as a solution providing freedom, but also as a problem, colliding to a large extent with the spatial and social stability searched for by many of the long-term or 'permanent' caravanners.

Among the British caravanners, constant reference is made to problems with regard to the nationality of the caravanners. At a patio party I attended one of the couples present communicated their frustration with Spanish caravanners coming for the weekend. This started a torrent of complaints around the table regarding 'the Spanish' lack of caring about their pitch neighbours. Sarah was particularly furious 'I just think it is rude … . I know we're in their country, but … ', she exclaims, raising her eyebrows. Among these British caravanners, 'the Spanish' are the most feared neighbours, framed as being numerous, bringing several ill-behaved children, throwing patio parties and in general being noisy. Annoyance with Spanish presence at the site enforces a view on the campsite as a contained unity, spatially and culturally cut off from the cultural context wherein it is located, where Spanish staff forms part of a necessary daily infrastructure maintaining life at the site, but where Spanish caravanners are regarded as potentially problematic elements.

Nevertheless, among Swedish and British caravanners, as well as within the caravan industry, a strong discourse of equality is maintained. Notions of equality are historically linked with democratic ideas of the campsite as an open ground for the modern citizen. Ideas of democratic equality are played out in sayings such as 'here we are all the same, directors or carpenters', or in the words of the Lake Camping caravanner, 'We camping people are all the same.' In this

Community: 'We have found here what we can't find at home anymore'   131

Figure 17 Campsite Panorama, Lake Camping (photo by the author).

chapter we see, however, how a move to the campsite is also a move towards the presumably 'like-minded'.

Away from a nation in decay

The notions of inside and outside in relation to the campsite community contain and entail visions of the world that include an explicit fear of – or frustration with – what is phrased as a European (in this case: British or Swedish) immigration problem. Some caravanners' articulations are closely related to the mobility narratives discussed earlier in this book. In these narratives, an urban-rural divide, wherein the campsite features as a semi-rural withdrawal, is reproduced. A negatively loaded urban discourse entails specific visions of ethnicity and immigration, which, depending on the national context, frame 'the other' as a central factor for the weakening of social ties and neighbourhood decline.

In 2011, when spending the winter months at Camping Mares, I would often sit in front of my run-down mobile home and write notes in between moments of socializing and interviews. The patio was facing the main road crossing Camping Mares, which also made it a good spot for engaging in conversations and observing daily life at the campsite. One of the families that often passed my mobile home was a boastful British heavy-built man in his sixties, with a disabled adult daughter and a quiet wife. When I once commented on their long absence from the site, he blinked while exclaiming that they had been back in England: 'The reason why we go home is only to make sure the Muslims don't take any of our property.' The British pensioner's statement reflects a common British working-class attitude in which property ownership 'signals continuity within a framework of a national identity seen to be threatened by outside forces, in the form of immigrants and the European Union', as Hazel Andrews (2011: 65) puts it.

During fieldwork on both Camping Mares and Lake Camping I would repeatedly be served similar comments, sometimes served in humorous wrappings, but nevertheless raising the question of what kind of societal context the campsite is believed to offer an alternative to, and why. My retired neighbour, as many of his friends at Camping Mares, had somewhat paradoxically solved what he sees as a problem of immigration by becoming a migrant himself. But in what ways is a withdrawal to the campsite phrased with reference to national politics and the unwanted outsider?

There are seventeen of us gathered on a sunny Saturday, drinking liquor, sangria, two-Euro bottles of wine obtained in the weekend quizzes and lotteries, and eating Peter's chilli con carne that he has made in the outdoor kitchen tent on the corner of the pitch. It is March 2011 and Peter and Laura have invited their closest friends and acquaintances on the site to a patio party. All my friends are present: Lucy's cheeks are red from the sangria, and some of the men regularly sneak off to the road to have a cigarette and a private talk. Present are also three couples that I have only met on a few occasions before. One of these couples is Rita and Kenneth, both in their fifties and travelling in a massive motorhome that, after having sold their house near Leicester, is now their only home. The sale of the house has financed the travelling that they always dreamt of doing, and each year they spend three months near Málaga and three months in Benidorm. During the summer they stay in the UK, where Rita's work in the reception of a campsite allows them extra income, but also free pitch rent. The last time we met, Rita and Kenneth both expressed their disapproval of British politicians' lack of concern with what they saw as a huge immigrant problem. Rita recalled visiting a hospital in Leicester where 'it didn't smell like an English

Community: 'We have found here what we can't find at home anymore' 133

hospital, it smelled of curry and spices …' and added promptly, 'I don't think it is supposed to be like that.' A heated conversation took shape between Rita and Kenneth, Peter and Laura and their friend Ron:

> *Kenneth*: 'Why we spend most of the time away from England is because we don't like what is happening in our country.'
> *Hege*: 'What do you mean?'
> *Kenneth*: 'First of all, the multiculturalism … that is obviously not working.'
> *Rita*: 'Muslims are taking over.'
> Peter and Laura keep quiet, but Ron nods and agrees.
> *Ron*: 'One of them ayatollahs said no, let's not have a revolution, just keep on having babies. They will take over!'

Kenneth points out that they all have babies and are 'born into a religion'.

> *Laura*: 'But we also have our children born into a religion, the Catholic one. It is the same. The Muslim religion is not a violent one. It is just these extremists, people can't see past the extremists. Even though it has nothing to do with the rest of the people.'
> *Kenneth*: 'The second problem is the politicians, they only think about themselves and their own pockets.'
> *Hege*: 'Has there been any change with the new Conservative government?'
> *Laura*: 'Conservatives, Labour … it is all the same. They only think about themselves.'
> *Kenneth*: 'This [the campsite] is becoming what England was 50 years ago.'
> *Hege*: 'What do you mean?'

Kenneth explains how they 'all take care and help each other' and that they spend their time outside. 'But there must be something more', I ask, 'apart from the fact that you spend time outdoors and help each other. What is the difference between this and living in an apartment?

> *Laura*: 'Hege, listen. The difference is that when you go into an apartment and you lock the door you won't have this', she points at all of us.
> *Peter*: 'Just that happened today. You drop in and we drink and we share our food. You wouldn't do that in England anymore. People come over and help each other here.'

At the Saturday patio party, like the last time we met, and in between the generous portions of wine and stronger liquor, Kenneth continues to express his concern for the bad state his country is in. 'Some years ago, I heard that Leicester was 50% Asian!' Kenneth and Rita, who are seated next to each other, both raise their eyebrows looking around the suddenly rather quiet table. 'To be honest, this is the reason we all are away, isn't it?' Kenneth says. 'They [the immigrants] care for their families. We English have stopped doing that. We don't care about each other anymore.' When there is no immediate response, he says 'oh, I'll shut up now … '. But soon others follow up; Sarah takes the lead saying that in England there is no sense of neighbourhood anymore. 'People won't help each other anymore, you are just afraid they are going to tell people you are going away so that they can rob you', one woman adds. 'People are just afraid and do not help each other. We are more egoistic.' While some of the guests remain silent, others nod and agree. Kenneth says, 'We have found here what we can't find at home anymore … . I mean, we have sold our home to do this.'

The conversation at the two patio gatherings stayed with me for a while. Not least, because of the many complex layers embedded in Kenneth's argument. Here we find a clear reference to the idealized and caring village neighbourhood, in which the 'English' are also presented as a people that have lost their networks of care through neighbourhood ties. This partly reflects the age of the caravanners, their concern with safety, and friendships based on acts of reciprocity. In Kenneth and Rita's exclamations, there are also clear references to those believed to alienate them from their hometown and their former neighbourhoods: 'the immigrants'. As Kenneth explains it, these 'immigrants' still care and provide family networks, but at the expense of the British, who are not able or willing to maintain the same basis of social relations.

Immigrants, Brexit and campsite withdrawal

An anti-immigration rhetoric, or what O'Reilly (2009) terms an 'anti-immigration tone', is recognizable within the research that deals with British lifestyle migrants in general. O'Reilly's (2000) writings on the British on the Costa del Sol illustrate this problematic well, showing that among the lower middle-class and working-class lifestyle migrants, a common and shared escape narrative is framed with reference to believed problems of immigration.[11] Hazel Andrews notes, with reference to British working-class charter tourists in Mallorca, how immigration criticism forms part of a wider reaction against what one sees as a loss of British identity: 'The reality of the home world for many of these tourists is one in which they are forced out of their homes, as these become centres for particular groups of the immigrant community, and some politicians are perceived to be "paki-lovers"' (2011: 16). Through a similar anti-immigration rhetoric, some caravanners at Camping Mares happily ignore the fact that they themselves have become migrants, benefiting from the facility of movement within the EU.

This anti-immigration rhetoric, recognized in the examples above, is however only part of a more general narrative of a nation in decay.[12] With recourse to 2013, when John was still fighting his cancer, John and Lucy continued to refer to the bad state of the UK. 'That country has gone to the dogs', John sighed. 'They have taken in too many immigrants, all those eastern Europeans, Polish and Romanian.' Lucy and John complained about how 'normal people' were going to soup kitchens. Part of the problem was the taxes, they thought. John was furious about a suggested tax on spare bedrooms.[13] 'Horrible! They wanted to take away pensions from people living abroad, but they can't do that. We have worked hard for this.' John and Lucy used to vote, faithfully supporting the Labour Party. But not anymore. 'We stopped voting years ago. We used to, but stopped when we started coming here. It didn't do any good did it? No matter whom you voted for they ended up making a mess anyway!' Lucy exclaimed, irritated.

When I returned to Camping Mares in 2017, it was less than a year since the British population had voted for an exit out of the EU and Brexit was a theme of conversation also among the caravanners. Lucy was still happy not having to engage with politics at all. Among other caravan dwellers at the site there were however diverse opinions about the reasons for Brexit and the possible consequences an exit from the EU would have for their own situation in Spain. Gary and Margaret had voted for staying and speculated in the practical chaos that would be the consequence of limiting the free access of Britons in the EU. 'It would be impossible', Gary said, referring to the high number of British living in and visiting Spain and their importance for the Spanish economy. But in terms of the reasons for Brexit, Gary could clearly see what argument had won. 'Immigration was the argument … the problem is that they have taken in too many eastern Europeans receiving benefits.'

If we look back at Kenneth's argumentations at the patio party, among the caravanners however, a possible answer to the believed problems of immigration and other societal changes has not been found in simply leaving the UK for an idealized Spain – as it is for the tourists and lifestyle migrants treated in the wider sociological and anthropological literature. Rather it has been to leave a house and the neighbourhood for the campsite where values of reciprocity and care – from an imagined British past – are believed to be still practised. In this setting, even if Spain is portrayed as laid-back, sunny and affordable, it is the campsite and the caravan sociality that offers the reciprocity, safety and imagined freedom that a house-led life cannot. The campsite is thus seen as offering a sphere that is different, but manageable and identifiable, protected and withdrawn from some of the problems associated with contemporary society.

It is interesting to observe then, that the route of withdrawal from a negatively portrayed immigrant neighbourhood reality is found not only by crossing national borders, but by placing oneself in a location where the same problems are believed to not exist, or are at least kept at a distance. And something similar occurs in Sweden. Kalle and Lena, who live all summer season in their caravan on Lake Camping, some kilometres away from their apartment, are happy to get away from the centre of Lake Town at least for four months a year. Kalle is particularly worried about the immigration situation in their neighbourhood: 'To put it this way, there are many "new Swedes" in the area … it has become a lot like that in the western areas of Lake Town.' Whereas Kalle is rather careful in his articulations of these comments, Kim, who is originally from south-western Sweden, but has lived in the Lake Town area for almost fifteen years, is openly frustrated about the current situation in the more segregated areas of Lake Town. In a morning conversation in his motorhome, serving me rolls and orange juice after a hard night's shift at the transport company, he describes the centre of Lake Town as a 'concrete ghetto' full of immigrants, 'even people in burkas and everything'.

An early morning fight

Whereas the patio parties and the Swedish caravanners' comments illustrate how certain logic around immigration and loss of 'community' operate in the discourses of caravanners on Camping Mares and Lake Camping, there are also episodes where the campsite itself becomes a place for contestation of belonging and inclusion. On an early, rather chilly Lake Town morning in August 2011, as I step out of my caravan awning to go to the toilet, I am surprised to hear a woman yelling and screaming from behind Kalle and Lena's caravan. Out from behind a cluster of trees comes Kim, followed by a short, heavily built woman, walking three small dogs while screaming loud insults including 'Nazi bastard, you shit, you civil police'.

I stand still outside my awning watching her furious attacks. When he spots me, Kim loafs over to say that the woman got angry when he told her not to throw the dog's excrements around at the site, but to use the bin. He just shakes his head, as if he can hardly believe what he has just witnessed. Louise has woken up and as she exits her awning, she simply laughs while witnessing the last part of the insults. Some minutes later, the woman and what seems to be her husband shows up at Kim's bus, and as Kim retells the story when I run into him at the reception shop later in the day, the man had taken a strangling grip around his neck and threatened to kill him. Kim calls on manager Gunnar, who is sent out to talk to both parties and tell them to calm down.

In the afternoon I pass Benny and Louise's pitch as they are sitting outside talking loudly, and I am invited to sit down for some wine. Benny shows me the manuals for the new awning they have bought. It looks awfully complex. Since my summer of camping is soon coming to an end, Louise wonders if I am ever going to go camping again. Benny thinks that taking the car and renting cabins is the best solution for me. You need to be handy to go caravanning, and I am definitely not. Kalle comes around to tell us that they have got an open fire outside the caravan, and as Benny and I sit with our backs to the fire in the chilly night, he says they are hoping for a warm late summer. Someone mentions the incident with Kim this morning, when Benny explains what really happened: that Kim had called the woman a whore and said it was a bad thing the Nazis were not around anymore to deal with people like her. Upon reading a mix of shock and confusion on my face, Louise explains to me that the couple were what she referred to as *Resande* – Swedish Travellers. What follows is an eager discussion about different Swedish Traveller families and who belongs to whom.

This uncomfortable episode is an extreme illustration of prejudice, but does to some degree resonate with a more common discourse around social order, belonging and social exclusion on the campsite. Benny puts it quite frankly, saying 'I don't want any gypsies on the site', while adding 'that they steal is a known fact'. Louise agrees: 'This is not something we make up, it is actually proven.' Benny and Louise are mostly concerned with what they identify as Irish Traveller families that some years ago used to frequent Lake Camping. The Lake Camping management's regulations restricting the possibility of one person paying for more than one family, the obligation of obtaining a Scandinavian Camping Card, and the requirement of prepayment with credit cards, had however stopped most Traveller families from coming to the site. Benny found this to be a relief. 'I almost scared the hell out of a little kid once', referring to how he thought the child had been trying to steal an item on the site.

Questioning the presence and practices of Travellers also takes place at Camping Mares. When I returned to the site after some months of absence in

2011, Lucy fills me in on the events I had missed, complaining about the presence of two Irish Traveller families that had been staying at the touring area of the site during a period when the men in the family had acquired construction work in the area. Lucy and her friends are shocked about the way 'the Travellers' had taken over the site, making noise and leaving the toilets dirty.

Simultaneously, as we saw in the Introduction, a reference to 'gypsy lifestyle' is made with frequency, embedding romanticized visions of freedom and mobility. As for nomads and other mobile groups, Euro-American modernity has placed 'the Gypsy' outside or at the peripheries of metropolitan locations.[14] The Gypsy-Travellers' relationship with caravans[15] is a long-standing and complex history that looks very different from the historical context of leisure caravanning referred to earlier in this book. However, in the case of both Sweden and the UK, there are clear examples of how these worlds also merge and collide due to the different groups' involvement with the same material object.[16] The complaints and reactions against the presence of Travellers at the sites, both in Sweden and Spain, reflect the inherent ambivalence between the Traveller and Gypsy as idealized figures of freedom and mobility, and actual experiences at

Figure 18 Home on Wheels (photo by Terje Tjærnås).

the campsites, where the sharing of space is framed in terms of a moralizing discourse of social order.

Withdrawing to the caravan community

This chapter has pointed to how specific visions of community, articulated in a celebration of village or neighbourhood sociality, as well as in acts of reciprocity, are central to how caravanners value caravan and campsite life. Notions of positively valued care, reciprocity and visibility, all crucial components in this creation of community, point to a two-sided face of care and control in which both watching and being watched (cf. Foucault 1977) are central to how daily life is constituted. Being seen by, and seeing, one's neighbours resonates with how the caravanners perceive of the qualities of social relationships necessary to create a good life, one often rooted in an imagined past. Familiarity and intimacy characterize such relationships – between neighbours and friends, but also in terms of spatial facilities and the availability of service. On the campsite, the knowledge and help of good neighbours is regarded a fundamental aspect of the camping phenomenon itself, a care for others that the caravanners repeatedly return to when being asked about their choice of living. In the case of the British caravanners at Camping Mares, it is not simply a revitalization of a village ideal that is performed, but a particular re-creation of central aspects of leisured sociality associated with the northern English industrial neighbourhood.

A campsite community is simultaneously envisioned in contrast to the original 'home' – whether this home is the apartment in centre of town, as in the case of Lake Town dwellers, or it is the 'home nation', as the imagined UK in decay. The 'home' that is left is one believed to be in trouble, not least because of what caravanners see as an immigrant presence that has caused frustration and alienation, but also because of a political situation that many describe as hopeless and run by selfish actors. One way forward is withdrawal – whether from the town to its outskirts, or by crossing national borders. The acts of withdrawal are therefore located on different levels. The Swedish caravanners that find the good life on a campsite in their hometown have considerably more faith in Swedish society than what is expressed among their British counterparts. Some of them, like Benny and Louise, see moving to a campsite abroad as a possibility after retirement, and even if they are reluctant to consider the idea of leaving Sweden completely, they could see an option of having one caravan in Spain and another in Sweden. Perhaps more importantly then, rather than the crossing of national borders, one answer is found in a particular materially practised way of living on wheels in a present continuous, located on campsites at the periphery of a nation state where worries of an economic, political and cultural nature seem less apparent. In this periphery, 'like-minded' people are believed to be easy to find, sharing values of reciprocity, care and a highly normative social order.

Yet, the material instability of the caravan, and the campsite with its comings and goings of people, nurtures and enforces forms of internal control and the maintenance of boundaries. As I have shown earlier in the book, social control is also part of the campsite infrastructure, through a gradually increasing building of gates and fences. These control mechanisms are part of keeping outside separate from inside through sharp categorizations. But as I have shown in this chapter, even the 'inside' is far from frictionless. Conflict arises around questions of social order, and on Camping Mares at times between groups of different nationalities. The campsite, as it appears, hold elements of both squatting and gating. We saw in the previous chapter how the 'temporary' is materially bent and adjusted, and a full-time caravan home located in a shady legal zone. Still, I argue there is a prevalent discourse of safety and security, where a 'gating from within' is nurtured not only by the caravanners' social control, but also by the pressure on campsite managers to increase security infrastructure.

From this perspective, one answer to the good life is found within a leisure infrastructure designed for, and based on, mobile and temporary dwelling. The good life as it appears in the present continuous at the campsite is located in the withdrawal: the act of ending or changing one's involvement with traditional infrastructures of reproduction in terms of formal work, family and political life. Following J. B. Jackson (1984), these tendencies are characteristics of the moveable dwelling, since the vernacular home is one 'dependent on the community not as a political entity but as a source of services' (1984: 86). Community, as it appears in the campsite setting, is nurtured – in discourse and practice – as a manageable unit of informal service, care and control in the periphery of the nation state. But where Jackson slips into framing such spaces as temporary, this ethnography shows that a simple dichotomy between the temporary and the more permanent and long-lasting is hard to maintain. Rather, experiences of stability and relationship with a particular place are searched for and (re)found within the temporary structures of homemaking in the infrastructural leisure sphere. Here, potential mobility is the fundamental basis for stability, and a prerequisite for the formation of the immobile mobile dwelling.

6

Conclusion: Troubling Temporalities

When in 1984 the landscape theorist John Brinkenhoff Jackson predicted that the mobile home in the form of the trailer would be the dwelling of the future, was he possibly right? Some current tendencies seem to indicate he was at least on to something. In the spring of 2017 a journalist from the Swedish national radio asked me for an analysis of the Tiny House Movement that had now reached Sweden. How can we, she wondered, explain the new interest in small and inventive dwellings, many of them on wheels? The question was one I had thought about before, and at an anthropological conference in the United States a few years back discussed with colleagues who worked on both tiny house dwellers and mobile home owners in North America. The past few years have seen an extensive design and architectural interest in mini-houses, container living and compact homes. What has become known in the United States as the Tiny House Movement has grown extensively as a social movement advocating downsizing to 'the simple life'.[1] Tiny houses come in a wide range of shapes; many of them are self-built on wheels and some are converted RVs or trucks. Downsizing to a tiny house is related to a wide range of concerns, including environmental and financial, but is also promoted by enthusiasts with reference to notions of 'adventure' and 'freedom'. Whereas the Tiny House Movement attracts people from different socio-economic backgrounds, there is little doubt it still remains a largely middle-class initiative.

Recent tendencies of so-called 'tiny living' thus both resonate and clash with how the caravan is being treated in the European industry, and with the configurations of home we find among the caravanners at Lake Camping and Camping Mares. Many of the people that have chosen a downsized life share a concern with self-sufficiency, and likewise share an understanding of how such self-containment is placed in relation to notions of 'freedom'. Through a focus on the positive sides of downsizing, on getting rid of things, living in a house that is easy to tidy, and on the financial freedom such downsizing entail, tiny house enthusiasts' – or boat

Figure 19 Caravans exhibited in Mediterranean Gardens, Caravan Salon Düsseldorf 2011 (photo by the author).

residents for that sake – references to freedom are, for instance, similar to those of the caravanners I have introduced in the past chapters. More importantly, what can be read from these recent tendencies is a general redefinition of – or wish to redefine – home in the contemporary Western world.

From temporary to permanent

But caravan dwellers' ideas about material downsizing only take us so far in trying to understand both the multiple causes and consequences of a life on wheels. In the past chapters I have pointed to the importance of the wider material and social *potential* of the domestic sphere when it comes to how caravans are both imagined and inhabited. While 'potential mobility' as a concept builds on ideas borne out of the current mobilities literature that perhaps in itself runs the risk of producing dubious portrayals of freedom and universal mobility, this term still pinpoints some of the central elements of caravan living. The 'static' and 'immobile' mobile dwelling shows that mobility in this context is socially significant, but that it can be the very potential of mobility, rather than its execution, that shapes experiences of 'freedom'.

We therefore need at this point to stress the first part of the term: *potential* rather than *mobility*. One of the mistakes made by sociologists and others associated with the mobility turn in the social sciences has been the continuous highlighting a general and taken-for-given category of mobility at the expense of what elements it is constituted of. Tim Cresswell (2010) makes a similar observation when asking researchers to look at the specific aspects of mobility in order to offer a more fine-tuned approach. But even in mobility scholar Kaufmann's (2002) launching of the concept of *motility*, mobility appears always as an explicit goal and necessary outcome. The analytical strength of the term *potential mobility* is rather a capacity to capture that which is unrealized, probably never to happen and that thus takes on fundamentally contradictory material and social forms (see Leivestad 2016). As an indication of something that has not yet happened, and perhaps never will, potentiality holds a critical temporal dimension. In naming this last chapter Troubling Temporalities I wish to address the ways in which a clash of different temporal scales has come to influence the creation and use of the mobile dwelling.

Caravans are still designed and built merely as leisure dwellings, but as the stories from Lake Camping and Camping Mares show, these prefabricated homes on wheels are appropriated, altered and changed in a range of different manners. Chapter 1 illustrated how the caravan's ambiguous character, located on a continuum between leisure and domesticity, between the vehicle and the static home – continues to be an object of negotiation within the caravan industry. Through their lightness, which enables mobility and reflects J. B. Jackson's (1984) portrayal of the mobile dwelling as a particular flexible domestic form, the materials used to build caravans and motorhomes also become associated with notions of 'weakness' and 'unstableness'. In a dedicated manner, caravan enthusiasts and potential buyers perform thorough testing and evaluations of mobile dwellings and what they see as material 'quality'. At the European trade fairs, manufacturers also engage in evaluations over quality, as they tend to associate it with particular national characteristics of design and production process. For actors in the caravan industry and caravanners alike, quality is linked with that which is regarded as stable, 'home-like' and enduring, thus reflecting how conventional ideas about proper domestic spheres interfere with the leisure-oriented caravan market.

It is when the leisure-built caravan is used as a full-time dwelling and appropriated in ways that go beyond its original intention that problems can occur. That is when bulges are discovered in the floor, or the smell of mould starts spreading in the caravan awning. What the past chapters have shown, are the multiple ways in which the 'temporary' and mobile dwelling gradually is turned 'permanent' and static. Such transformations happen through a range of material alterations and rebuilding of the caravan, and through extending its exterior living space, based on a 'house-like' aesthetics. Many of the caravan dwellers we have met in the previous chapter make sure caravans doors are concealed, awnings cladded and wheels hidden. Still, these disguised caravan wheels are what somehow ironically keep the mobile dwelling firmly in place. These wheels are a requirement for the caravan's placement on a campsite, carrying with them a legal expectation of a temporal hook-up.

Ambiguous homes

In the bestseller *Two Caravans* (2007), Marina Lewycka describes how a group of migrant workers from three continents, all in the search of a better future, are assigned to pick strawberries on the field of a mean farmer, and thus are forced to share the narrow space of two caravans. The limited caravan space provokes the most intimate of encounters, but its residents have taken the utmost care in trying to create a homely sphere. 'A particularly charming feature of their caravan is the clever storage space: there are compact cupboards, cunning head-level lockers and drawers with delightful decorative handles where everything can be hidden away', as one of Lewycka's main characters describes it (2007: 2).

When home meets mobility – or at least the potential for it – clashes between human aspirations for change and needs of stability become curiously visible. Caravans and other mobile dwellings may however become troublesome objects when the use of them passes the expected time frame of a leisure infrastructure landscape. But also historically, the caravan appears as an object of both love and hatred. One reason for the caravan's ambiguous position in popular imaginary is its association with groups of society usually thought of as geographically mobile, while simultaneously conceived of as deeply socially immobile. As we have seen in the previous chapters, 'the gypsy' appears as a mythical figure of mobility among other caravan dwellers, but in less symbolic forms also as a highly undesirable campsite neighbour. In media and popular representations, the caravan home is at the same time frequently visible to us as a home for groups of society for whom life has left few options. Perhaps it is the presumed linkage between mobile dwellings and 'troublesome' figures of society that has caused the leisure caravan to occupy such an ambivalent role in relation to the nation state. Its potential mobility and facility to be inhabited full-time clash with the static categories of stable homes and residence produced within a nation state grid. That is why caravans continue to be placed in ambiguous zones of both economy and politics, even when occupied by people that have chosen these dwellings as part of a lifestyle change.

Earlier in this book I noted how caravans slip through both national and European housing registries, leaving an open knowledge gap in relation to how many people actually live their lives on wheels.[2] European Census data via *Eurostat* reveals that the categories used to separate forms of dwelling are broad, leaving caravans and mobile homes in an unspecified category of 'Other Housing Unit and the Homeless'. But in both Sweden, the UK and Spain, caravans as full-time housing is furthermore enabled by other economic, political and legal voids in which objects legally registered as vehicles or private property are used and treated as real estate. In this sense, their legal ambiguity can become an asset for caravan dwellers who see their withdrawal to a mobile dwelling also as a downsizing of expenses and liberation from legal ties related to the property realm.

Inhabiting caravans that are legally categorized as mobile leisure vehicles thus also involves a convenient avoidance of property taxes, shedding yet more light on the 'freedom' and flexibility caravanners associate with the mobile dwelling. And despite an emphasis on social control, the campsite is a space whose location in the legal periphery opens up for the flourishing of informal economies and housing practices. These informal modes of regulating daily life shape, as we have seen, a fragile sense of community that is based on face-to-face relationships, an experience of short-distance service, manual labour and a cash economy. But when the 'temporal' dwelling crosses the expected time frames of what is seen as appropriate leisure, set up by authorities and campsite managers, we also need to ask for *whom* it becomes a 'permanent' housing solution. What forms of social relations and distinctions are being shaped – and perhaps reproduced – in the fully furnished awnings and among neighbours in the campsite club?

Figure 20 Between Squatting and Gating (photo by Terje Tjærnås).

The classed campsite

In a Swedish hotel bar in September 2011, celebrating the end of a long day inside the trade fair building next door, I find myself among a group of middle aged suit-dressed men, all managers and owners of the largest caravan manufacturers in Sweden. In between the generous portions of beer, and eagerly offering me an explanation of the economic particularities of the caravanning industry, one of them leans over the table, literally whispering: 'Where are all the non-western immigrants in this business? There aren't any of them. This is the last bastion.' Even if bluntly put, the industry actor's observation was certainly accurate, and during the following years I came to realize that the whiteness of the industry also reflected the very whiteness of the campsite population in general. Explanations for an absence of people with non-western migrant background are complex, and need also to be found in the historical development of camping and campsites that I briefly outlined in Chapter 2. But one of the things I discovered when studying the campsite in more detail, was that caravan enthusiasts' own claims of heterogeneity expressed in terms such as 'here you find everyone ... from managers to carpenters', seemed to me to be out of tune with reality. To me it rather became more and more clear, that it was what a social scientist would call a white working class that occupied the neat rows of white and grey caravans, no matter what campsite I travelled to.

One of the most pressing challenges found in the social sciences today is how to conceptualize and find a language for social class, to provide a vocabulary that reflects its societal relevance (Walley 2013: 167). During years of economic crisis we have witnessed class return to the political agenda, appearing, as the philosopher Peter Thompson puts it, 'on the scene as a political determinant' (Thompson 2013: 2). The Europe that we have vaguely seen the contours of in this book is a changing Europe. It is a Europe that, during the time of my campsite fieldwork, was marked by economic recession, political turmoil and general insecurity, not least in the UK and Spain.

In this book we have only seen the traces of this crisis and insecurity, through houses that have been difficult to sell and dropping prices on caravans, but also through people whose permanent caravan life started after finding themselves without fixed employment. But in 2016 and 2017 it was also a Europe that witnessed a range of political changes, where it was exactly a white working class that suddenly was seen as a politically influential group (if somewhat difficult to define as such). Withdrawal, as I have used it in the past chapters, can for some provide an accessible answer in times of political and economic frustration. It is in many ways an apolitical move, but in its attempt to achieve a distance to anything perceived of as political it thus becomes political in its own sense. Or as Lucy puts it, when in spring 2015 she was commenting upon the UK parliamentary elections, 'It's got nothing to do with me anymore!'

In her writings on gated communities, Setha Low argues that 'the "perversion" of dwelling in the postcivil society' is that 'it takes the holiday as a model, a vacation from ordinary life, a leave from the disorder of the everyday and, in a sense, from society altogether' (Low 2008b: 162). In times of what we might term a general uncertainty, what Jane Guyer calls an 'enforced presentism' (Guyer 2007: 410) seems particularly enduring, and can even gain new fuel. It is precisely these elements of an enforced presentism that forms part of what I have described as a present continuous. Withdrawal, as I have used it throughout the past chapters, involves taking a step back from an undesirable or unwanted context, from homes or work where one feels 'stuck', or from neighbourhoods one does not recognize anymore or from what the caravanners see as failed multiculturalism. But withdrawal is also a step into a manageable sphere of routines, predictability and control.

Withdrawal is a way to the good life – a particular version of it, that is. As it comes out in the caravanners' stories and practices on Camping Mares and Lake Camping, it is a good life that strongly builds on a value of 'freedom' as potential mobility as well as an ideology of democratic equality that has gradually been transformed into a moral notion of 'like-mindedness'. It is a conception of the good life that nurtures community ideals through an emphasis on care and friendship, and as Chapters 2 and 5 discussed more extensively, on visibility and control. Campsite life appears to be a quiet retreat, away from the politics of the middle class, but also into a sphere where class seems to matter even more. In a similar vein, at Lake Camping and Camping Mares, one can observe an explicit reproduction of a strong work–leisure dichotomy, reflecting not only the caravanners' socio-economic background, but also a refashioning of an industrial economic model that, to a large extent, differs from current observations of the flexibility of the new economy. On the campsite, 'work' is 'drudgery' (Clarke and Critcher 1985: 10), and camping life is portrayed as an idealized version of living in the present continuous.

While the gated community Low is referring to is a residential area planned and constructed on a specific holiday-business model, the campsite, a place designed for temporary leisure, is gradually transformed by caravanners themselves into a location for full-time housing. The means of financing a full-time caravan life are, however, deeply rooted in Western welfare systems, extend into the workings and crises of the property market and interrelate with the informal economy developed within campsite gates. The caravan home, through its potential mobility, opens up a sense of possibility (Hage 1997), but simultaneously embeds a risk of downward mobility, a fear of falling that is visible not least in the referral to family members' scepticism towards the mobile dwelling as an acceptable housing option. In both the UK and Sweden, the caravan has come to be attached with ridiculing portrayals of working-class leisure, and in media coverage the caravan is still 'uncool' in the broadest sense. The stigma of the caravan is thus very much alive, also among its residents that see it as a path to the 'good life'.

But the caravan dwellers that appear in this book are all part of what Lynsey Hanley, in her raging account of the British council estate and its history, calls a 'society of homeowners' (2007: 212). Many of them were also homeowners before moving into a caravan on a campsite or investing their savings in a motorhome. But somewhat ironically, the importance invested in owning one's home sometimes neglects the risks attached to a flexible and mobile home. In the past pages I have referred to some of these risks. I have described the lack of rights the campsite tenant has concerning the plot of land where their dwelling is parked and the risk of investing money in a dwelling whose shelf-life remains somewhat limited.

Before this book ends, let's for a moment return to the analysis of the Tiny House Movement I was asked to give on the Swedish radio. One of the questions I was asked was one that curiously resonated with J. B Jackson's prediction in the early eighties: 'What do you see for the future?' Will we have more of these small and mobile dwellings?' I was probably not the right person to predict the future housing situation. But returning to John and Lucy, or Benny and Louise for that sake, perhaps one answer is found in the way these caravan dwellers centre their everyday on the 'the good life' through a quiet withdrawal to a safe community on static wheels. Throughout this book I have sought to demonstrate how new modes of housing are established within an infrastructural sphere designed and planned for leisure. The potential mobility of the caravan is the actual prerequisite for its stability. Or put differently, a potential for movement is what keeps the caravan standing still in the peripheries of Europe.

Epilogue

After a few years living on the site, Petra and Edward left Lake Camping. According to their neighbours the couple had packed up in a hurry, selling their caravan and awning to a neighbour at a low price and re-installing themselves in a small rental apartment in the outskirts of Lake Town. As the summer season of 2017 was approaching, the refugees had been moved elsewhere and the streets of Lake Camping were full of seasonal guests, with more than thirty of the units on full-year contracts. As Benny saw it, the campsite was becoming increasingly popular. Together with his brother Kalle he had bought an automatic lawn mower that Benny from the veranda now could be watching neatly cutting the grass between their two caravans. Whereas Kalle and Lena were thinking of buying a new caravan, Benny would not mind doing like his new campsite neighbours next door: buy a static caravan in Spain to spend the winters, while enjoying the summer season at Lake Camping, and thus get rid of their expensive rental apartment in town. Benny and Louise had visited their neighbours in Spain in February, and were fascinated with the campsite that was just like a village on its own, with all thinkable infrastructure. At Camping Mares, caravan prices were rising after years of recession, and the campsite was full even off-season. Caravans were again sold for up to 30, 000 pounds. The management had moved several of the caravanners from their regular pitches, replacing them with a bungalow area with tropic plants and balconies in the shade. At a meeting in winter, the management had promised a redoing of the restaurant building, and British full-timers such as Gary and Margaret were still waiting to see the results of a new club. Rumours of a more restrictive policy regarding caravan rentals and the building of extensions had made Lucy's neighbours move from the site. The new couple next door were in their early fifties from northern England and were cooking for Lucy every day. In 2015 Lucy finally got her house in England sold and invested in redoing her awning at Camping Mares, where she continues to live, moving around in a new mobility scooter.

Notes

Introduction

1. In order to protect the integrity and privacy of my informants, I will use pseudonyms on all my informants throughout this book, and I have also anonymized the names of the two campsites: Camping Mares and Lake Camping. Benidorm is a well-known tourist destination in Spain and due to the high number of campsites in the area I have not anonymized the name of the town.
2. Lake Camping and Lake Town are both pseudonyms. See note 1.
3. See the European Caravan Federation. www.e-c-f.com
4. The ethnographic reality of the British Camping Mares residents reveals similarities with recent forms of Western *lifestyle mobility* (Cohen et al. 2015). Attempting to overcome the limits of previous umbrella conceptualizations such as retirement migration, leisure migration, second home ownership and seasonal migration, some researchers have proposed *lifestyle migration* as a conceptual framework for dealing with people who relocate in the pursuit of a better way of life elsewhere (Benson and O'Reilly 2009a,b). In the context of international retirement and seasonal migration, the northern European and Scandinavian presence on the Spanish coast is among the best documented (Casado-Díaz 2006, 2009; Gustafson 2001, 2008, 2009; Huber and O'Reilly 2004; Janoschka 2011), with several in-depth studies dealing specifically with British nationals in southern Spain (Casado-Diaz 2009; King et al. 2000; Oliver 2008; O'Reilly 2000, 2003, 2009). In the lifestyle migration literature, the search for a particular type of destination and longing for community is commonly referred to in terms of 'escape', linking historical notions of 'escapism' both to Bauman's idea of utopia, tourism theory and the quest for authenticity (Benson and Osbaldiston 2014). What a theoretical discourse of 'escape' attempts to illuminate is how relocation in search of the good life implies both a turn to – but also away from – something. The lifestyle migration literature tends to address mobility as a highly individualistic quest for the good life. This approach evokes problematic links between mobility and modernity that come as a result of a theoretical grounding in the sociological work of Bauman and Giddens (see Huete, Mantecón and Estévez 2013 and Salazar and Zhang 2013 for more extensive critiques).
5. For the concept of motility, see also Flamm and Kaufmann 2006; Kaufmann 2011; Kaufmann, Bergman and Joyce 2004; Kaufmann and Montulet 2008; and Kesselring 2006. I have in Leivestad 2016 offered a more extensive discussion of the concept.

6   An early example being Bourdieu's (1990) seminal study of the Kabyle house.
7   See however public policy researcher Alan Wallis' (1991) extensive work about the history of the mobile home in the United States, *Wheel Estate,* in where he shows how manufacturers, park owner, users and institutions have shaped the form and meaning of the American mobile home. The anthropologist Nicholas Shapiro (2014, 2015) interestingly accounts for the use and spread of the FEMA trailers and domestic formaldehyde exposure. The anthropologists Dorothy Ayers Counts and David R Counts (1992, 2009) discuss in the monograph *Over the Next Hill* the use of Recreational Vehicles (RVs) as retirement option in the United States. RV culture in the United States and Australia (where RVers are commonly referred to as 'grey nomads') has also been studied by sociologists and tourism scholars (see Jobes 1984; Hardy, Gretzel and Hanson 2012, 2013; Hartwigsen and Null 1989, 1990; Hillman 2013; Mchugh and Mings 1995; Onyx and Leonard 2005). See also media scholar Viallon (2012) on French RVers in Morocco. There also exists a few studies about caravan parks and mobile home parks in the United States and Australia (Brooker and Joppe 2014; Caldicott and Scherrer 2013; Hurley 2001; Kusenbach 2009; Newton 2006). In Europe, the research on camping and caravans is sparse. We find Löfgren's lucid work *On Holiday*, which I frequently refer to throughout this book. See also Østby (2014) on campsite history in Norway, Southerton et al. (2001) on the campsite as a social world, Bevan (2010) on park-home living in England, Blichfeldt and Mikkelsen (2009, 2013) as well as Mikkelsen and Cohen (2015) on sociality on Danish campsites, and Triantafillidou and Siomkos (2013) on Greek camping.
8   Tim Ingold (2007) argues that material culture studies, merely as a result of their focus on consumption, overlook actual materials and their properties. Ingold's critique is based in a phenomenological metaphysics where humans and things are ontologically inseparable and where 'materials of the most diverse kind … undergo continual generation and transformation' (2007: 7). A different strain of critique worth mentioning has claimed that material culture studies use objects merely as illustration to other arguments and has called for an approach that sees things and concepts as ontologically the same (cf. Henare, Holbraad and Wastell 2007). I will not delve in these critiques, but for the purpose of this chapter note the need of finding ways to go beyond material culture understood as simply human representations of things.
9   The *Guardian* 'Caravanning is most popular UK holiday' (15 January 2007). https://www.theguardian.com/travel/2007/jan/15/travelnews.uk.camping
10 *Carry on Camping* is a 1968 British comedy featuring two couples who thinking they were heading for a nudist camp called Paradise end up at a badly run family campsite on a damp open field.

11 *Huffington Post*, 'Three recent changes that have helped the caravan holiday's resurgence' (7 September 2013).
12 The *Guardian* 13 August 2009 'Recession-hit Britons abandon foreign holidays in favour of "staycations"' https://www.theguardian.com/travel/2009/aug/13/uk-recession-travel-holidays-staycation.
13 The most popular of these shows were *Böda Camping* (Swedish TV4), which followed caravanners at a large campsite on the island of Öland through several seasons.
14 Motorized caravanning holidays existed in the UK as early as in the 1920s, and camping history on the British Isles is better documented than in other areas of Europe. In the book *Gypsies and Gentlemen* (1986), Nerissa Wilson links early camping to the new movement for compulsory holidays taking place in the UK. In the late 1920s, UK incomes were rising, and more people were able to own private cars; still it was mainly a phenomenon among the more economically privileged classes. In the early 1930s, despite there being only a few thousand touring caravans around, caravanners were already causing public frustration; 'motorists loathed trailers', as speed limits were made less restrictive on UK roads and motorists who wanted to enjoy their driving found themselves stuck behind slow caravans, Wilson says (1986: 171). However, holidaying along the British sea coast was expensive, and one of the initiatives in favour of the working classes was the establishment of holiday camps, where tents still were the most popular form of accommodation. The US camping expansion had a major impact on European development. Motorized camping spread in the United States in the 1920s and, in his vivid account of the history of vacationing, Swedish ethnologist Orvar Löfgren (1999) describes how America was becoming *the* camping nation of the world, having already been quite extensive in the pre-war period. The history of motorized camping in Europe cannot be viewed in isolation from the twentieth-century expansion of automobiles and the infrastructures of roads that facilitated their use (Counts and Counts 2009: 65). In Scandinavia, Germany, France and the Netherlands, motorized caravanning as a widespread phenomenon came later than in the United States and United Kingdom. In France and Germany, car leisure developed first as middle and upper classes went touring, spending the night in hotels (Sachs 1992: 153). In large parts of Europe, the real boost of camping and caravanning came in the period after the Second World War. More groups of workers were now entitled to holidays, and with increased time for leisure, an ever-increasing number of people found their way to the countryside and the sea. While motorized camping was well established as a leisure and holiday form in large parts of western Europe by the 1950s, countries in southern Europe saw this development come much later. In the case of Spain, there are few reliable sources that can document the history of camping in the country (Miranda Montero 1985;

Feo Parrondo 2003), and as late as the mid-1980s camping was a recent, and still developing, form of tourism on the Spanish peninsula.

15 The constitution of what we can identify as the caravan unit, consisting of white, heterosexual couples, also had methodological implications. During fieldwork in this project I have met and talked to hundreds of caravanners, but also carried out longer semi-structured interviews with approximately 110 individuals in 60 caravan units in Spain and Sweden, the majority of them couples. Other social happenings, on caravan patios or in the campsite restaurant, usually took shape as gatherings of several couples, where the majority of them were about the age of, or even older than, my own parents. The age difference became dramatically visible when three of my closest informants at Camping Mares died before the project was completed.

16 Fieldwork took me to a range of different caravan settings such as attending the European Caravan Park association's annual meeting in Stockholm in 2010, attending the Swedish annual Caravan Club Rally and a field visit to a caravan manufacturer in 2011. The trade fairs, however, remained the most important setting for examining the marketing, sales and distribution of caravans and motorhomes. The largest caravanning trade fair in Scandinavia at Elmia in Jönköping in 2010 and 2011, the regional trade fair in Stockholm in 2011, 2013 and 2015, the Caravan Show at the Mets in London in 2012, and the German megaevent at Düsseldorf's Caravan Salon in 2011, introduced me not only to central actors in the industry, but also to situations and instances in which the material qualities of the caravans are evaluated and negotiated among manufacturers, retailers and customers. For analysis of the trade fair, see Aspers and Darr 2011; Leivestad 2017b; Moeran 2010; Skov 2006).

17 I recognize the difficulties of referring to Britishness, British and the United Kingdom, acknowledging that Scottish, Welsh, Northern Irish and English national identities all comprise part of these categories (see also Andrews 2011). For the purpose of finding a collective conceptual hanger, I will frequently employ the terms *British*, *Brits*, *Britain* and *the UK* throughout this book.

18 The excessive building in Benidorm started in late 1950s, and with Dictator Franco's decision to allow for tourism in the area and with the arrival of bikini-clad northern Europeans, Benidorm transformed from a sleepy fishing village into a metropolis of sun, beach and party. Figures from 2011 identified a population of 75,000 registered inhabitants, most of them working in the tourism sector and public administration, 37 per cent of which were foreigners (Ivars Baidal et al. 2013: 184). In terms of tourist accommodation, Benidorm hotels alone register about 10 million overnight stays a year, with foreign guests accounting for half of them; in addition there are about 18,000 second homes registered in the area (Ivars Baidal et al. 2013: 185). The award-winning British sitcom *Benidorm* (where some of my camping informants worked as extras), airing its ninth season in March 2017, reproduces the image of

Benidorm as a working-class holiday Mecca. Situated in an all-inclusive Benidorm hotel, it follows holidaymakers chasing low prices in the sun, reconstituting the image of a resort 'where sangria still flows freely', as a *Daily Mail* article read in 2013. Benidorm's micro-climate makes it a popular holiday resort all year round, with less seasonal changes than other destinations and with a high average length of stay (Ivars Baidal et al. 2013: 185).

19 During the 1900s, Lake Town grew from a quiet countryside town to one of Sweden's most busy industrial centres with the establishment of several large electricity, metal and power plants. The number of inhabitants grew rapidly, most dramatically during the post-war industrial expansion in Sweden when it rose from less than 63,000 in 1945 to almost 117,000 in 1970. While the early immigration to Lake Town mainly came from Europe, and was managed by the industry to meet the needs for labour, immigration after 1970 came from a range of countries. In the early 1980s, Lake Town was one of the municipalities in Sweden with the highest percentage of immigrants, and already then one could see tendencies towards segregation with some areas of town hosting large immigrant populations.

Chapter 1

1 Around the same time, one could find the first examples of motorhomes in Britain. While Gordon Stables is considered a pioneer of the leisure caravan, the first streamlined caravan for motorcars has been credited to Frederick Alcock, who built a vehicle to be towed behind his 1913 Lanchester. Motor caravanning was still in its infancy and Alcock's invention was to remain unique until after the First World War (Pressnell 1991: 3).

2 In a booklet on the history of the touring caravan, Pressnell (1991) reports of 'ramshackle sites' and shantytowns of caravans being established, which led to a dubious reputation for the mobile dwelling in the UK. 'The caravan, which before the war had been adjunct to motor touring, now became primarily a permanent and non-mobile residence', Pressnell writes, referring to how industry sources in 1950 estimated that 80 per cent of all caravans built after the war were used for permanent housing (Pressnell 1991: 17; The Caravan Club 2011: 48).

3 The secretary general of EFC, Hans-Karl Sternberg, expressed his worries about the German leisure vehicle industry, which prior to the crisis had exported 60 per cent of all their products, a number that by January 2013 had sunk to 50 per cent. Even if Sweden in this period was struck less hard than the southern European markets in Italy, Portugal and Spain, the Swedish caravan manufacturer also noted drops in sales. A year later, in January 2014, the EFC expressed a continuous worry about what they termed 'unfavourable market conditions'.

4 After several years of strained liquidity, in 2015 Cabby Caravan was forced into official receivership.
5 Some caravans, though, are so heavy that they require not only more stable chassis, but also a tandem axle, which consists of four wheels on twin axles, instead of the regular construction with one axle.
6 In the 1950s, aluminium was used instead of hardboard and canvas to construct exterior walls and roof. Aluminium and hardboard, however, were objects of continuous alternation well into the 1950s, depending on the availability of aluminium and the capacity of the manufacturers to handle the qualities of this new material (see Sheller 2014).
7 This building technique goes under the name of 'Sandwich construction'. First seeing light in the 1960s, the Sandwich construction is considered one of the major developments in caravan technology.
8 A chemical toilet is a self-contained toilet with a sealed tank that holds waste material and that needs to be periodically emptied. There are chemical fluids that help break down the waste and prevent odours.
9 Showers appeared in Swedish caravan models as early as in the 1970s, but it was originally standard mostly in the motorhomes, which can provide bigger water tanks and the water can be filled and emptied directly from the car.
10 In Kalle and Lena's case, we see however that living arrangements are extended into the awning, giving room for freezing, cooling and storing facilities that the spatial limitations of the caravan do not enable.
11 This differs from country to country though; in Germany, where this source of energy is cheap, it is common to heat the whole caravan with gas (Eriksson 2006: 119).
12 During my fieldwork on caravan shows and trade fairs in Sweden and Germany, the non-presence of UK-based manufacturers was notable. The UK caravanning industry described above has historically been focused on the home market. This is in stark contrast to the German company Hobby, who export nearly 70 per cent of their caravans every year.
13 The anthropologist Krisztina Fehérváry (2013) offers a useful framework for attempting to understand material qualities and their links to ideas about Swedishness. By employing a Piercean semiotic approach, she shows that when a 'qualia' such as colour appears in several different realms of objects, substances and bodies it becomes a 'qualisign' (2013: 8). Through their inherent qualities, apparently unrelated objects thus become united into a common aesthetic (ibid.).
14 See for instance Garvey (2008) or Müller (2007) on the Nordic second homes.
15 The lighter the car, the heavier the caravan can be, but the outfit cannot exceed 3,500 kg. European driver's licence legislation also puts limits on the total weight a driver is allowed to tow or drive (in case of the motorhome).

16 Well into the twenty-first century, this conventional caravan is facing its greatest challenge in the motorhome: a product in which the industry itself sees its future. It is mobile, and seems to attract other users, they claim – those less 'traditional'. But in terms of design, also the European manufactured motorhome meets similar restrictions on weight and space and thereby reproduces conventional caravan aesthetics.

Chapter 2

1 The car has, to use the words of Dennis and Urry, 'redefined movement, affect and emotion in the contemporary world' (2009: 41), bringing about important social, cultural and material changes (Monroe 2014: 517; Miller 2001b). But the car is also a system that has created distances through its separation of home, work, business and places of pleasure (Dennis and Urry 2009: 41). The private car changed American tourism and made motorized camping a central part of holidaying. With the car, Löfgren argues, came speed and distance, and the development of a landscape in transit through the establishment of tourist camps, cabins and alternative stopovers (1999: 58). Löfgren furthermore shows how the introduction of the car in many ways made tourism more privatized, and it provided the middle classes with the possibility of reaching new and untouched places. For the working classes, on the other hand, motorized camping opened up the possibility of leaving home on weekends and short holidays where one could sleep in the car or in a tent with no need for long-term planning or saving (Löfgren 1999: 63). In the early 1900s, organized tent-camps were established as a cheap leisure alternative, and according to Löfgren this contributed to the institutionalization of several aspects of American camping life such as campfire evenings and sing-alongs, features we also recognize from the scouts movement.

2 Camping as leisure phenomenon has roots back in the 1800s and the beginning of the 1900s, when growing urban areas spurred a need to leave the town on weekends on a bicycle, to go hiking, fishing and tenting in the countryside. The spread of camping during the 1920s and 1930s was furthermore intimately linked to the increased rights for holidays among European workers. An international convention of the right to holidays was passed in 1936, and the same year France introduced holiday legislation. Towards the end of the 1930s, holidays were included in Swedish and Danish law and the Swedish 1938 holiday legislation gave workers the right to two weeks of holiday per year; in 1978, these two weeks had become four. In Scandinavia, the growth of camping is also partly a result of customary law regarding fundamental rights to access to nature. In Sweden and Norway, the principle of public right to access to nature has even been included

in the constitution. This right to access to nature made tenting an important part of leisure life in the 1920s and the 1930s; it was affordable and relatively easy. In Scandinavia, camping provided an alternative for those who did not have access to land by the sea in countries where middle-class ownership of second homes and cabins hold a visible position in the leisure landscape.
3. Online Etymology Dictionary.
4. See for example Agamben (1998) and Malkki (1995) on the camp as a social and political formation of power and control.
5. Campsite infrastructures are 'things and also the relation between things' (Larkin 2013: 329) that form a material basis of services consisting of electricity hook-up points, water points, sanitary facilities, the actual pitches themselves and the drainage, cable and sewage systems built underground. See the expanding literature on infrastructure in anthropology (for instance Anand 2011; Harvey et al. 2017; Larkin 2013; Star 1999).
6. Approximately 3, 5 million Euro (June 2017).
7. During the rebuilding period all caravan dwellers were removed from the site, where the ground was entirely dug up to enable a new laying of cables, sewage and drains, 200 pitches with electrical hook-ups, the construction of a new reception building containing a restaurant and a small shop, two-storey cabins for rental, a children's playground, as well as service buildings with room for fully equipped kitchen sections with microwaves, stoves and dishing facilities, a toilet section with separate showers, a laundry section, an outdoor dog shower, and a separate sauna and jacuzzi. The neighbourhood planning of the old site was also gone, leaving spacious pitches with no vegetation between them.
8. A report from the Swedish Research Institute of Tourism 2006 indicated that about 20 per cent of caravanners on Swedish campsites rent pitches on a seasonal basis.
9. See Blomkvist (2001) and O'Dell (1997, 2001) for discussions about the car and politics in Sweden. Löfgren also emphasizes the role of leisure as a symbol of modernity for the Social Democrats when they came into power in Sweden in the early 1930s: 'Biking through Sweden, camping in the woods, or mingling on the beach was supposed to foster a new and classless breed of modern citizens, in healthy tanned bodies, overalls and sandals' (1999: 271).
10. Camping in the countryside was 'a privilege, an opportunity and an education' Nina Morris (2003: 304) writes about the caravan clubs' role.
11. The large caravan clubs still play a central role in the organization of caravanning through their commitment to rallies, club tours and the running of own caravan sites – most of which is based on the members' volunteer work. What later has become the UK-based *The Camping and Caravanning Club* was founded in 1901 first as a cycle camping association by an outdoor enthusiast, Thomas Hiram Holding, usually presented as one of the pioneers of European camping life

(Constance 2001) A few years later, in 1907, *The Caravan Club* was founded and its 1,000 members in 1939 grew to 10,000 in 1945 and 100,000 in 1971.

12 The first Spanish statistics from the early 1960s indicate an existence of somewhere around 200 campsites spread around the different autonomous regions. In 2002 this number had passed 1,100 as Spanish tourism has grown extensively (Feo Parrondo 2003). More than 50 per cent of the guests at Spanish campsites are registered as foreign nationals.

13 Among the caravanner and motorhomers on the site's touring area, the connection remains one of potential mobility, where the mobile dwelling is unhooked from the campsite through the simple removal of a cable.

14 See Von Schnitzler (2013) about the history of the metre in South Africa.

15 See Brenda Chalfin's (2014) discussion about public toilets and infrastructure in Ghana for an interesting comparison.

16 Approximately 2 million Euro (June 2017).

17 Taking advantage of the need for housing, the campsites were often poorly run and were seen as undesirable from the point of view of local authorities (Wilson: 190). This all changed gradually however, not least with legislation that aimed to secure the sanitary conditions of the campsite.

18 Writing on Los Angeles, Mike Davis (1990) has argued that US gated communities are part of a 'militarization' of the city, where building the fortress city is a way of regulating and controlling the poor minorities. Today, one finds gated communities increasingly popular, not only in the United States, but also in Latin America, parts of urban Africa (cf. Appel 2012), and in Europe, for instance in so-called *urbanizaciónes* (urbanizations) on the Spanish coast. Even if gating through the use of walls, gates, locks and guards exists cross-culturally, their histories and causation vary, from for instance South African racism to fear of property vandalism in Accra or kidnapping and robbery in Mexico City (Low 2001: 46). As Low (2003, 2008a) notes, the speculation and theories on the reasons for gated communities' increased popularity are many. She argues that the gated community is 'a response to transformations in the political economy of the late 20th century urban America' (2008a: 51). When tracing this transformation to the 'Reaganomics' of the 1980s, with enforced economic restructuring and a shift towards free market capitalism, Low identifies increasing inequalities of neighbourhood resources and a general weakening of existing social relations and social control (ibid). The gated community, Low argues, should also be seen as an extension of the already existing tendency of middle-class and upper middle-class residents to separate themselves as a class through the building of fences and avoidance of neighbours and potential conflicts (ibid.: 52). In the US urban and suburban context, Low turns to racism as a general contributor to materialized exclusion practices, and in many of the

Chapter 3

1. Annual test required for motor vehicles.
2. See for instance Garsten (2008) on this latter point.
3. Approximately 800 Euro (June 2017).
4. In this sense, their caravan mobilities can be seen in relation to how second homes have been theorized and understood in a growing body of literature. Hall and Müller (2004) use second homes as an umbrella category, encapsulating various types of dwelling: vacation homes, cottages, summer homes and weekend homes. In their approach, the authors categorize second homes into three different groups: stationary, semi-mobile and mobile, separated through their relation to mobility (2004: 5). The semi-mobile group consists of what Hall and Müller identify as camping, in forms of caravans, mobile homes, RVs and tents. Whereas Hall and Müller concentrate on what they term the non-mobile second home, specifically on the privately owned rural second home (ibid.), the way dwellings are categorized in terms of an undefined category of mobility is certainly problematic. One of the issues raised here however, is how the term second home also evokes problematic connotations through its establishment of hierarchical relationships between dwellings and their users. See also Bendix and Löfgren (2007) on the problem of first and second dwellings.
5. See Benson and O'Reilly (2009a).

Chapter 4

1. Chevalier (2002) notes that the fireplace was always the central focus of the room in English homes. Even if central heating and the television have changed this, it is only to a minor degree compared to what Chevalier finds in the case of France.
2. See for instance Bevan (2014) or Cresswell and Martin (2012) for further analysis of the container.
3. See Warnier (2006) for a more comprehensive analysis of containers as metaphors.
4. First screened on BBC in 2002, *Cash in the Attic* looks for antiques in a family's house and value assesses them with the help of experts, helping the family to arrange an auction.

5 See Leivestad (2017c) for a discussion about the handyman jobs performed at the campsite. Morris (2012) offers a fruitful case of comparison, when discussing the exchange of practical skills among Russian workers.
6 *Decreto 119/2002*, de 30 de Julio del gobierno Valenciano, regulador de los Campamentos de Turismo de la Comunidad Valenciana.
7 In 2013 the annual rent was 3,842.45 Euro, with an IVA of 10 per cent, bringing it 4,226.70 Euro. Water and electricity are added, and to be paid monthly, according to the counter installed on every pitch.
8 'Se prohibe expresamente la instalación por parte de los clientes de elementos que no se correspondan con los de uso temporal, propio y habitual de la estancia en los campings y/o perjudiquen la imagen turística del establecimiento'.

Chapter 5

1 It needs to be noted that community is a much debated term within anthropology. See for instance Amit and Rapport (2002) and Ortner (1997).
2 See Matthew Hull's (2011) interesting discussion on the term neighbourhood and its history.
3 As Miller (2001c) notes, *Coronation Street* is the most popular television show in Britain. Many of my informants at Camping Mares watched the show on a weekly basis.
4 EastEnders, about an East London neighbourhood, has been broadcasted on BBC One since 1985.
5 Gossip, Luise White (2000) argues, is 'talk about people when they are not present, but it is not just any kind of talk: it reports behaviour; it rests on evaluating reputation' (2000: 60). See also Gluckman (1963) and Hannerz (1967).
6 White (2000) finds 'rumour' to be a weak term 'with which to discuss stories that the storytellers think of as true' (2000: 58).
7 See also Hazel Andrews' (2011) research on British working-class holidaymakers on Mallorca.
8 Some caravan dwellers did however have contact with the wider British community in the area through their membership of expat clubs, or more commonly, through frequenting a British-run pub in Benidorm.
9 Working men clubs are member-run non-profit organizations. Lately, many clubs are facing a great decrease in memberships and struggle for their existence.
10 A north–south divide was repeatedly manifested in daily talk at the campsite as a general dislike of Londoners or the few caravanners that came from the London area, or presumed 'posh' areas of Britain such as Surrey.

11 An anti-immigration debate gained new fuel during the time of my fieldwork, especially in 2013, when the political party UKIP entered the political arena in the UK.
12 Discussing the migration motivations of working-class British in Turkey, Nudrali and O'Reilly (2009) show how in a similar context, 'Britain is depicted as unhealthy, cold, depressing, isolated and lonely, unaffordable, highly regulated and taxed, and as offering no sense of future security or control over one's life' (2009: 142). In this more general negative portrayal, what is experienced as an immigration problem is a major issue of concern. As the authors rightly point out in the case of British in Turkey, one's own mobility is positively valued in this context, compared to those that are immobile and 'stuck' in the UK (2009: 142). Andrews reads the realities of British working-class tourists in a similar vein, emphasizing how 'British identity' is presumed to be under threat, caused by the EU's intervention in British life, loss of British sovereignty and independence, and a decrease in British global importance (2011: 8).
13 'The bedroom tax' or rather the 'under-occupancy penalty', came into force in April 2013 as part of the Welfare Reform Act 2012. The change reduced the benefits paid to people living in housing association property that were deemed to have too much living space, and caused a spur of angry debate in the UK. Not a tax per se, the penalty has been called 'the bedroom tax' in media and by representatives of the Labour Party.
14 Kaplan argues that as romanticized figures, the nomad and the Gypsy are positioned and believed to be 'closer to nature, purer or simpler, and near to vanishing' (Kaplan 1996: 90).
15 There is no word for caravan in the Romany language, and in her classical ethnographic study of the *Traveller-Gypsies* in the 1970s UK, Okely (1983) notes that Traveller-Gypsies would refer to the household or home dwelling as the trailer, while employing the term caravan only in conversation with *Gorgios* (non-gypsy people). As Okely (1983) and others have demonstrated, the history of the Gypsy population in Europe is one that is marked by dominant society's attempts to 'exoticise, disperse, control, assimilate or destroy them'. Many of the measures used to control the Gypsy population, especially well-documented in the UK, have been related to the control of mobility and the Gypsy caravan life. Nomadic lifestyle, Taylor (2008) argues, was seen as the result of failure and social inadequacy, not as a positive and desirable choice.
16 In her book *Gypsies and Gentlemen*, Wilson (1986) clearly demonstrates that the ambivalent relation between leisure caravanning and gypsy lifestyle is far from new. In 1933, the first real caravan magazine, *Caravan and Trailer*, was published in the UK with the subtitle 'The only magazine for those who love the gypsy life' (1986: 171). This subtitle was soon to be dropped, 'perhaps because the public image of the

gypsy was reverting to the old notion of a shifty traveller who would leave rubbish behind him and clutter up the view with his ugly van', Wilson suggests (ibid.).

Chapter 6

1 *The Tiny House Movement* and *The Small House Movement* gained fuel in the United States after the 2007–8 financial crisis.
2 Mobile homes don't come without the problems I have pointed to in this book, and one possible consequence of a 'no fixed abode' is that a lack of postcode can exclude you from official registries. See for instance *The Independent* (29 March 2015) *'Floating Voters: How Living on a Houseboat meant I didn't officially Exist'*.

References

Adam, Barbara. 1995. *Timewatch. The Social Analysis of Time*. Cambridge: Polity Press.
Adam, Barbara. 1990. *Time and Social Theory*. Cambridge: Polity Press.
Adey, Peter. 2010. *Mobility*. London and New York: Routledge.
Agamben, Giorgio. 1998. *Homo Sacer: Sovereign Power and Bare Life*. Translated by Daniel Heller-Roazen. Stanford: Stanford University Press.
Amit, Vered and Nigel Rapport. 2002. *The Trouble with Community. Anthropological Reflections on Movement, Identity and Collectivity*. London: Pluto Press.
Anand, Nikhil. 2011. 'Pressure: The Politechnics of Water Supply in Mumbai', *Cultural Anthropology* 26 (4): 542–64.
Andrews, Hazel. 2011. *The British on Holiday. Charter Tourism, Identity and Consumption*. Bristol: Channel View Publications.
Appel, Hannah C. 2012. 'Walls and White Elephants: Oil Extraction, Responsibility, and Infrastructural Violence in Equatorial Guinea', *Ethnography* 13 (4): 439–65.
Aspers, Patrik and Asaf Darr. 2011. 'Trade Shows and the Creation of Market and Industry', *Sociological Review* 59 (4): 758–78.
Attfield, Judy. 1999. 'Bringing Modernity Home: Open Plan in the British Domestic Interior', in Irene Cieraad (ed.), *At Home. An Anthropology of Domestic Space*, 73–82. New York: Cyracuse University Press.
Bauman, Zygmunt. 2007. *Liquid Times: Living in an Age of Uncertainty*. Cambridge: Polity Press.
Bell, Sandra and Simon Coleman. 1999. 'The Anthropology of Friendship: Enduring Times and Future Possibilities', in Sandra Bell and Simon Coleman (eds), *The Anthropology of Friendship*, 1–20. Oxford: Berg.
Benson, Michaela and Nick Osbaldiston (eds). 2014. *Understanding Lifestyle Migration. Theoretical Approaches to Migration and the Quest for a Better Way of Life*. Basingstoke: Palgrave Macmillan.
Benson, Michaela and Karen O' Reilly. 2009a. 'Lifestyle Migration. Escaping to the Good Life', in *Lifestyle Migration: Expectations, Aspirations and Experiences*, 1–13. Aldershot: Ashgate.
Benson, Michaela and Karen O' Reilly. 2009b. 'Migration and the Search for a Better Way of Life: A Critical Exploration of Lifestyle Migration', *The Sociological Review* 57 (4): 608–25.
Bevan, Andrew. 2014. 'Mediterranean Containerization', *Current Anthropology* 55 (4): 387–418.
Bevan, Mark. 2010. 'Retirement Lifestyles in a Niche Housing Market: Park-Home Living in England', *Ageing and Society* 30: 965–85.

Birdwell-Pheasant, Donna and Denise Lawrence-Zuñega. 1999. 'Introduction: Houses and Families in Europe', in Donna Birdwell-Pheasant and Denise Lawrence-Zuñega (eds), *House Life: Space, Place and Family in Europe*, 1–35. Oxford and New York: Berg.

Blichfeldt, Bodil S. 2009. 'Innovation and Entrepreneurship in Tourism: The Case of a Danish Caravan site', *Pasos. Revista de Turismo y Patrimonio Cultural* 7 (3): 415–31.

Blichfeldt, Bodil S. and Marie Mikkelsen. 2013. 'Vacability and Sociability as Touristic Attraction', *Tourist Studies* 13 (3): 235–50.

Blomkvist, Pär. 2001. *Den goda vägens vänner: Väg- och billobbyn och framväxten av det Svenska bilsamhället 1914-1959*. Stockholm: Symposion.

Bourdieu, Pierre. 1990. 'The Kabyle House or the World Reversed', in Pierre Bourdieu (ed.), *The Logic of Practice*, 271–83. Stanford: Stanford University Press.

Brooker, Ed and Marion Joppe. 2014. 'A Critical Review of Camping Research and Directions for Future Studies'. *Journal of Vacation Marketing* 20 (4): 335–351.

Buchli, Victor. 2013. *An Anthropology of Architecture*. London: Bloomsbury.

Caldicott, Rod and Pascal Scherrer. 2013. 'The Lifecycle of Caravan Parks in Australia: The Case of Northern New South Wales', *Australian Geographer* 44 (1): 63–80.

Carsten, Janet and Stephen Hugh-Jones. 1995. 'Introduction', in Janet Carsten and Stephen Hugh-Jones (eds), *About the House*, 1–46. Cambridge: University Press.

Casado-Diaz, Maria Ángeles. 2009. 'Social Capital in the Sun: Bonding and Bridging Social Capital among British Retirees', in Michaela Benson and Karen O' Reilly (eds), *Lifestyle Migration: Expectations, Aspirations and Experiences*, 87–102. Aldershot: Ashgate.

Casado-Diaz, Maria Ángeles. 2006. 'Retiring to Spain: An Analysis of Difference among North European Nationals', *Journal of Ethnic and Migration Studies* 32 (8): 1321–39.

Castells, Manuel and Alejandro Portes. 1989. 'World Underneath: The Origins, Dynamics, and Effects of the Informal Economy', in Alejandro Portes, Manuel Castells and Lauren A. Benton (eds), *The Informal Economy. Studies in Advanced and Less Developed Countries*, 11–40. Baltimore and London: The John Hopkins University Press.

Chalfin, Brenda. 2014. 'Public Things, Excremental Politics and the Infrastructure of Bare Life in Ghana's City of Tema', *American Ethnologist* 41 (1): 92–109.

Chevalier, Sophie. 2002. 'The Cultural Construction of Domestic Space in France and Great Britain', *Signs* 27 (3): 847–56.

Chu, Julie. 2010. *Cosmologies of Credit: Transnational Mobility and the Politics of Destination in China*. Durham and London: Duke University Press.

Clarke, John and Chas Critcher. 1985. *The Devil Makes Work: Leisure in Capitalist Britain*. Basingstoke and London: Macmillan.

Cohen, Scott A., Tara Duncan and Maria Thulemark. 2015. 'Lifestyle Mobilities: The Crossroads of Travel, Leisure and Migration', *Mobilities* 10 (1): 155–72.

Coleman, Simon and Tamara Kohn. 2007. *The Discipline of Leisure. Embodying Cultures of 'Recreation'*. New York and Oxford: Berghahn.

Constance, Hazel. 2001. *First in the Field: A Century of the Camping and Caravanning Club*. Coventry: The Camping and Caravanning Club.

Counts, Dorothy Ayers and David R. Counts. 2009. *Over The Next Hill: An Ethnography of RVing Seniors in North America. Second Edition*. Ontario: University of Toronto Press.

Counts, Dorothy Ayers and David R. Counts.1992. 'They're my Family Now: The Creation of Community among RVers', *Anthropologica* 34 (2): 153-182.

Crapanzano, Vincent. 2010. 'Textualization, Mystification and the Power of the Frame', in Olav Zenker and Karsten Kumoll (eds), *Beyond Writing Culture*. Oxford: Berghahn.

Cresswell, Tim. 2010. 'Towards a Politics of Mobility', *Environment and Planning D: Society and Space* 28: 17–31.

Cresswell, Tim. 2006. *On the Move. Mobility in the Modern Western World*. Abingdon and New York: Routledge.

Cresswell, Tim and Craig Martin. 2012. 'On Turbulence; Entanglements of Disorder and Order on a Devon Beach', *Tijdschrift voor Economische en Sociale Geografie* 103 (5): 516–29.

Dalakoglou, Dimitris. 2010a. 'Migrating-Remitting – "Building"-Dwelling: House Making as "Proxy" Presence in Postsocialist Albania', *Journal of the Royal Anthropological Institute* 16: 761–77.

Dalakoglou, Dimitris. 2009. 'Building and Ordering Transnationalism: The "Greek House" in Albania as Material Process', in Daniel Miller (ed.), *Anthropology and the Individual: A Material Culture Perspective*, 51–68. Oxford: Berg.

Daniels, Inge. 2010. *The Japanese House. Material Culture in the Modern Home*. Oxford and New York: Berg.

Daniels, Inge. 2009. 'Seasonal and Commercial Rhythms of Domestic Consumption. A Japanese Case Study', in (eds), Elisabeth Shove, Frank Trentmann and Richard Wilk *Time, Consumption and Everyday Life. Practice, Materiality and Culture*. Oxford: Berg.

Daniels, Inge. 2008. 'Japanese Homes Inside Out', *Home Cultures* 5 (2): 115–40.

Davis, Mike. 1990. *City of Quartz: Excavating the Future in Los Angeles*. New York: Vintage Books.

Dickens, Charles. 1840. *The Old Curiosity Shop*. London: Chapman and Hall Strand.

Dolan, John A. 1999. '"I've Always Fancied Owning me Own Lion": Ideological Motivations in External House Decoration by Recent Homeowners', in Irene Cireaad (ed.), *At Home. An Anthropology of Domestic Space*, 60–72. New York: Cyracuse University Press.

Dennis, Kingsley and John Urry. 2009. *After the Car*. Cambridge: Polity Press.

Eriksson, Leif. 2006. *Camping. Vem, Hur och Varför?* Stockholm: Wahlström och Widstrand.

Fehérváry, Krisztina. 2013. *Politics in Color and Concrete*. Bloomington and Indianapolis: Indiana University Press.

Feo Parrondo, Fransisco. 2003. 'Los Campings en España', *Cuadernos de Turismo* 11: 83–96.

Flamm, Michael and Vincent Kaufmann. 2006. 'Operationalising the Concept of Motility: A Qualitative Study', *Mobilities* 1 (2): 167–89.

Foucault, Michel. 1977. *Discipline and Punish: the Birth of the Prison*. New York: Pantheon Books.

Garsten, Christina. 2008. *Workplace Vagabonds. Career and Community in Changing Worlds of Work*. Basingstoke: Palgrave Macmillan.

Garvey, Pauline. 2008. 'The Norwegian Country Cabin and Functionalism: A Tale of Two Modernities', *Social Anthropology* 16 (2): 203–20.

Glick-Schiller Nina and Noel Salazar. 2013. 'Regimes of Mobility Across the Globe', *Journal of Ethic and Migration Studies* 39 (2): 183–200.

Gluckman, Max. 1963. 'Gossip and Scandal', *Current Anthropology* 4 (3): 307–16.

Gregson, Nicky and Vikki Beale. 2004. 'Wardrobe Matter: The Sorting, Displacement and Circulation of Women's Clothing', *Geoforum* 35: 689–700.

Gregson, Nicky, Alan Metcalfe and Louise Crewe. 2007. 'Identity, Mobility, and the Throwaway Society', *Environment and Planning D: Society and Space* 25: 682–700.

Gustafson, Per. 2009. 'Your Home in Spain. Residential Strategies in International Retirement Migration', in Michaela Benson and Karen O' Reilly (eds), *Lifestyle Migration: Escaping to the Good Life. Lifestyle Migration. Expectations, Aspirations and Experiences*, 69–86. Aldershot: Ashgate.

Gustafson, Per. 2008. 'Transnationalism in Retirement Migration: The Case of North European Retirees in Spain', *Ethnic and Racial Studies* 31 (3): 451–71.

Gustafson, Per. 2001. 'Retirement Migration and Transnational Lifestyles', *Ageing and Society* 21 (4): 371–94.

Guyer, Jane I. 2007. 'Prophecy and the Near Future: Thoughts on Macroeconomic, Evangelical, and Punctuated Time', *American Ethnologist* 34 (3): 409–21.

Hage, Ghassan. 2009. 'Waiting Out the Crisis: On Stuckedness and Governmentality', in Ghassan Hage (ed.), *Waiting*. Melbourne: Melbourne University Press, 97–103.

Hage, Ghassan. 2005. 'A Not so Multi-Sited Ethnography of a Not so Imagined Community', *Anthropological Theory* 5 (4): 463–75.

Hage, Ghassan. 1997. 'At Home in the Entrails of the West: Multiculturalism, "Ethnic Food", and Migrant Home Building', in Helen Grace, Ghassan Hage, Leslie Johnson, Julie Langsworth and Michael Symonds (eds), *Home/World: Space, Community and Marginality in Sydney's West*, 99–153. Annandale: Pluto Press.

Hall, Michael C. and Dieter Müller. 2004. 'Introduction: Second Homes, Curse or Blessing? Revisited', in Michael C. Hall and Dieter Müller (eds), *Tourism, Mobility and Second Homes: Between Elite Landscape and Common Ground*, 3–14. Clevedon: Channel View Publications.

Hanley, Lynsey. 2007. *Estates. An Intimate History*. London: Granta Books.

Hannam, Kevin, Mimi Sheller and John Urry. 2006. 'Editorial: Mobilities, Immobilities and Moorings', *Mobilities* 1 (1): 1–22.

Hannerz, Ulf. 1967. 'Gossip, Network and Culture in a Black American Ghetto', *Ethnos* 32: 35–60.

Hardy, Anne, Ulrike Gretzel and Dallas Hanson. 2013. 'Travelling Neo-Tribes: Conceptualizing Recreational Vehicle Users', *Journal of Tourism and Cultural Change* 11 (1–2): 48–60.

Hardy, Anne, Dallas Hanson and Ulrike Gretzel. 2012. 'Online Representations of RVing Neo-Tribes in the USA and Australia', *Journal of Tourism and Cultural Change* 10 (3): 219–32.

Hart, Keith. 1973. 'Informal Income Opportunities and Urban Employment in Ghana', *Journal of Modern African Studies* 11 (1): 61–89.

Hartwigsen, Gail and Roberta Null. 1990. 'Full Timers: Who are these Older People Who are Living in their RVs?', *Journal of Housing for the Elderly* 7 (1): 133–47.

Hartwigsen, Gail and Roberta Null. 1989. 'Full-timing: A Housing Alternative for Older People', *International Journal of Aging and Human Development* 29: 317–28.

Harvey, David. 2011. 'The Future of the Commons', *Radical History Review* 109: 101–7.

Harvey, Penelope, Casper Bruun Jensen and Atsuro Morita (eds). 2017. *Infrastructures and Social Complexity: A Companion*. London: Routledge.

Henare, Amaria, Martin Holbraad and Sari Wastell (eds). 2007. *Thinking through Things: Theorising Artefacts Ethnographically*. London: Routledge.

Hetherington, Kevin. 1997. *The Badlands of Modernity: Heterotopia and Social Ordering*. London and New York: Routledge.

Helliwell, Christine. 1996. 'Space and Sociality in a Dayak Longhouse', in Michael Jackson (ed.), *Things as They Are: New Directions in Phenomenological Anthropology*, 128–48. Bloomington and Indianapolis: Indiana University Press.

Hill, David W. 2012. 'Total Gating: Sociality and the Fortification of Networked Spaces', *Mobilities* 7 (1): 115–29.

Hillman, Wendy. 2013. 'Grey Nomads travelling in Queensland, Australia: Social and Health Needs', *Ageing and Society* 33: 579–97.

Huber, Andreas and Karen O'Reilly. 2004. 'The Construction of Heimat under Conditions of Individualised Modernity: Swiss and British Elderly Migrants in Spain', *Ageing and Society* 24: 327–51.

Huete, Raquel, Alejandro Mantecón and Jesús Estévez. 2013. 'Challenges in Lifestyle Migration Research: Reflections and Findings about the Spanish Crisis', *Mobilities* 8 (3): 331–48.

Hull, Matthew S. 2011. 'Communities of Place, Not Kind: American Technologies of Neighbourhood in Postcolonial Delhi', *Comparative Studies in Society and History* 53 (4): 757–90.

Humphrey, Caroline 2005a. 'Ideology in Infrastructure: Architecture and Soviet Imagination', *Journal of the Royal Anthropological Institute* 11 (1): 39–58.

Humphrey, Caroline. 2005b. 'Alternative Freedoms', *Proceedings of the American Philosophical Society* 151 (1): 1–10.

Hurley, Andrew. 2001. *Diners, Bowling Alleys and Trailer Parks: Chasing the American Dream in the Postwar Consumer Culture*. New York: Basic.

Ingold, Tim. 2007. 'Materials against Materiality', *Archaeological Dialogues* 14 (1): 1–16.
Ivars, Baidal, Josep A. Trueta, I. Rodríguez Sánchez and J. F. Vera Rebollo. 2013. 'The Evolution of Mass Tourism Destinations: New Approaches Beyond Deterministic Models in Benidorm (Spain)', *Journal of Tourism Management* 34: 184–95.
Jackson, John Brinckerhoff. 1984. *Discovering the Vernacular Landscape*. New Haven and London: Yale University Press.
Janoschka, Michael. 2011. 'Habitus and Radical Reflexivity: A Conceptual Approach to study Political Articulations of Lifestyle- and Tourism-related Mobilities', *Journal of Policy Research in Tourism, Leisure and Events* 3 (3): 224–36.
Jenkinson, Andrew. 2001. 'Pioneer Caravans', in Hazel Constance (ed.), *First in the field. A Century of the Camping and Caravanning Club*, 60–1. Coventry: The Camping and Caravanning Club.
Jobes, Patrick C. 1984. 'Old Timers and New Mobile Lifestyles', *Annals of Tourism Research* 11: 181–98.
Johnson, Mark. 1987. *The Body in the Mind: The Bodily Basis of Meaning, Imagination, and Reason*. Chicago: University of Chicago Press.
Kaplan, Caren. 1996. *Questions of Travel. Postmodern Discourses of Displacement*. Durham and London: Duke University Press.
Kaufmann, Vincent. 2011. *Re-Thinking the City. Urban Dynamics and Motility*. Oxford: Routledge.
Kaufmann, Vincent. 2002. *Re-Thinking Mobility: Contemporary Sociology*. Aldershot: Ashgate.
Kaufmann, Vincent, and Bertrand Montulet. 2008. 'Between Social and Spatial Mobilities: The Issue of Social Fluidity', in Weert Canzler, Vincent Kaufmann and Sven Kesselring (eds), *Tracing Mobilities: Towards a Cosmopolitan Perspective*, 37–55. Aldershot: Ashgate.
Kaufmann, Vincent, Manfred Max Bergman and Dominique Joyce. 2004. 'Motility: Mobility as Capital', *International Journal of Urban and Regional Research* 28 (4): 745–56.
Kellerman, Aharon. 2012. 'Potential Mobilities', *Mobilities* 7 (1): 171–83.
Kesselring, Sven. 2006. 'Pioneering Mobilities: New Pattern of Movement and Motility in a Mobile World', *Environment and Planning A* 38 (2): 269–79.
King, Russel, A. M. Warnes, Tony Warnes and Allan M. Williams. 2000. *Sunset Lives: British Retirement to Southern Europe*. Oxford: Berg.
Kusenbach, Margarethe. 2009. 'Salvaging Decency: Mobile Home Residents' Strategies of Managing Stigma of "Trailer" Living', *Qualitative Sociology* 32: 399–428.
Lakoff, George. 1987. *Women, Fire and Dangerous Things: What Categories Reveal about the Mind*. Chicago and London: University of Chicago Press.
Larkin, Brian. 2013. 'The Politics and Poetics of Infrastructure', *Annual Review of Anthropology* 42: 327–43.
Latour, Bruno. 2005. *Reassembling the Social. An Introduction to Actor-Network-Theory*. Oxford: Oxford University Press.

Lawrence Denise L. and Setha Low. 1990. 'The Built Environment and Spatial Form', *Annual Review of Anthropology* 19: 453–505.

Lea, Tess and Paul Pholeros. 2010. 'This is Not a Pipe: The Treacheries of Indigenous Housing', *Public Culture* 22 (1): 187–209.

Leivestad, Hege Høyer. 2018 (forthcoming). 'Caravan Cultures: Second Homes on Wheels', in Michael Hall and Dieter Müller (eds), *Routledge Handbook of Second Homes*. London: Routledge.

Leivestad, Hege Høyer. 2017a. 'Inventorying Mobility: Methodology on Wheels', in Alice Elliott, Noel Salazar and Roger Norum (eds), *Methodologies of Mobility. Ethnography and Experiment*, 47–67. Oxford: Berghahn books.

Leivestad, Hege Høyer. 2017b. 'Beyond Informality: Intimacy and Commerce at the Caravanning Trade Fair', in Hege Høyer Leivestad and Anette Nyqvist (eds), *Ethnographies of Conferences and Trade Fairs: Shaping Industries, Creating Professionals*, 129–45. New York: Palgrave MacMillan.

Leivestad, Hege Høyer. 2017c. 'Campsite Migrants: British Caravanners and Homemaking in Benidorm', *Nordic Journal of Migration Research* 7 (3): 181–88.

Leivestad, Hege Høyer. 2016. 'Motility', in Kiran Jayaram and Noel Salazar (eds), *The Keywords of Mobility: Critical Engagements*, 133–51. Oxford: Berghahn.

Lewycka, Marina. 2007. *Two Caravans*. London: Penguin Books.

Lindquist, Johan A. 2009. *The Anxieties of Mobility: Migration and Tourism in the Indonesian Borderlands*. Honolulu: University of Hawai'i Press.

Low, Setha M. 2008a. 'Fortification of Residential Neighbourhoods and the New Emotions of Home', *Housing, Theory and Society* 25 (1): 47–65.

Low, Setha M. 2008b. 'The Gated Community as Heterotopia', in Michiel Dehaene and Lieven De Cauter (eds), *Heterotopia and the City: Public Space in a Postcivil Society*, 153–63. Oxford and New York: Routledge.

Low, Setha M. 2003. *Behind the Gates: Life, Security and the Pursuit of Happiness in Fortress America*. New York and London: Routledge.

Low, Setha M. 2001. 'The Edge and the Center: Gated Communities and the Discourse of Urban Fear', *American Anthropologist* 103 (1): 45–58.

Lundin, Per. 2013. 'Confronting Class: the American Motel in Early Post-War Sweden', *Journal of Tourism History* 5 (3): 305–24.

Löfgren, Orvar. 1999. *On Holiday: A History of Vacationing*. Berkeley: University of California Press.

Löfgren, Orvar and Regina Bendix. 2007. 'Double Homes, Double Lives?', *Ethnologia Europaea* 37: 7–16.

MacDougall, David. 1999. 'Social Aesthetics and the Doon School', *Visual Anthropology Review* 15 (1): 3–20.

Malkki, Liisa. 1995. *Purity and Exile: Violence, Memory, and National Cosmology amongst Hutu Refugees in Tanzania*. Chicago: Chicago University Press.

Marcoux, Jean-Sébastien. 2001a. 'The "Casser Maison" Ritual: Constructing the Self by Emptying the Home', *Journal of Material Culture* 6 (2): 213–35.

Marcoux, Jean-Sébastien. 2001b. 'The Refurbishment of Memory', in Daniel Miller (ed.), *Home Possessions. Material Culture Behind Closed Doors*, 69–86. Oxford: Berg.
Mauss, Marcel and Henri Beuchat. 1979. *Seasonal Variations of the Eskimo. A Study in Social Morphology*. London, Boston and Henley: Routledge and Kegan Paul.
McHugh, Kevin E. and Robert C. Mings. 1995. 'Wintering in American Sunbelt: Linking Place and Behaviour', *The Journal of Tourism Studies* 6 (2): 56–61.
Merriman, Peter. 2014. 'Rethinking Mobile Methods', *Mobilities* 9 (2): 167–87.
Mikkelsen, Marie and Scott A. Cohen. 2015. 'Freedom in Mundane Mobilities: Caravanning in Denmark', *Tourism Geographies* 17 (5): 663–81.
Miller, Daniel (ed.). 2005. *Materiality*. Durham and London: Duke University Press.
Miller, Daniel. 2001a. 'Behind Closed Doors', in Daniel Miller (ed.), *Home Possessions*, 1–19. Oxford: Berg.
Miller, Daniel (ed.). 2001b. *Car Cultures*. Oxford: Berg.
Miller, Daniel. 2001c. *The Dialectics of Shopping*. Chicago and London: Chicago University Press.
Miranda Montero, Maria Jesús. 1985. 'El Camping, la Forma Más Reciente de Turismo', *Cuadernos de Geografía* 37: 157–74.
Moeran, Brian. 2010. 'The Book Fair as a Tournament of Values', *Journal of the Royal Anthropological Institute* 16: 138–54.
Moeran, Brian. 2007. 'Marketing Scents and the Anthropology of Smell', *Social Anthropology* 15: 153–68.
Monroe, Kristin V. 2014. 'Automobility and Citizenship in Interwar Lebanon', *Comparative Studies of South Asia, Africa and the Middle East* 34 (3): 518–31.
Morris, Jeremy. 2012. 'Beyond Coping? Alternatives to Consumption within a Social Network of Russian Workers', *Ethnography* 14 (1): 85–103.
Morris, Nina. 2003. *Feeling Nature: Naturism, Camping, Environment and the Body in Britain, 1920-1960*. Unpublished PhD Thesis. University of Hull.
Müller, Dieter. 2007. 'Second Homes in the Nordic Countries: Between Common Heritage and Exclusive Commodity', *Scandinavian Journal of Hospitality and Tourism* 7 (3): 193–201.
Newton, Janice. 2006. 'Permanent Residents in Caravan Parks, Managers and the Persistence of the Social', *Health Sociology Review* 15 (2): 221–31.
Nóvoa, André. 2014. 'A Country on Wheels: A Mobile Ethnography of Portuguese Lorry Drivers', *Environment and Planning A* 46 (12): 2834–47.
Nudrali, Ozlem and Karen O'Reilly. 2009. 'Taking the Risk: The Britons of Didim, Turkey', in Michaela Benson and Karen O' Reilly (eds), *Lifestyle Migration. Expectations, Aspirations and Experiences*, 137–52. Aldershot: Ashgate.
O'Dell, Tom. 2001. 'Raggare and the Panic of Mobility', in Daniel Miller (ed.), *Car Cultures*, 105–32. Oxford: Berg.
O'Dell, Tom. 1997. *Culture Unbound: Americanization and Everyday Life in Sweden*. Lund: Nordic Academic Press.
Okely, Judith. 1983. *The Traveller-Gypsies*. Cambridge: Cambridge University Press.

Oliver, Caroline. 2008. *Retirement Migration: Paradoxes of Ageing*. New York: Routledge.
Oliver, Caroline. 2007. 'Imagined Communitas. Older Migrants and Aspirational Mobility', in Vered Amit (ed.), *Going First Class? New Approaches to Privileged Travel and Movement*, 126–43. New York and Oxford: Berghahn Books.
O'Reilly, Karen. 2009. 'The Children of the Hunters: Self-Realization Projects and Class Reproduction', in Michaela Benson and Karen O' Reilly (eds), *Lifestyle Migration. Expectations, Aspirations and Experiences*, 103–19. Aldershot: Ashgate.
O'Reilly, Karen. 2003. 'When Is a Tourist? The Articulation of Tourism and Migration in Spain's Costa del Sol', *Tourist Studies* 3 (3): 301–17.
O'Reilly, Karen. 2000. *The British on the Costa Del Sol*. London: Routledge.
Ortner, Sherry. 1997. 'Fieldwork in the Postcommunity', *Anthropology and Humanism* 22 (1): 61–80.
Onyx, Jenny and Rosemary Leonard. 2005. 'Australian Grey Nomads and American Snowbirds: Similarities and Differences', *Journal of Tourism Studies* 16 (1): 61–8.
Østby, Per. 2014. 'Car Mobility and Camping Tourism in Norway, 1950-1970', *Journal of Tourism History* 5 (3): 287–304.
Pinney, Christopher. 2005. 'Things Happen: Or, From Which Moment does that Object Come?', in Daniel Miller (ed.), *Materiality*, 256–72. Durham and London: Duke University Press.
Pressnell, Jon. 1991. *Touring Caravans*. Oxford: Shire Publications Ltd.
Sachs, Wolfgang. 1992. *For Love of the Automobile: Looking Back into the History of our Desires*. Oxford: University of California Press.
Salazar, Noel B. 2016 'Keywords of Mobility: What's in a Name?', in Noel Salazar and Kiran Jayaram (eds), *Keywords of Mobility. Critical Engagements*, 1–12. Oxford: Berghahn.
Salazar, Noel and Yang Zhang. 2013. 'Seasonal Lifestyle Tourism: The Case of Chinese Elites', *Annals of Tourism Research*, 43: 81–99.
Savage, Mike. 2015. *Social Class in the 21st Century*. London: Penguin Press.
Shapiro, Nicholas. 2014. *Spaces of Uneventful Disaster: Tracking Emergence Housing and Domestic Chemical Exposures from New Orleans to National Crises*. Unpublished PhD Thesis. Oxford University.
Shapiro, Nicholas. 2015. 'Attuning to the Chemosphere: Domestic Formaldehyde, Bodily Reasoning, and the Chemical Sublime', *Cultural Anthropology* 30 (3): 368–393.
Sheller, Mimi. 2014. *Aluminium Dreams: The Making of Light Modernity*. Cambridge, MA: MIT Press.
Sheller, Mimi and John Urry. 2006. 'New Mobilities Paradigm', *Environment and Planning A* 38 (2): 207–26.
Skeggs, Beverley. 2006. *Class, Self, Culture*. London and New York: Routledge.
Skov, Lise. 2006. 'The Role of Trade Fairs in the Global Fashion Business', *Current Sociology* 54: 764–83.
Sneath, David, Martin Holbraad and Morten Axel Pedersen. 2009. 'Technologies of the Imagination: An Introduction', *Ethnos: Journal of Anthropology* 74 (1): 5–30.

Southerton, Dale, Elizabeth Shove, Alan Warde and Rosemary Deem. 2001. 'The Social Worlds of Caravanning: Objects, Scripts and Practices', *Sociological Research Online* 6: 2.

Star, Susan Leigh. 1999. 'The Ethnography of Infrastructure', *American Behavioral Scientist* 43 (3): 377–91.

Strathern, Marilyn. 1992. *After Nature: English Kinship in the Late Twentieth Century*. Cambridge: Cambridge University Press.

Taylor, Becky. 2008. *A Minority and the State: Travellers in Britain in the Twentieth Century*. Manchester: Manchester University Press.

The Caravan Club. 2011. *Little Book of Caravans*. G2 entertainment Limited.

Thompson, Peter. 2013. 'Introduction: The Privatization of Hope and the Crisis of Negation', in Peter Thompson and Slavoj Zizek (eds), *The Privatization of Hope: Ernst Bloch and the Future of Utopia*, 1–20. Durham and London: Duke University Press.

Triantafillidou, Amalia and George Siomkos. 2013. 'Summer Camping: An Extraordinary, Nostalgic, and Interpersonal Experience', *Journal of Vacation Marketing* 19 (3): 197–208.

Turner, Victor. 1982. *From Ritual to Theatre: The Human Seriousness of Play*. New York: Performing Arts Journal Publications.

Urry, John. 2007. *Mobilities*. Cambridge: Polity Press.

Urry, John. 2006. 'Inhabiting the Car', *The Sociological Review Monograph Series: Against Automobility* 54: 17–31.

Viallon, Philippe. 2012. 'Retired Snowbirds', *Annals of Tourism Research* 39 (4): 2073–91.

Von Schnitzler, Antina. 2013. 'Traveling Technologies: Infrastructure, Ethical Regimes, and the Materiality of Politics in South Africa', *Cultural Anthropology* 28 (4): 670–93.

Wallis, Allan D. 1991. *Wheel Estate: The Rise and Decline of Mobile Homes*. Baltimore and London: The John Hopkins University Press.

Walley, Christine J. 2013. *Exit Zero: Family and Class in Postindustrial Chicago*. Chicago and London: Chicago University Press.

Warnier, Jean-Pierre. 2006. 'Ch 12: Inside and Outside: Surfaces and Containers', in Christopher Tilley, Webb Keane, Susanne Küchler, Michael Rowlands and Patricia Spyer (eds), *Handbook of Material Culture*. London: Sage, 186–195.

William, Gordon Staples. 1886. *The Cruise of the Land Yacht Wanderer, Or, Thirteen Hundred Miles in My Caravan*. London: Hodder and Stoughton.

Wilson, Nerissa. 1986. *Gypsies and Gentlemen: The Life and Times of the Leisure Caravan*. London: Columbus Books.

White, Luise. 2000. *Speaking with Vampires. Rumor and History in Colonial Africa*. Berkeley and London: University of California Press.

Xiang, Biao and Johan Lindquist. 2014. 'Migration Infrastructure', *International Migration Review* 48 (1): 122–48.

Young, Diana. 2004. 'The Material Value of Color: The Estate Agent's Tale', *Home Cultures* 1 (1): 5–22.

Index

Adey, Peter 6
aesthetics
    cabin 31
    'real home' 101
agency 4, 8, 35, 64, 96
Alicante 104
ambiguity 3, 7, 35, 100–1, 144–5
Andrews, Hazel 123, 128–9, 132, 134, 163
Appel, Hannah 103, 160
aspirations
    life 16, 60, 118
    mobility 6, 88, 144

Bauman, Zygmunt 5, 88, 152
Benidorm
    camping in 11, 43, 53, 60
    and economic crisis 53, 86–7
    health care 117, 122
    history 11, 155–6
    and lifestyle migration 79, 84, 132
    tourism 11, 79, 126
    and working-class 79, 155–6
boundaries
    campsite 38, 42
    domestic 92–3, 102, 105–6
    national 129, 140
Bourdieu, Pierre 92, 153
break-ins 49–56
Brexit 134–5
Britishness 129, 155

Cabby Caravan 21–33, 157
cabins 29–31, 40, 49, 137, 158–9. *See also* aesthetics
camp
    control 15, 40–3, 50–8
    etymology 36
    history 15, 37, 40
    planning 40
    spatiality 43–6, 159
camping
    clubs 9, 41–2, 59, 159

history 26, 37–8, 40–1, 58, 62, 154–62
industry 3, 21, 40
media 9–10
Camping and Caravanning Club, the 59, 159
cancer 65–6, 121–2
Caravan Club, the 155, 160
care
    community 56, 118, 122–3, 134–9
    economy 123
    health system 122
    mobility 122
cars 19, 52, 83, 154
Chu, Julie 6
Clarkson, Jeremy 9
class
    and camping 19, 37, 40, 76, 154
    middle class 9–10, 54, 148, 158, 160
    theories of 3, 10, 146–8, 159
    working class 9–10, 40, 58, 126–8, 148, 156, 160, 162–3
colour 29–32, 35, 157
community
    in anthropology 162
    aspirations of 1, 4, 70, 75–6, 84, 88
    conflict 54–6, 126, 128–31, 136–48
    standards 118, 124, 126
consumption 62, 126–8
containers 92–3, 161
control
    social 2, 48, 56, 140, 145
    systems of 42, 15, 38–42, 51–6
Crapanzano, Vincent 4
Cresswell, Tim 143, 161
crisis
    economic crisis 4, 9, 20, 53, 147, 156, 164
    mobility narratives 62
    recession 59, 80, 85–6

Dalakoglou, Dimitris 7
Daniels, Inge 98, 106

decay
    material   26, 34, 110
    national   131, 135, 139
democracy   15, 41, 84, 130, 148
design
    caravan   92, 109–10, 141, 143, 148
    infrastructure   140
    interior   27–32, 102, 158
Dickens, Charles   17
disposal   92–6
divestment   94–5
domesticity   57, 114, 143
downsizing   33, 63, 88, 94–9, 141–5

economy
    cash   85, 145
    household   63
    informal   103, 112, 123, 148
    new   67, 148
    Spanish   135
England   123, 132–4
equality. *See* democracy
escape   4, 134, 152
European Union   3, 132. *See also* Brexit
exchange   29–30, 33–4

family
    and camping   41, 66–8, 72, 75, 96, 100–1
    friendship   122, 134
    unit   98
Féhervary, Krisztina   26, 157
fieldwork   10–11, 155
food   108–9, 126
Franco, Dictator   43, 155
freedom
    camping   41, 62, 67, 84, 148
    economic   63, 84–5, 141, 145
    material   38, 64, 68, 74, 141
    mobility   76, 78, 88, 138, 141–3
    narratives   61, 63, 68
friendship   75, 78–9, 82, 101, 118. *See also* family

gated community   54–6, 148, 160
gender   46, 63
'Gentlemen Gypsies'   19
Giddens, Anthony   5, 152
'Glamping'   40

'good life'   1–4, 15–16, 83, 139–40, 148–52
Guyer, Jane   65, 84, 147
Gypsy
    discrimination of   163–4
    gypsy metaphor   10, 138, 144–5, 163–4
    Gypsy-Travellers   15, 138

Hage, Ghassan   4, 61, 68, 89, 148
Hammond, Richard   9
Hanley, Lynsey   10, 148
Hannam, Kevin   5
Helliwell, Christine   105
hobby   20, 27, 157
holiday legislation   158, 160
home. *See also* domesticity; aesthetics
    aspirations of   2, 25, 68, 91–2, 94
    and class   10, 147
    conceptualization of   4, 7, 14, 19, 91, 139
    making   3, 15, 94–115
    mobility   7, 16, 25–7, 50, 61, 77, 88, 142–3
    ownership   63, 82, 84–9, 141, 148
housing
    campsite   56–8, 64, 67, 75–6, 148–9, 145–8
    economy   1–3, 21, 49, 65, 80–6, 92
    social housing   13, 39, 49
humidity   34, 105, 107, 109–10
hybridity   7
hygiene politics   41–2

identity   106, 126–34, 163
imaginaries   5
immigration   4, 48, 131–6, 156, 163
immobility   5, 68, 78, 115
infrastructure
    campsite   39, 43–5, 57, 140, 144
    electrical   24–5
    motorway   10, 154
    sanitary   47, 57
Ingold, Tim   8, 153
insecurity   15, 53, 99, 121, 147

Jackson, John Brinckerhoff   7, 67–8, 115, 140, 143

Kabe   21, 29

Index

Kaufmann, Vincent   5–6, 143, 152
knowledge   24, 63, 118, 113

labour   10, 102–3, 145, 148
Labour Party   133, 135, 163
'Lake Town'   12, 38–9, 111, 136, 156
Latour, Bruno   6
Lawrence-Zuñiga, Denise   7, 73, 108
leisure
   camping and   10, 20, 39–41, 57–8, 158–9
   class   3, 19, 37, 126–7, 139–40, 148
   domesticity   2, 106, 143, 145
   work and   67–8, 148
liberal ideas   15, 85
lifestyle migration   152
Lindquist, Johan   6
Löfgren, Orvar   31, 38–40, 153–4, 158–9, 161
Low, Setha   54–5, 147–8, 160

markets
   caravan   20–1, 143, 156, 29–35
   informal   103
   marketing   14, 19, 41, 155
   property   15, 29, 49, 65, 80, 85–6, 89, 148
material culture   18, 153. *See also* materiality
materiality, theories of   8, 153
Mauss, Marcel   73–4
Mediterranean   12, 79
Miller, Daniel   8, 18, 124, 162
mobility turn   5, 143
Moeran, Brian   47, 109
morality
   campsite   4, 48, 38, 42
   community   106, 119, 139, 148
   and materiality   37–8, 68, 95
motility   5–6, 143, 152
multiculturalism   133, 147
municipality   12, 38–9

nature   15, 26, 31–47, 62, 158–9
neighbourhood   2–4, 54–6, 119–39, 147, 159–62
network   122–3, 134
new mobilities paradigm   5

Okely, Judith   6, 163
O'reilly, Karen   134, 152, 163

photographs   95–6
privacy   8, 70, 76, 105–6
privatization   37, 39, 125
property. *See* home, ownership
public space   46–7

recession. *See* crisis
reciprocity   123, 134–6, 139–40
refugees   48–9
Roma   32, 39, 42, 163
retirement   54–5, 65–7, 99, 135, 152–3

safety. *See* security
Salazar, Noel   5, 79, 152
Savage, Mike   10
seasonality   49, 73, 79
second homes   155, 161
security. *See also* break-ins; gated community
   campsite   15, 43, 140
   economic   88–9, 99
   measurements   48–56
Sheller, Mimi   5, 157
Skeggs, Beverley   10
smell   35, 47, 105, 107–9
Social Democratic Party   26, 41, 84, 159
sound   8, 16, 105–7
Staples, Gordon   19, 156
stasis   5, 45, 107, 115
surveillance   38, 43, 53–6, 106. *See also* security
Svensk Camping (SCR)   41

Taylor, Becky   9, 163
temporality
   logics of   4–8, 89, 92, 101
   material   7–8
   notions of   16, 34, 110, 114
Thatcher regime   84–5
Thompson, Peter   147
Tiny House Movement   141, 149, 164
Top Gear   9
tourism
   Benidorm   155
   charter   11

    domestic   10, 41
    industry   3, 57, 86–7
trade fairs   2, 10, 14, 18, 23–34

uncertainty   5, 86, 88, 147
Urry, John   5, 158

vernacular   7, 115–16, 140
visibility   16, 51, 56, 74–6, 139

Wallis, Alan D.   3, 7, 25, 115, 153
war
    First World War   19, 126, 154, 156
    post-war   21, 31, 41, 49, 156
    Second World War   20, 35, 49, 60
Wilson, Nerissa   19, 154, 163–4
wood   20, 22, 25–35
working men's club   65, 120, 126–7

Lightning Source UK Ltd.
Milton Keynes UK
UKHW022026281119
354411UK00006B/563/P